Alexander of Aphrodisias
Quaestiones 2.16-3.15

Alexander of Aphrodisias
Quaestiones 2.16-3.15

Translated by R.W. Sharples

B L O O M S B U R Y
LONDON · NEW DELHI · NEW YORK · SYDNEY

Bloomsbury Academic

An imprint of Bloomsbury Publishing Plc

50 Bedford Square
London
WC1B 3DP
UK

1385 Broadway
New York
NY 10018
USA

www.bloomsbury.com

First published in 1994 by Gerald Duckworth & Co. Ltd.
Paperback edition first published 2014

British Library Cataloguing-in-Publication Data
A catalogue record for this book is available from the British Library.

ISBN HB: 978-0-7156-2615-3
PB: 978-1-7809-3459-4
ePDF: 978-1-7809-3460-0

Acknowledgements
The present translations have been made possible by generous and imaginative funding from
the following sources: the National Endowment for the Humanities, Division of
Research Programs, an independent federal agency of the USA; the Leverhulme
Trust; the British Academy; the Jowett Copyright Trustees; the
Royal Society (UK); Centro Internazionale A. Beltrame di Storia dello
Spazio e del Tempo (Padua); Mario Mignucci; Liverpool University. The editor
wishes to thank Ian Crystal and Dirk Baltzly for their help in preparing
the volume for press.

Typeset by Ray Davies
Printed and bound by CPI Group (UK) Ltd, Croydon, CR0 4YY

Contents

Introduction[1]

Alexander and the *Quaestiones*

The *Quaestiones* attributed to the Aristotelian commentator Alexander of Aphrodisias, known by later generations as *the* commentator on Aristotle,[2] who lived in the latter part of the second and the first part of the third century AD,[3] have been the subject of increasing study in recent years. The present volume and its predecessor however form, to the best of my knowledge, the first translation of the whole collection into English or into any other modern language. Like the other minor works attributed to Alexander,[4] these texts have their apparent origin in discussion and debate of Aristotle's works and thought by Alexander himself and his associates or pupils. They thus throw light, even if a dimmer and more fitful light than we might wish, on the functioning of a philosophical 'school' in the early years of the third century AD;[5] and, in their concern to remove apparent contradictions and anomalies, they exemplify an aspect of the process by which Aristotle's thought was, over the centuries, organised and formulated into Aristotelia*nism*. They also, in varying degrees, show how the interpretation of Aristotle was influenced, consciously or unconsciously, by familiarity with the doctrines of Hellenistic philosophy. The direct or indirect influence of Aristotle and of those who have sought to interpret him extends to a great part of European thought; and these *Quaestiones* are important documents in the history of that influence.

Their interest for the student of Aristotle is not however purely historical. Of the many topics with which they deal, some are of more interest to us today than others; nevertheless, many of these texts can still be of use to us in our own attempts to interpret Aristotle's views, whether we find the interpretations advanced here plausible or whether we are provoked to new insights by our reactions against them. In a very real sense we who try to interpret Aristotle now are engaged in the same enterprise as Alexander and his associates. And, given the importance of Aristotle in the history of thought, these texts should be of interest to all those who share a belief that reasoned consideration and argument are the best methods of advancing the *eudaimonia* of mankind at large.

Nor is the interest of these texts confined to the student of European thought. Versions of some of them were translated, with more or less alteration, into Arabic, and in some cases from Arabic into Latin; they thus have a part in the history of the transmission of ancient Greek philosophy to the Islamic world and thence to the medieval Latin West. In the present translation account is taken of Arabic versions of the texts preserved in Greek where these have been accessible, but a complete edition and translation of all the Arabic texts so far discovered, both those that are parallel to surviving Greek texts and those that are not, is much to be desired.[6]

Most of the minor texts attributed to Alexander that survive in Greek are arranged in collections apparently made in antiquity. Three books of these collected discussions are entitled *phusikai skholikai aporiai kai luseis*, 'School-discussion problems and solutions on nature' (often cited in modern literature as Alexander's *Quaestiones*); it is with these that the present volume and its predecessor are concerned. A fourth book is titled 'Problems on Ethics' but sub-titled, no doubt in imitation of the preceding three books when it was united with them,[7] *skholikai êthikai aporiai kai luseis*, 'school-discussion problems and solutions on ethics'.[8] A further collection was transmitted as the second book of Alexander's treatise *On the Soul*, and labelled *mantissa* or 'makeweight' by the Berlin editor Bruns. Other texts essentially similar to those in these collections survive, some in Greek[9] and some only in Arabic; and there is evidence that there were other collections now lost.[10] The circumstances in which these collections were put together are unclear; it was not always expertly done, and while some of the titles attached to particular pieces seem to preserve valuable additional information,[11] others are inept or unhelpful.[12] Nor is it clear at what date the collections were assembled.[13] In a few cases the views expressed in a particular text are so different from those in other works by Alexander that it is difficult to believe that they are those of Alexander himself;[14] more often there are no very clear reasons to suppose a text is not by Alexander himself, but equally no way of proving conclusively that it is. In the notes I have sometimes for the sake of convenience referred to the author of a particular text as 'Alexander', without thereby intending to express a definite view as to its authenticity.

A classification of the types of texts found in these collections was undertaken by Bruns in the preface to his edition.[15] In addition to (i) 'problems' in the strict sense[16] with their solutions, these minor works include (ii) expositions (*exêgêseis*) of particularly problematic Aristotelian texts, (iii) short expositions of Aristotelian doctrine on a particular topic, and (iv) straightforward and sometimes tedious paraphrases of passages in Aristotle's writings; both (iii) and (iv) alike seem to be described as *epidromai* or 'summaries'. There are also (v) collections, one might almost say batteries, of arguments for a particular Aristotelian position;[17] and (vi) what appear to be fragments of more elaborate literary works apparently never finished. It seems likely that (iii), (iv) and (v), in particular, reflect teaching activity; it is difficult in some cases to see why else they might have been written. Some of these texts may be Alexander's own expositions of particular topics, while some may be more in the nature of exercises by his students.[18] There are references to discussion and enquiry which in some cases seem to reflect actual school-discussions.[19]

Some of the short texts attributed to Alexander are clearly related either to his monographs[20]or to Aristotelian works on which he wrote full-scale commentaries. The *Quaestiones* include a number of discussions of passages in Aristotle's *de Anima*, and Moraux pointed out that these actually follow the sequence of Aristotle's own treatise, though interspersed with other material in the collections as they now exist.[21] Other groupings of texts are connected with particular themes or particular Aristotelian works.[22]It has sometimes been suggested that some of these texts may be extracts from full-length commentaries now lost to us; but there is none of which this can conclusively be proved, and a number of which it can apparently be disproved.[23]

The present volume, a sequel to Sharples (1992), includes

the second half of the second book of the *Quaestiones* and the third book. This arrangement has resulted from the requirements of the present series – much as ancient book-divisions often depended on nothing more than the size of a papyrus roll; it involves breaking up the series of texts relating to the *de Anima*, but so would a division by books, and the present arrangement does keep together a number of groups of closely related texts (1.8, 1.17, 1.26, and 1.19 and 2.15 in the previous volume; 2.22 and 3.5 in this one).

To discuss in this Introduction Alexander's position on the philosophical questions raised by these *Quaestiones* would in general be superfluous; the texts themselves, supplemented by the notes and references there to Alexander's commentaries, set out the issues clearly enough. One point which it may be appropriate to mention here, however, since it concerns a number of the texts in the present volume, is Alexander's explanation of divine providence in terms of the effect of the movement of the heavens in preserving the continuity of sublunary coming-to-be and passing away. The physical theory itself is Aristotelian;[24] characteristically, Alexander's contribution is to take existing doctrine and apply it to a problem which scarcely arose for Aristotle himself. By limiting providence to the preservation of sublunary species[25] he is enabled to steer a middle course between, on the one hand, asserting that sublunary individuals are the primary concern of divine providence, and on the other denying providential concern for the sublunary altogether. The difficulties and nuances of Alexander's position are developed partly in texts surviving in Greek, especially *Quaest.* 2.21,[26] and partly in the treatise *On Providence* surviving, apart from a few fragments, only in Arabic;[27] how far he succeeds in resolving them, and how far he can escape from the charge – levelled by Moraux before all the texts now available to us were known – that his conception of providence is essentially mechanistic,[28] are issues that the reader will want to consider.[29]

Bruns argued that the Greek text of the *Quaestiones*, as of all Alexander's *scripta minora* apart from the *de Mixtione*, ultimately depended on one late ninth- or tenth-century MS, Ven. Marc. gr. 258 (V).[30] However, a fourteenth-century Florence MS, Riccard. gr. 63, not only contains two fragments of Alexander absent from V (below, pp. 89-94) but also a text of *Quaest.* 2.7 superior to that of V, and one of part of the *de Mixtione* independent of any extant MS of that work.[31] A planned series of critical editions of all the other *scripta minora* in the Budé collection will provide an opportunity to re-examine the whole textual tradition.

In addition to corrections made when V was copied, there are later corrections by a hand (Bruns' V[2]) which Bruns (1887) viii dated to the twelfth century but Thillet (1982) 28 identifies in the *de Fato* as that of Bessarion (1395-1472); however, V[2]'s corrections are fewer in the latter part of *Quaestiones* book 2 and in book 3 than earlier (Bruns [1892,1] xviii). Further fifteenth-century conjectures are represented by the second hands in MSS B and S, followed by the Aldine edition of Trincavelli (1536); cf. Bruns (1892) xxiii-xxiv. B (Ven. Marc. gr. 261) was a copy of V made for Bessarion, the first hand in B incorporating the corrections of V[2]; Thillet (1982) 29-31. Thillet considers the possibility that some of the conjectures of B[2] may also be due to Bessarion, but remains tentative on this matter.[32]

The present translation

Something should be said here about the procedures followed in the present translation. I have endeavoured – with what success, the reader must judge – to produce a translation that is close to the original Greek while still being readable. One immediate difficulty is the length and complexity of sentences that is characteristic both of Alexander's own writings and of those attributed to him. The long sentences found in these texts have here been broken up into more manageable units.

A second and greater difficulty is consistency in the translation of particular Greek words. The range of meanings of a word in one language does not correspond exactly to that of any one word in any other language. It is desirable to translate the same Greek word by the same English word as far as possible, in order to indicate – especially to the Greekless reader – that there is a single Greek word in question; and this applies especially in the case of texts like those with which we are here concerned, replete with technical terminology in the original language. I have therefore endeavoured to follow this principle as far as I judged possible; but it is a principle which sometimes needs to be tempered in the interests of readability. In general, I have sought consistency within a given *quaestio* rather than between different *quaestiones* with different subject-matter; but exceptions even to this have proved necessary.[33] The Indexes may help to clarify these and similar points. I have also sometimes translated the optative with *an* by a present or future indicative; the tentativeness of the potential form sometimes seems to be little more than a mannerism which it would be misleading to reproduce literally in English.[34] A notable stylistic feature of these texts is carelessness over the reference of pronouns.[35]

The present translation is rather more heavily annotated than some other volumes in this series. This seemed desirable, since we are here concerned not with the continuous exposition of a single Aristotelian text, but with relatively short and self-contained sections of argument which stand in need of some indication of their context in ancient, and especially Aristotelian, discussion generally. The Textual Emendations (on pp. 100-9) list places where I have diverged from Bruns' text; these divergences are indicated by * in the translation. Where I have followed Bruns' text I have not generally noted the foundations on which it rests even where these are themselves conjectural, except in major cases where the interpretation is substantially affected or where there is real doubt. I have taken the opportunity to record in the Textual Emendations all subsequent conjectures known to me, even those I have not adopted, in the hope that this will be of service to readers.

My interest in these texts began in the context of my research for my Ph.D. thesis *Studies on the De Fato of Alexander of Aphrodisias* (Cambridge, 1977), my concern then being especially with those relating to the topics of fate, possibility and divine providence. My thanks are due to the supervisors of my research then, the late Professor W.K.C. Guthrie and Professors J.D.G. Evans and G.E.R. Lloyd. Some of the translations in this volume are revised versions of ones that have appeared elsewhere, and I am grateful to Gerald Duckworth and Co. and to the editor of the *Bulletin of the Institute of Classical Studies of the University of London* for permission to re-use those translations here in revised form.[36] I am also grateful to the readers for the Ancient Commentators series, and to many other people for their comments and advice. It would be impossible to name all the latter, but my thanks are particularly due to Jonathan Barnes, Silvia Fazzo, Alan Lacey, Eric Lewis, Robert Todd, Hillary Wiesner and Fritz Zimmermann, and to an anonymous reader. I am also grateful to André Laks, Katerina Ierodiakonou and Fritz Zimmermann for letting me see work of theirs in advance of publication, and for permission to refer to it, and especially to Robert Todd for allowing me to see and to make use of his unpublished annotated translation of *Quaest.* 3.12. The responsibility for the use or misuse I have made of the advice of others is of course my own. I have been able to confirm certain readings in the principal MS, V, with the aid of a microfilm in the library of the Institute of Classical Studies purchased from the Joyce Southan Memorial Fund; I am also grateful to Jonathan Barnes for information on cod. Riccard. 63, which he has examined in Florence. To avoid misunderstandings, I should perhaps mention that I do not myself know Arabic, and that statements made here about the Arabic versions of the *Quaestiones* are based on the published translations unless otherwise indicated.

There is much more still to be discovered and said about these texts, the positions adopted in them, and the relation of those positions to other ancient commentaries on Aristotle. If the present translation helps to stimulate and facilitate such discussion, it will fulfil its purpose. Above all, however, my thanks are due to my wife Grace and daughter Elizabeth for their unfailing interest and support.

University College London   R.W.S.

Alexander of Aphrodisias
Quaestiones 2.16-3.15

Translation

The school-puzzles and solutions on nature*[—] of Alexander of Aphrodisias:[37] chapter-headings of the second book

... 16.[38] How other arts will not, in a similar way to the stochastic arts, have as their end making every effort towards achieving their objective.

17. That, if there is some other fire hotter than the heavenly fire (which [heavenly fire] is, moreover, an element), [the heavenly fire] is not for that reason such [as it is] through mixture with the opposite.

18. Concerning nature's being a principle of movement.

19. That, if the universe is eternal and it is its ordering that [constitutes] its being the universe, this too will be [included] in its own proper being.

20. How that which changes into something in accordance with the potentiality that it possesses, preserves the potentiality even after changing into that into which it changes.

21. That providence is not accidental according to Aristotle.

22. Explanation of a passage from the second [book] of *On Coming-to-be and Passing Away*,[39] differing from that in the commentary on it.

23. About the stone from Heracleia.[40]

24. Explanation of a passage from the second book of *On the Soul* a little after the beginning.[41]

25. Explanation of another passage from the same [book].[42]

26. <Another passage from the same [book].>[43]

27. <Another passage from the same [book].>[44]

28. That matter is not genus.

80,1   The school-puzzles and solutions on nature*
            of Alexander of Aphrodisias: chapter-
            headings of the third book[45]

1. What recollection is.

2. Explanation of a passage from the second [book] *On the
   Soul*, in which [Aristotle] says 'For what possesses knowledge comes to be [actually] contemplating, and this is not
5 an alteration; for the progression is towards itself[46] and
   towards actuality'.[47]

3. Explanation of a passage likewise from the second [book]
   On the Soul,[48] in which [Aristotle] speaks about sensation.

4. How both the approach and the receding of the sun are[49]
   alike causes of coming-to-be and passing away. For the
   coming-to-be of one thing is the passing away of another.

10 5. That coming to be of necessity without qualification, and
   not conditionally, [is] in the things that come to be always,
   in a cycle.

14 6.*[50] Explanation of a passage from the third [book] *On the
   Soul*, in which [Aristotle] showed that there are not more
   than the five senses.[51]

12 7.*Explanation of a passage from the third [book] *On the Soul*,
   in which [Aristotle] enquires how self-awareness comes
   about when we sense [things].[52]

16 8. Whether that which is capable of being sensed by all the
   senses *per accidens*, is capable of being sensed.

9. Explanation of a passage from the third [book] *On the Soul*,
   through which [Aristotle] shows that there is something
   with which we sense everything simultaneously.[53]

10. About the sea, from the *Meteorology*.

20 11. An attempt to show that names [are] by [our] laying [them]
   down.

12. That reality is not unlimited.

13. Some [points] concerning that which depends on us.

14. Summary of the contents of the fourth book of the *Meteorology*, unfinished.

15. About what is as it were without parts.

2.16. How it is not in a similar way to the stochastic arts 61,1
that the other arts too will have, as their end, making
every effort towards achieving their objective.[54]

If someone were to say (I) that the end of the stochastic arts is
to make every effort towards achieving their objective, how will 5
these not achieve their proper end in a similar way to the arts
that are not stochastic?[55] But this, that they do not achieve
their end in a similar way, seems to be the greatest difference
between the stochastic [arts] and the others. Now, according to
those for whom (II) the end of [the stochastic arts] is to *achieve*
their objective, they *will* differ in this way;[56] but according to
those for whom (I) what has previously been mentioned* [*making every effort* to achieve their objective] is their end, [then,] 10
although [the stochastic arts] *achieve** their end in a similar
way [to the other arts], they will differ* from them in not having
a similar *end* to them.[57]

For those [non-stochastic] arts have achieving their objective
as their end, because the things that come about in accordance
with the art are followed by that for the sake of which they come
about, and their failure to achieve their objective follows
through error in the things that come about, when they do not
do so in accordance with the art. For in those cases making 15
every effort towards achieving the end, and actually achieving
it, are equivalent; for these things come about when [the
agents] make every effort.[58] But in the case of the stochastic
[arts] the things that come about in accordance with the art are
not in every case followed by that for the sake of which [they
come about], because to achieve it they need many things which
do not depend on the art alone. Moreover the things that come
about in accordance with the art are themselves not [com- 20
pletely] determinate, and they do not always produce the same
[results] because they are not applied to [objects] that are in a
similar condition in every way; but all or at any rate some of
the things [included] in them will be different and not as was
expected. So [for these, stochastic arts] the end is not the
achieving of their objective, but the completion of what belongs
to the art [itself].

Or: (III) in the case of these too their *end* is to achieve that
for the sake of which they make every effort, [and to do so]

25   *through* making every effort; but their own proper *task* is to
      make every effort towards achieving their objective. For this
      alone is not sufficient for achieving their objective, but they also
      need certain other things, which do not depend on the art.

      2.17. That, if there is some other fire hotter than the
30   heavenly fire[59] (which [heavenly fire] is, moreover, an
      element), [the heavenly fire is] <not>[60] for that reason
      such [as it is] through mixture with the opposite.

The effervescence of fire, which is what the fire in our region is
like, is hotter than the elemental fire which is also called
heavenly fire. But it is not the case that, just for this reason,
62,1 the lesser heat in the latter is [caused] by mixture with the
      opposite. At any rate, a flame is less hot than red-hot iron, but
      this is not by the admixture of coldness; rather, the intensifi-
      cation [of heat] in the iron results from the solidity and un-
      yielding [quality] of the matter. For by being resistant and
5   unyielding [itself], it also makes the heat in it like this.[61]
      Moreover elemental fire, which is by nature rare and dry and
      unmixed with [the] matter capable of providing a supply [of
      fuel] to fire of this [burning] sort, is hot in this way [i.e. the way
      appropriate to it].[62] At any rate, the things that are kindled
      here [on earth] are those which have in themselves a certain
      compression and density and nourishment for this sort of fire.
      And for this reason one might more reasonably say that it is
      this [terrestrial, burning] sort of fire that is mixed with its
10   opposite. For this [fire] needs nourishment and is preserved for
      as long as it has it, and it is the opposite that nourishes a thing.
      Moreover, since this [terrestrial] sort of fire depends on
matter*, it will also have something opposite to itself which it
conveys into itself and changes [sc. into its own nature]. The
other sort of fire which does not depend on nourishment, but is
unalloyed and pure, unmixed with its opposite, [is] the [fire]
that exists in its own right, as does each of the other elements
too.

2.18. Concerning nature's being a principle of move-   15
ment.[63]

That nature is a principle of movement is clear from the fact
that it is by their principle of movement that natural bodies
differ from ones that are not natural, and that by which natural
bodies, differing from those that are not natural, *are* natural is
nature. So as many bodies as are subject to coming-to-be, being
natural, have their coming-to-be in places other than their own,   20
and their movement contributes to their coming to be[64] in their
proper place; when they come to be in this they stay at rest with
regard to place, and are complete* as far as their coming-to-be
is concerned; for they also have in themselves the principle of
movement towards this.[65]

As for bodies that are not subject to coming-to-be, complete
by their own nature and in their natural place,[66] for these
nature, that is the principle of movement in them, does not   25
contribute to a change from incompleteness to completeness,
nor to being carried towards the place that is natural for them;
for they are complete and never depart from the place that is
natural for them. Rather, [their nature contributes] to their
being made like the best of beings, on account of their activity
in accordance with it, by their eternal and continuous and
unvarying movement, imitating its always* being in actual-   30
ity[67] and its [being] unmoved and at rest. It is through their
movement [that they are in imitation of] its being in actuality,
for* movement is a sort of actuality;[68] for the things that imitate
what is in actuality without qualification, and in no way shares
in potentiality, had to do this by means of the activity which is
natural for them. And it is through being moved continuously
and in an ordered way and always in a similar fashion that
they are in imitation of its eternal nature. For neither would
that which is most properly body[69] be a natural body if it did   35
not move, nor, [seeing that] it does move, does it have a
reasonable cause for ever being at rest and not moving continuously, neither as a result of the place [it occupies],[70] nor as a
result of its moving unnaturally, nor as a result of the weakness   63,1
that arises from mortality. And for this reason [the heavens],[71]
moving continuously on account of the nature that is in them,

imitate, through the permanence in their movement, the being
at rest of [the supreme being].

That it is not only being moved, but being moved in a
continuous and eternal movement, that is natural for [the
5   heavens] is also shown by their having a spherical shape, since
the best and most complete of shapes is natural for the best of
bodies, and for such a shape rest is contrary to nature; and for
this reason it has no base on which it will be at rest.

2.19. That, if the world is eternal and it is its ordering
that [constitutes] its being the world, this too will[72] be
[included] in its own proper being.[73]

10   If the world is eternal by its own nature, and [its] being the
world is [its] being in an order of a certain particular sort, it
will derive its ordering, too, from its own nature. If so, it will
have no need, either for its being or for the ordering which it
has, of [some being] exercising providence over it. But everything which exercises providence is concerned either with the
15   being of the thing over which providence is exercised, or with
its well-being; so that the world, not being in need of [some
being] exercising providence over it for either [of these], would
not be an object of providence at all.

Or rather:[74] the whole world does not need some [being] to
exercise providence [over it], neither for its being nor for its
well-being, but the providence that comes about in the world
does so by a certain part in the world exercising providence,
and another being the object of providence. For as much of it
as is body not subject to coming-to-be and passing away, and
20   is always ordered in accordance with its own nature and soul,[75]
and moves with the movement [proper to] itself through desire
for imitation of the first god,[76] this [part] is in no need of [some
being] to exercise providence [over it], having in its own proper
nature perfection with respect both to being and to well-being.
But as much of it as is subject to coming-to-be and passing
away, and needs assistance from something else both for being
and for the eternity in species [that comes about] through
25   orderly change,[77] this is that over which providence is exercised, being governed by the orderly movement of the divine
part of the world and [its being] in a certain relation[78] to it.

Participating in this ordering to the extent that is possible for something that is mortal, it obtains it from those [heavenly bodies] and through it preserves imperishability in species.

2.20. How that which changes into something in accordance with the potentiality that it possesses, preserves the potentiality[79] even after changing into that into which it changes.   30

How does that, which changes into something by possessing the potentiality for change into it before it changes into it, preserve the potentiality of becoming again that from which it changed? And it becomes that thing again, as Aristotle says   64,1 concerning the world,[80] if it is a thing that has come to be; for on account of this, he says, it will also pass away. [But there is a problem:] for the things that come to be are not seen to be like this. For the bench which has come to be from a log like this no longer keeps the potentiality for becoming such a log, nor is the change and passing-away to the same thing [as that from which it originally came to be], nor does the human being who came   5 to be by change from certain things pass away again into those things from which he had his coming to be, [namely] these menses and this seed.[81]

Or rather:[82] those things that come to be in accordance with the arts do not return again to their matter, because the matter, from which [the art] was making the product, was not [itself] a product of the art, and was not even the *opposite* of the product that was coming to be, into which the thing that was coming to be had its change.[83] The underlying [matter], being   10 natural, possesses the potentiality for receiving this form or not, and, if it receives it, it keeps the potentiality for being separated from the form which it received. [Accordingly] it is separated from it and passes away, and its passing away, like its coming-to-be, is brought about by something outside or something like this, if it passes away *qua* product of an art, or by nature, if the underlying body passes away naturally and the product of the art passes away along with it.[84]   15

In the case of things that come to be by nature, however, just as the thing that comes to be is by nature, so too is that which underlies.[85] And the first thing that underlies is matter, which

never exists in actuality in itself,[86] while that which underlies
in actuality is the elements, which already involve a certain
[degree of] qualification and opposition, and change into one
another in accordance with the oppositions which they have to
20   one another, the matter which underlies them being all common, and altering its form according as [one or other] of the
opposed qualities gains the upper hand. For it is by having
become *this*, but possessing the potentiality also for being in
the opposite [state] to this, that, keeping the potentiality, it
sometimes also changes into *that*; and for this reason none of
the simple bodies that come to be[87] is imperishable. And from
25   these simple bodies the composite [bodies] too come to be, in
accordance with a certain mixing and blending and proportioning of their potentialities,[88] according to which change comes
about not into a particular one of the simple [bodies], but into
something intermediate which shares in all the qualities and
potentialities which underlie in the simple bodies. But the
simple bodies possess the potentiality also for being separated
from one another again, and so they are dissolved and sepa-
30   rated from a mixture of this sort.[89] And for this reason it is not
possible for any of the things that are composed of them to be
imperishable.

And the coming-to-be of living creatures, too, comes about in
accordance with a proportioning of certain bodies which are
themselves already mixed (for the menses are not a simple
body), and in accordance with this proportioning [the living
creatures] come to possess soul and be unified and in possession
of certain particular potentialities.[90] [But] when this proportioning is dissolved, since the things from which [the creatures]
35   came to be change and do not preserve the potentialities in
regard to which the proportioning [took place], there comes
about a dissolution and breaking up [of the creatures], *not* into
the things which are no longer preserved in* them, like the
menses (for these themselves too were composite, and this
composition [took place] after the first mixing and joining
together of the [ingredients] from which the bodies of living
65,1   creatures are composed). But, when there is a change in the
things from which these bodies [were composed] (and these
were the elements, which *were* preserved [in the compounds]),
they are dissolved apart from one another, when a dispropor-

tion is brought about between them by the one of them that gains the upper hand (since they do not have the power to keep this proportioning indefinitely), and the passing away of living creatures and other composite bodies[91] leads to the dissolution 5 of those elements from which their coming to be and composition [took place] in accordance with a certain proportioning of the elements to one another.

And if*[92] the world, too, came to be by some change from certain bodies existing in actuality, it is clear that those bodies, by the change of which it* came to be, are preserved in it;[93] and that being preserved, and being able also to be in that state in 10 which [they were when] they changed* into being the world, they might change back again, into a state* [such that, if] they changed into it the world would no longer exist;[94] just as we see the simple bodies changing into one another first [of all] – since* the matter that underlies them is receptive of those [qualities] that give the first bodies their forms – and the composite bodies too [changing], whenever, either on account of nature or on account of some outside circumstance, some- 15 thing gains the upper hand in them and dissolves the proportioning that [the constituents][95] have to one another, and in accordance with which the composite body has its being.

2.21. That providence is not accidental according to Aristotle.[96]

Recently I was[97] discussing providence with my companions, and I tried to show both that there is some concern and providence from the divine [beings] about mortal ones, accord- 20 ing to Aristotle, and what it is. I was ready to say in what way it comes about when one of those who were present said that it was worth learning first what response one should give to those who ask whether one must say that the divine [beings][98] exercise providence* over these things here in a primary way according to us too*, or [only] accidentally. For those who deny that the providence we say occurs is [providence]*[99] say that it 25 is spoken of as providence [only] accidentally.*[100] But if in everything to which it is added 'accidentally' is a sign that these things are not in the proper sense what they are said to be, and what is not in the proper sense in a way is not even being,[101]

then what is spoken of as accidental providence will not even
be providence, if it is spoken of with such an addition. For it is
the things that are not moved in the proper sense and *per se*
30   that are said to have been moved accidentally, and accidental
causes are those from which there is no contribution in a
primary way towards the things of which they are said to be
the causes. So if we say that providence too comes about with
this addition, from what we ourselves say about providence we
would I suppose be doing away with the existence of providence. For just as it is not possible to say that a counterfeit
35   drachma coin is a drachma coin, because the addition [of
'counterfeit'] does away with it[s nature], so one cannot say that
66,1 accidental providence is providence, either, because 'accidental' is in all things added on the condition that it does away
with that with which it is combined.

And I said to him, 'Well, then, does it seem to you necessary
for providence to be combined with one or other of these, and
5   that in answering someone who asks such a question one must
either say that it comes about in a primary way and *per se* or
[that it does so] accidentally?'

And he [said], 'What else could someone say apart from these
and [still] seem to be giving a reasonable answer?'

'It's clear', I said, 'that, if it should become apparent that
10   there can be nothing intermediate between what is *per se* and
what is accidental, then it is necessary for the person who gives
a sound answer to the question to place providence in one or
other of these [classes]. But if there can be something intermediate between these, it is apparent that the person who has
shown this will show that the question is not inevitable, because it has not included all the types of providence that can
be mentioned.'

15   'And what sort of thing would this be', he said, 'which has
been left out and so removes the inevitability of answering [sc.
in the terms in which the dilemma was put]?'

And I [said], 'It seems to me that it will be clear whether this
is so or not, if we first remind ourselves what each of these
20   indicates*, I mean '*per se*' and "accidental".' He said that what
I was saying was right, and I tried to set out what is indicated
by each of the [terms] assumed in the question. I said that the
person who is said to exercise forethought[102] concerning some-

thing *per se* is the person who makes his end the benefit of the object of his forethought*, and performs, for the sake of this, those actions through which he thinks he will achieve the goal that is his objective, making the end of his activities the benefit of the object of his forethought. 'Somebody is said to exercise forethought concerning something accidentally, however', [I went on,] 'when the person who is said to exercise forethought in this way does nothing for the benefit of the object of fore-thought, but it happens as a result of some of the things brought about that it receives some benefit, the person who exercises forethought in this way not even being aware of the result in the first place. For the man who is thought to have found a treasure accidentally is the one who first dug for some other reason, not expecting to find [the treasure];[103] and someone* was killed by a thunderbolt accidentally because the thunder-bolt did not hurtle [downwards] for this reason, and no thought that this would happen occurred to the maker, or perhaps the Craftsman, of the thunderbolt.[104] For knowledge of some one of the things that will follow on things that come about for some other reason removes the accidental [quality of their] coming about, since what is accidental is what is thought to come about contrary to rational [expectation],[105] while foreknowledge is thought to be a sign of things that come about in accordance with reason. Or is it not to these things and those that come about in this way that we apply "accidental"?'

And he [said], 'No, not to anything else. At any rate, when we say that luck is a cause *per accidens*, we define it no less by [its being] unforeseen than by its occurring infrequently.'[106]

'Well', I said, 'if forethought that is *per se* and that which is accidental are like this, I do not think you will need many more arguments in order to think that the question, which demands that providence be divided* into that which is *per se* and that which is accidental, only, is not adequate.'

'What you say is right', he said; 'for if someone is aware of the benefit that will be brought about for someone from the things that he himself brings about for some other reason, it is clear from what has been said already that it is neither *per se* nor accidentally that this man exercises forethought concern-ing the one who receives benefit in this way from some one of the things which he [himself] brings about.'

25

30

35

67,1

5

10

'What', I said, 'if, in addition to [his] being aware of the
15 benefit that is brought about for someone, it is also brought
about in accordance with his own wish? Will you not say that
forethought that comes about in this way is much further still
removed from that which is accidental?'

And he [replied] 'Yes, certainly. I suppose that [forethought]
that comes about in this way <is neither *per se* nor accidental;
for>* to exercise forethought for something *per se* is to do
everything for the sake of the object of the forethought, while
to do so accidentally is to act for the sake of something else
20 without even being aware of the benefit that comes about for
[the object of one's accidental forethought] through that, and
not wishing [it] either. But what does not act for the sake of
[the object of forethought], while yet being aware of and wishing the benefit to it, will exercise forethought concerning it, but
will not do so either *per se* or accidentally.

['And, if he benefits the thing, but relates the benefit to
himself, concerning this thing too he does not exercise forethought either *per se* or accidentally. And if something
25 [exercises forethought] *per se* concerning universals, but
accidentally concerning the particulars, this too will not exercise providence over the individuals either *per se* or accidentally without qualification; not *per se*, because it is not for their
sake, and not accidentally, because the universal is not different from the particulars (for it is in these that it has its being);
but it falls a little short* of coming about *per se** in a primary
way.']¹⁰⁷

30 'What would you say', I said, 'about one who exercises forethought concerning certain things, but relates the benefit from
the objects of his forethought to himself? In the way in which
we see shepherds exercising forethought* about their sheep,
and cowherds about their cattle and goatherds about their
goats, and similarly horse-trainers and swineherds about the
creatures that are herded and grazed by them.'

68,1 'Well, these', he said, 'and all forethought that comes about
in this way differs little from that which does so in a primary
way and *per se*. For everything else [in these cases] comes about
in a similar way [to that in which it would if the benefit of the
creatures was the primary concern], and it is only the change

in the goal[108] that creates the difference between this sort of forethought and that which is *per se*.'

'How about this?' I said. 'Suppose someone says that fore- 5
thought in one respect comes about *per se* and in another accidentally, and that [it does so] *per se* for universals, but accidentally for the things that fall under them. Isn't he too speaking of some other type of forethought besides those mentioned at the beginning?'

'Yes of course', he said, 'if what is common is other than each of the things that fall under it, but* having in these its being 10
some one thing,[109] and on account of this in a way sharing with them the things that come about primarily with a view to itself?'

And I said to him, 'So it is clear from what has been agreed, that in whichever of the ways stated subsequently [i.e. after the original dilemma] one says providence and forethought comes about, one will be saying that it does so neither in a primary way nor accidentally.'

'Yes, it's clear', he said. 15

'But', I said, 'since this has become clear it is clear both that the first question* which you said some people ask does not deserve an answer, and also that the person who says that providence comes about in some one of these ways does not do away with providence, as the person who says that it comes about accidentally seems to do.

'For to give up assigning to some one of these types the 20
providence of the divine over what is subject to coming-to-be and mortal, and to say that the gods perform their own proper activities for the preservation of mortals, is completely inappropriate to gods. For this is just like a person who says that free men and masters exist for the sake of their servants, and perform their own proper activities for the sake of [the servants'] preservation and good order, if the gods are masters of 25
all other things. For in all cases that, for the sake of which something is, is more honourable than that which is for the sake of something else, if the end is more honourable than the things that precede it; and so according to those who speak in this way the servant and slave will be more honourable than his master, and mortal things [more honourable] than divine ones.[110]

'And yet, in the case of slaves and masters, it is possible to
30   say that there a certain reciprocity comes about between them
through the activities which they perform. For the activities of
the masters come about* for the sake of the preservation of the
slaves, but contribute in return to the preservation of the
masters. For the preservation of the masters depends on the
activity of the slaves; so that in a way each is the end of the
other. But to say that the preservation of the gods requires the
35   activity of mortals would seem to be altogether absurd.'[111]
      'Yes, of course.'
69,1   'And just like this it is absurd to say that the end and good
for the gods is located in the ordering of mortals and providence
[concerning them], especially when one sees that many of the
things that occur concerning them are not worthy of a divine[112]
ordering. If the divine is going to perform its own proper
activities for the sake of the preservation of mortals, and not
5   for its own sake, then it will seem altogether to exist for the
sake of mortals. But it will do this according to those who locate
its [very] being in the exercising of providence. For what else
will the divine be according to the person[113] who writes, 'for
what is left of snow, for example*, if someone* takes away the
white and the cold? What of fire, if you quench its heat, or of
honey [if you remove] its sweetness, the soul [if you remove]
10   movement, or god [if you remove] the exercise of providence?'
For if the being of god consists in the exercise of providence,
according to the person who speaks and writes in this way, and
everything that exercises providence exercises it over something, and to exercise providence is to perform one's own proper
activities for the sake of the object of providence, of necessity
every activity that god [performs] as god will come about for
the sake of the objects of providence. Or what do you think?'
15   And he [said], 'Yes, for what else is the person saying who
locates the being of the gods in the exercising of providence in
the way that that of fire is in heat?'
      'Well', I said, 'in every case aren't the things that contribute
to the end less perfect than the end itself?'
      'Yes, of course', he said.
20   'Well, then, isn't it necessary to say that everything that
performs its own proper and natural activities for the sake of

something else exists for the sake of that thing, especially if something like this is part of its [very] being?'

'Yes, certainly.'

'But if a thing has some other end as its objective*, for the sake of which it does what it does, and if a thing has in its own proper being the fact that it is for the sake of something else, it is necessary for this to be imperfect and second in honour to that for the sake of which it is.'   25

'Yes', he said.

'It is necessary, then, for those who say that the providence from the divine [beings] for mortals is like this to say* that the divine is less perfect* than mortals and exists for [mortals']   30 sake. What could be more impious than this, or more alien to the being of the gods and [our] conception [of them]?'

And he said, 'What you say is true, and it is necessary both for these [consequences] and for others just like them to follow for those who say that providence is like this and comes about in this way. For many of the things that occur here [on earth]   70,1 will not seem worth knowing about in the first place, nor* to be brought about by the providence of those [divine beings].[114] And an absurdity will follow for those who attribute everything to providence, but say that only what is fine is good, and suppose that this depends on us. For of what good for human beings is it possible* for the divine providence, in which they   5 say the being of the gods consists, to be the cause* according to them? [115]

'For this reason let us postpone discussion of these matters until we have longer leisure; the argument now set before us seems to ask, in what way we must say providence comes about according to Aristotle, since we assert that we say it does so neither *per se* nor accidentally, but we have found several other   10 types of providence or forethought besides these; one might ask which of these we say is proper to the gods.'

And I [said] to him, 'What? Wasn't our objective to show that the question, posed by those who say that the divine [beings] exercise providence in a primary way over things subject to coming-to-be and passing away, was indeed* empty and not worthy of an answer in the first place, if there are more ways   15 in which it is possible to say that providence comes about, but this [question] was about only two of them, and it has been

shown that it is not possible for the providence from the gods
that we are looking for to come about in either of these ways?'

'It was indeed so', he said, 'but since you have sufficiently
established what I proposed, your reply to them is completed;
20   for our sake it is right for you to add the things that follow on
what has been shown. For if it should be apparent that, in the
case of providence as it is spoken of by Aristotle,[116] all the
[difficulties] which have been shown to follow from the previously mentioned opinions are done away with, this too if it
occurred would be not a small piece of evidence for the establishing of this [Aristotelian] opinion as being true.'

'Well', I said, 'an account of these matters is not easy, espe-
25   cially since none of our predecessors made it his business to
show this. At any rate, it will seem that no one of those who
have developed Aristotle's account – as far as I know, [given
that I have] not [considered the matter] as a primary object of
concern[117] – have determined this problem in such a way as to
show that what Aristotle said is in harmony with what they
themselves say. But you request it, and I think it is a fine thing
30   for us to develop the account as far as we are able to determine
[the problem]. I think it is better to gain even a small advantage
in terms of what it is possible to say about [the matter], than,
for fear of not being able to complete [the solution of] the
problem, to stand aloof from even minor [suggestions]. So we
must not shrink back from [the problem.] But I will try, together with [giving] an account of these matters, also to show
that those who profess the position of Plato,[118] and have
71,1   strongly persuaded themselves that Aristotle said nothing
about providence, do not say anything with attention or reflection.'[119]

2.22. Explanation of a passage from the second [book] of
Aristotle's 'On Coming-to-Be and Passing Away', differing
5   from that in the commentary on it. The passage is this: 'If
then it goes on to infinity in a downwards direction, that
this particular one of the things that are later should come
to be will not be necessary without qualification, but
conditionally.[120] For it will always be necessary [that there

be][121] something else in front, on account of which it is necessary for that thing to come to be.'[122]

If [i] it were shown that it is only <in> those cases where what is later is of necessity that 'if what is first, of necessity what is later' is true,[123] and [ii] in the case of coming-to-be to infinity that which is later is not of necessity, because it does not even come to be the same*;[124] [then] [iii] neither would anything before that which came to be last[125] come to be of necessity without qualification, [iv] because the things that precede the final [member of the series]*[126] only derive necessity without qualification from the end if this comes to be of necessity without qualification.*[127] For *if* that [is] of necessity without qualification, then the things before it will be of necessity, each of the intermediate [members] of the [series] that comes to be to infinity possessing necessity conditionally. For if the one thing is to be of a certain sort, what precedes it must be of a certain sort; and that thing, again [the earlier one], will possess necessity in a similar way [sc. without qualification]; for that thing will be of necessity <without qualification>, if that which is after it [literally, after this] [is to be]; and so continuing. <But> since there is [in fact] no last member of the infinite [series] – [if there was and] if <it> was going to come to be of necessity, the things preceding it would come to be of necessity without qualification, and [if] these came to be of necessity it would conversely follow on them that the final [member of the series] would come to be of necessity, if the first ones did – [but since there is in fact no last member] it will no longer be possible in the case of things that come to be in this way to assume a consequence of this sort, 'if what is first, of necessity what is later'.

'So that, if there is no beginning of what is infinite, neither will there be any first thing on account of which it will be necessary [for the other members of the series] to come to be'[128] is equivalent to 'so that, if there is no end of what is infinite'.[129] For [Aristotle] here called the end 'beginning', because it is from such a thing that there is a beginning [i.e., 'such a thing is the source'], if it comes to be necessarily, of* all the things before it as well having to come to be of necessity. But if this does not exist, neither is that consequence true of it[130] that says 'if what

is first, [then] what is later'; for such a consequence becomes
30   true in those cases where there is some last [member of the
sequence] which comes to be of necessity, since it follows on this
thing* that comes to be of necessity that the things before it
too* come to be of necessity and that 'if what is first [then] also
what is later' is true of each of them. For it is necessary, if this
sort of consequence is going to be true, for there to be some limit
in the [terms] that are taken. And that [Aristotle] calls the limit
too 'beginning' he showed through what he said a little after-
72,1 wards as follows: 'And of these, if it is to be everlasting, it is not
possible for it to be in a straight line because there is in no way
a beginning, neither of things taken in a downwards direction,
applying to things that will be, nor in an upwards direction,
applying to those that are coming to be [already].'[131] For 'neither in a downwards direction applying to things that will be'
is indicative of 'beginning' in the sense of 'limit'. So there must
5   be a beginning in a downwards direction if the things that are
coming to be are going to possess necessity without qualification; because it was by the supposition, that this [sc. the last
member of the series] will be necessarily without qualification,
that this*, 'if what is first, of necessity what is later' became
true; and [there must be] a [beginning] in an upwards direction
because we will be able to take 'if what is first, [then] what is
later' in this way.

2.23.   About why the stone from Heracleia[132] attracts iron.

10   Empedocles[133] says that the iron is carried towards the magnet
by the effluences from both and the pores of the magnet which
are commensurate with the [effluences] from the iron. For the
effluences from [the magnet]* push away the air on the pores
of the iron and move [the air] which rests on them like a lid;
and when this is removed the iron follows the effluence which
15   flows all together. And the effluences from [the iron] travel to
the pores of the magnet, and because they are commensurate
with them and fit into them, the iron too follows the effluences
and is carried [along]. But someone might ask, even if the
[theory] of effluences were granted, why indeed the magnet
does not follow its own proper effluences and is [not] moved
towards the iron. For from what has been said the iron will not

be moved towards the magnet any more than the magnet   20
towards the iron.[134] Moreover, why will the iron not sometimes
be moved even without the magnet, when the effluences from
it travel all together towards some other thing? For why is it
only the effluences from the magnet that are able to move the
air which rests on the pores of the iron like a lid and holds back
the effluences? Moreover, why is nothing else carried towards
anything else in this way, although he says that many things   25
have pores commensurate to one another with regard to their
effluences? At any rate, he says 'water has more of an affinity
to* wine, but it is not willing [to mix] with olive-oil'.[135] And yet
neither of these things is moved towards the other.

Democritus[136] too postulates that effluences occur and that
like things are moved towards like, but also that all things are
moved towards the void*. Supposing this, he assumes that the   30
magnet and the iron are composed of similar atoms, but that
the magnet is composed of finer ones; and he thinks* that it is
rarer and contains more void, and that for this reason its atoms,
being more easily moved*, are carried towards the iron more   73,1
swiftly (for [things are] carried towards what is similar), and,
penetrating the pores of the iron, move the bodies within it,
spreading out through them because of their fineness. The
[bodies] when they have been moved are carried outside, [form-
ing] an effluence, and [are carried] towards the stone, both   5
because of [their] similarity [to it] and because it has more void
[spaces]; the iron follows these because they are all at once both
separated out [from it] and carried along, [and so] it too is itself
carried towards the magnet. The magnet is not also carried
towards the iron, because the iron does not have as many void
[spaces in itself] as the magnet. – Well, someone might accept
that the magnet and the iron are composed of similar [bodies],
but how [could anyone accept this of] amber and chaff? Even if
he gives* this reason in the case of these too, still there are
many [other] things that are attracted by amber; if it were   10
composed of similar [bodies] to all of these, then these too, being
composed of similar [bodies] to one another, would attract one
another.

Diogenes of Apollonia[137] says that all the things that are
malleable both naturally emit a certain moisture from themselves and attract it from outside, some more and some less,

but that bronze and iron emit most, a sign of which is both that
something is burnt off and consumed from them in fire, and

15   also that when they are smeared with vinegar and olive-oil they
rust; they are affected in this way because the vinegar attracts
the moisture out of them. For the fire, too, burns that part of
them which it burns* by penetrating into each and attracting
and consuming the moisture in them. The iron both attracts
and emits more moisture; the magnet, being rarer and more
earthy than the iron, attracts more moisture from the adjacent

20   air than it emits. Well, it admits into itself that [moisture]
which it attracts that is akin to it, but rejects that which is not.
The iron is akin to it, and for this reason it attracts [the
moisture] from [the iron] and admits it into itself, and through
its attracting of this it draws the iron too [towards itself], on
account of the continual attraction of the moisture in it. The
iron does not also attract the magnet, because the iron is not

25   so rare as to be able to admit the moisture from it all together.

    But if this is so, why is it just the magnet that attracts the
iron, while nothing else [is attracted] by what is akin to it – for
example bronze and lead? For these too emit and attract
moisture, and there are certain things that are akin to these
too, as the magnet is to the iron. Moreover, why does the
magnet not also attract certain other solid things, which emit

30   more moisture, among which is bronze? For that from which
there flows the [moisture] that is attracted [by the magnet]
does not follow it because what is attracted *remains* [in the
magnet] on account of its commensurateness, but rather [just]

74,1 because [the moisture] *is attracted*; and it [would be] more
reasonable for those things, the moisture from which does not
remain in what attracts it but is rejected, to be moved more.
For it is likely that more is attracted from these, since [what
attracts] <does not retain>* in itself what is attracted and is
not filled by it as it attracts, but remains like [it was].

    Similarly, it is in general necessary for the person who
5   speaks about this first of all to have enquired what is the
manner of the attraction. For some things attract by force and
contact; and these are moved themselves when they cause
movement. But the magnet does not [attract] in this way, for
it is unmoved. And it neither comes into contact with the iron
nor draws it to itself by means of the intervening air or water,

drawing [them to itself]. For it would attract the things that are on the surface of [the iron] and lighter by drawing the intervening air towards itself, as amber and the cupping-glass do by the hot within themselves. But [the magnet] does not [attract things] in this way.[138] For in those cases the fire, being moved and passing outwards, draws in the adjacent moisture, and, coming into contact, attracts what is adjacent by what it draws in; but the magnet only [attracts] the iron. For if it drew in the intervening air, all the things in the air that are lighter than the iron would be carried towards the magnet before the iron.

The womb, too, seems to attract the seed, and the veins and limbs [seem to attract] the nourishment. But the magnet does not attract the iron in this way. For of these things too those that attract by first drawing in the intervening air and mois- ture do this accidentally. The sun, too, seems[139] not to attract water in the same way as the magnet [attracts the iron]; for being changed by the heat of the sun [the water] is carried up to the natural place for [such] things, which is above, where the sun too is. [But the magnet] does not change the iron.

Nourishment*, too, and everything that is an object of desire and appetite attracts a living creature, not by making what is between itself and the object of appetite like itself (for what is between does not become nourishment,[140] nor is this attracted), but rather, what intervenes is set in motion by the object of appetite and transmits the form to what is set in motion, as occurs in the case of seeing. It is in this way that the iron, too, is carried towards the magnet; [the magnet] does not attract [the iron] to itself forcibly, but rather by desire for that which it lacks itself but the magnet possesses. For the magnet too seems to be iron-like,[141] but to have had its moisture dried out either by time or for some other reason. For it is not only things that possess sensation and soul that have a desire for what is natural to them; this is so with many things that are without soul, too.[142]

10

15

20

25

30

2.24. Explanation of a passage from the second [book] of Aristotle's *On the Soul* stated a little after the beginning: 'We say that one kind of the things[143] that there are is substance, and that of this one [sort we call substance] as matter, which in itself is not a definite something;[144] another is shape and form, according to which [a thing] is now called a definite something; and thirdly there is the product of these.'[145]

75,1

If matter in itself is not a definite something (*tode ti*), but is called 'this' (*tode*) something inasmuch as it receives and possesses shape and form, it is from this form that each of the things that possess matter will [derive] its being [the sort of thing it is]. In the case of the simple and primary bodies[146] their matter is not at all a definite something in itself, because it is prime matter and matter in the proper sense that underlies these proximately. In the case of composite bodies it is no longer prime matter and matter in the proper sense that underlies these proximately; rather, the matter is bodies that underlie these things, if it is the so-called elements that are their matter. So the matter of these things will be a definite something, but what comes to be from them does not derive its being what it has come to be from the matter and from the form of the matter, but rather from the form which has come to be in a certain sort of composition and mixture of the bodies which underlie it.

For it is not the case that, since fire and air, water and earth are the matter of flesh, flesh is and is called flesh as a result of *these*, but [rather] as a result of the form that has come to be in these, according to which the flesh that has come to be from them possesses its being. For those [simple bodies] are not even preserved any more in the flesh in the first place. In the case of the coming-to-be of simple bodies the matter that underlies them – that is, prime matter – was not a definite something in itself, and yet it was in existence, being in relation to some other form and being a definite something in accordance with this; for the fire that comes to be does so in accordance with a change of the matter, which loses the form that existed in it beforehand and changes into the [form] of fire. It is not the case that, because this change is from air, if it so happens, the fire possesses its being in respect of the air, just as the change of

5

10

15

20

matter to fire is not [change of it *qua* air,] either. Similarly composite bodies too, which already possess proximate matter which is a definite something, do not derive *their* being a definite something from some form of the bodies that underlie   25
them, but from that [form] which comes to be from them and out of them.

And for this reason it is universally true that every composite substance derives its being what it is from its form; and this being so it is true that that, in accordance with which each compound[147] substance possesses* its being and its being said [to be what it is], is its form. So, since a living creature is a   30
compound substance, and its being and being said to be a living creature derives from its soul and is in respect of its soul, the soul of living creatures will be their form, and so too with other things possessing soul apart from living creatures.[148]

That the soul is form, [Aristotle] showed using a route like the following. Of substance one [sort] is matter, another form, and another compound; and the compound [substance], which is composed of matter and form, derives its [being] a definite   35
something not from its matter, but from the form that is in it.   76,1
He supposed that natural bodies are substances (for they act, and what is active is substance); and, because [they are] composite substance, when he had distinguished natural body by [whether] it possesses life, he supposed that the natural body which possesses life is a compound substance; not because natural body is not also in itself composite and compound substance, but rather because it is already clear of what this   5
itself is composed, [namely], from a natural body and [from] life, which is the soul. He supposed that the body which possesses life is a compound substance [made up] of matter and form, and showed that the soul is neither a body nor what underlies in the living creature; [and thus] he showed that it is the substance in the sense of form that is the soul. For it must be present in [the living creature] either as form or as matter.   10

2.25. Explanation of another passage from the second [book] of Aristotle's *De anima*.

'The soul is not the essence and account of a body of this sort, but of a natural [body][149] that possesses a principle of move-
15   ment and rest in itself.'[150]
        What is the point of 'that possesses a principle of movement and rest in itself'? If this is what that which is natural is like, how will the divine [body][151] still be natural, since it possesses no principle of rest in itself?
        Or rather:[152] it possesses a principle of rest [in itself] in a way, if, you see, it is moved in respect of its parts, but the whole, *as* a whole, is at rest. For it is always in the same [place].
20   Or rather: he did not speak about every natural body, but about that in which soul comes to be.[153] Or else he says 'that possesses a principle of movement and rest in itself' not about *natural* body [as such], but about [body] that possesses soul. For in these things the soul is the principle of movement and rest.

2.26. Another passage from the same [book].

25   'The seed and the fruit are what is a body of this particular sort in potentiality.'[154]
        The soul can most of all be shown not to be in a substrate[155] by this passage. For if the organic body, in which the soul is, derives its being organic from the soul, and was not organic before it possessed the soul and is not so when the soul has
30   departed, [the soul] will not be in it as in a substrate. But it is not in any other body than this. For the seed is ensouled in potentiality since it is able to come to be a body of this particular sort, of which the soul is the perfection, and which derives from the soul its being what it is.

77,1   **2.27.** Another passage from the same [book].[156]

'Let us speak, then, taking it as the beginning of the consideration of the matter that what possesses soul is distinguished
from what is without soul by the [fact of] being alive.'[157]
        By taking it that the body which possesses soul is a com-

pound substance, and that every compound substance is com- 5
posed of matter and form, [Aristotle] shows* that the body is
not in something that underlies but is itself what underlies. He
gives [his] account of the soul as 'the first actuality of an organic
natural body',[158] since it has not yet been adequately shown
that the soul is a form, because in the account that has been
given there does not even appear the reason why the soul is the
form and actuality of a body of this sort. 10

[Then], resuming again from [what he said] above, he tries
to show this very thing. First of all he sets out the powers of
the soul, and shows[159] that some of them are primary and can
be separated from the others, and that others are secondary.[160]
He shows that there is a certain order among them, and that
things that possess soul derive their being *alive* from the
nutritive soul, but being *a living creature*[161] from the sensory. 15
He also shows that there is a certain order in the case of the
sensory [faculties][162] too, and that some are primary and are
separated from the others, others secondary and inseparable
from those before them.[163] He also enquires whether one must
say that each power of soul [possesses] soul or [only] a part of
soul,[164] and if a part, whether one that can be separated only
in the account [of it] or also in place; and he shows that most
of its powers are separated only in the account; but he says that 20
there is some dispute about intellect. He also says that there
are differences in kind among things possessing soul, in that
some possess all the powers [of soul], others some, and others
only one. And after this he showed how the soul is a form and
an actuality, because, by being something [that is] *of* the body
that underlies, it is similar to it and can be separated from it.[165]

The demonstration is like this: he takes it that, in the case 25
of all things that are said to be such as they are in a primary
and in a secondary way, the respect in which they are said to
be in a primary way is their form, and that in which [they are
said to be] in a secondary way is what underlies and the matter
which comprises that form.[166] And having established this by
induction he also supposes that [creatures] possessing soul are
said to be alive in respect of their soul primarily, <and secon-
darily in respect of the body that> possesses <the soul>*.
<This>* being so the soul has been shown to be the form of the 30
body that possesses it, and the body the matter.[167]

2.28. That matter is not genus.[168]

It is common to genus and matter that they are common to
several things, and that they are by nature primary in relation
to the things that [fall] under them and to which they are
78,1 common, and that they take on differences by the combination
of some species or form (*eidos*)[169] with them. For matter is
common, and the forms that come to be in it make the compound [of form and matter], too, different in accordance with
their own difference from each other; and just so genus is
common, and the species and differences,[170] being combined
with it, produce the difference within genera in accordance
5   with the difference in themselves. For things which are the
same come to be other by combination with things that are
different.

Or rather;[171] the difference of [matter and genus] from one
another is because what is common is not in a similar relation
to the species or forms to which it is common. For matter is
common as underlying the things to which it is common; for it
underlies the forms. But genus is common as being predicated
of the things to which it is common. For forms come to be in
10   matter which underlies, in the way that shapes do in bronze,
but not so are species in the genus; genera are predicated of the
things of which they are genera.

Also matter, taken altogether, is common because it has in
itself all enmattered forms, but each part of it is also itself
common in itself, because it is able to receive all the opposites
15   in turn.[172] Genus however is itself common to its proper species,
but its particular [aspect] is not common; for it is not possible
for the living creature in Socrates to come to be in some other
[living creature].[173]

Also matter is a [real] thing and underlies [by] contributing
to each of [the things it underlies] being a definite something;
but genus taken as genus is not a [real] thing that underlies,
but only a name, and it possesses the [property of] being
20   common in its being thought of, not in some reality.

Also matter is imperishable even individually,[174] but genus
possesses imperishability in kind and by the uninterrupted
succession of the things that come to be,[175] while its particular
[aspect] is perishable.

Also the matter which is one part of the compound being[176] is separated and preserved in the ceasing-to-be of the compound [being]. Genus is present even in simple [beings],[177] for this is what the genera of species and accidents are like; neither qualities nor quantities nor anything besides the genera of substances, is composite and compounded as from form and what underlies [it].[178]* But in compound and enmattered being the genus and what is common are composite, as being composite in it. For just as the particulars in [the genus of] living creature are composite, so too are their species and genera. For 'living creature' indicates a form accompanied by matter, and is not one part of the compound like matter; being for a living creature is itself being [composed] of both [form and matter]. And for this reason it is[179] not separated from matter in a similar way.[180] For it possesses something of the species or form in its proper definition;[181]* and [so] in the ceasing-to-be of the whole [compound being], which comes about in the ceasing-to-be of the form, it too itself ceases to be through its sharing in what is perishable. And for this reason the living creature in Socrates, which is in a way a part of the genus, does not remain when Socrates ceases to be. In this way if all particular living creatures actually ceased to be the living creature which is as a genus, too, would be done away with; but matter is not affected in any such way.[182]

Nor are species or forms in matter and in genus in a similar way. For every form comes to be in matter which exists apart from form as far as its own account is concerned;[183] but in the genus [that] form which is more common [than the particular species], and [which is] in all the species under the genus, is included as something that exists already.[184] And for this reason it is not the case either that every species comes to be in the genus, through the fact that part of it, which exists already, completes the nature of the genus,[185] but the differences which divide what is common in the form are those which are combined with the genus. For this reason the genus is inseparable from the things of which it is the genus and passes away along with them, and it is able to receive not species but a part of species; and it is not even able to receive these as a thing that underlies, but being apprehended by intellect and separated from the things in company with which it possesses

10   its being. Matter [however] is primary in every enmattered
      body. For [matter], which in a way is not in actuality in its own
      right,[186] comes to be a definite something by having received
      the form, and is itself the first principle of the definite some-
      thing and the compound;[187] [but] the genus takes on* its being
      from these enmattered and particular things, on account of the
      separation of the things that indicate and produce the differ-
15   ence in it.[188] Matter is a cause of the being and existence of all
      the things that are subject to coming-to-be and ceasing-to-be;
      genera supervene, in the things which have their being and
      existence on account of matter, as the product of that which
      puts them together through separation in thought from the
      other things which exist along with them.[189]

81,1   **3.1.** What recollection is.[190]

      Recollection is the discovery by searching of an impression
      which once came about in the body in which the soul capable
      of sensation [is].[191]

      3.2. Explanation of a passage from the second book of
5   Aristotle's *On the Soul*, in which he says 'For what pos-
      sesses the understanding comes to be [actually] contem-
      plating, and this is not[192] an alteration; for the progression
      is towards the very thing and towards actuality'.[193]

      Aristotle has spoken in the second [book] *On the Soul* about
      <the activity>* resulting from the disposition, which he called
10   second potentiality; for the first potentiality was suitability for
      taking on the disposition.[194] So he has spoken about it as
      follows: 'For what possesses understanding comes to be [actu-
      ally] contemplating, and this is not[195] an alteration (for the
      progression is towards the very thing and towards actuality),
      or [if it is alteration] it is another kind of alteration. And for
      this reason it is not right to say that what thinks is altered
      when it thinks, just as the builder [is not altered] when he
15   builds. So it is right that what leads to actuality from being
      potentially, in respect of exercising intellect and thinking,[196]
      should be called not "teaching" but by some other name.'
      Well, [Aristotle] having said this, it was enquired in general

by the commentary[197] whether the transition to actuality is a change.[198] For if [it is] not an alteration, much less[199] will it be any of the other [types of] change instead.*[200] For making the transition* from the intellectual disposition[201] to actually exer- 20 cising intellect[202] will not be some sort of alteration, if alteration is transition in respect of an affection, and this is not transition in respect of an affection, if it is progression towards what is the same.[203] And the activity that results from the disposition preserves the disposition and is its completion, if the end for each thing is that for the sake of which it is, and every disposition comes about for the sake of the activity that is in accordance with it.

If the person who is active in this way does not undergo 25 change in the sense of alteration, much less[204] will he do so in respect of place or increase; for it is bodies that [undergo] changes of these sorts. For the activities that result from the dispositions [of possessing] arts, too, come about *through* change, since they need the service of the body, but they themselves*, in so far as they are completions of the dispositions,[205] will not be changes.

Is it then perhaps better to call them comings-to-be of some 30 [sort], since they contribute to the completeness of the beings of which they are? For in* every thing that possesses its being through coming-to-be, the progression to completion is a part 82,1 of its coming-to-be. So in a certain way the transition from the disposition to the activity is a part of the coming-to-be of the art, coming to be through certain changes, since every coming-to-be seems to come about through changes.

But, if one must say this in the case of the arts, should one say this same thing also in the case of [such changes] relating 5 to the theoretical sciences, which are certain activities themselves too? For in the case of these it is much more reasonable that there not be any change. If however one should call these too comings-to-be, and every coming-to-be is through change, through the change of what* things would such coming-to-be come about?

Or rather: it must first become clear to the completion of 10 what thing this sort of activity contributes. <Activities> in respect of the arts <will contribute to the completion>* of the arts and of those that possess them, *qua* artisans. But in the

case of intellect and the virtues and dispositions relating to
theoretical [understanding], it is to the completeness of the
human being [as such] that the activity resulting from these
dispositions will contribute, if at least these dispositions too are
completions of the nature of a human being *qua* human being.
For a human being in the proper sense is one who both pos-
15   sesses the dispositions and is active in accordance with those
in respect of which there belongs to a human being what it is
to be a human being most of all and in the proper sense. So the
[kinds of] teaching which are changes and alterations of the
dispositions, creating those things through which the completion of the human being comes about, will also be causes of the
activities that result from these, if, that is, everything that
possesses a disposition is active in accordance with it at once,
provided that something* does not impede it; [for] the removal
20   of the things that impede the activities* itself comes about*
together with some change.

3.3. Explanation of a passage likewise from the second
[book] *On the Soul*, in which [Aristotle] speaks about
sensation; the passage is this: 'Having made these distinctions, let us speak in general about all sensation.'[206]

Having spoken about the nutritive capacity of the soul he goes
25   on to the discussion of sensation, and first speaks universally
and generally about sensation; he will then go on to speak about
each [type of sensation] individually.[207] Well, he first notes
(416b33) that sensation comes about in the course of something's[208] being changed and affected (for it seems to come
about through some change and affection), and having noted
that sensation comes about through alteration and affection,
he remarked about how affection and being affected come
30   about, that some think that like is affected by like, others that
a thing [is affected] by its opposite. He remarked about this
because, in order to explain what sensation is, it is useful for
him for it to have been laid down by what things that are
affected are affected; for it has been laid down that sensation,
too, is a certain affection and [comes about] through an affection.
      Before discussing this in detail he first (417a2) raised a

difficulty concerning sensation why, if the things sensed are in   35
the sense-organs, sensation does not sense these [the sense-
organs] but only outside objects; and he resolved the difficulty
by the fact that sensation is then [only] potential. For sensation   83,1
is related to what is sensed, and what is sensed by it is what is
separate [from it]. For nothing is affected by itself, and sensation [comes about] through being affected; so as long as the
thing sensed is not present, the sensation is [only] potential.
Noting that 'to sense' is said in two ways, both potentially and
actually, he noted that of sensation one [sort] is potential and   5
the other actual, and similarly with the thing sensed. And
having noted that sensation comes about through being affected, one [sort of it] potentially and the other actually, he next
(417a14) speaks about what that which is affected is affected
by, the [point] he raised a little before.

Having noted that everything that is affected is affected by
that which causes change and is in actuality that which the   10
thing affected by it is able to become, he showed from this that
'there is a way in which' what is affected 'is affected by what is
like [it], and a way in which it is affected by what is unlike [it].
For it is affected [as] being unlike,[209] but when it has been
affected it is like' (417b18-20). This again is useful for him also
in relation to potential sensation, if it comes about through
being affected, being unlike what acts [upon it], that is the
thing sensed, when it is being affected, but like it when it has   15
been affected and has come to be.

Next after this he noted in addition (417b21) that of sensation some is potential and some actual, and makes a distinction
[concerning] the potential and the actual,[210] wishing to show
through [doing so] that it is not in the proper sense that
sensation is called being affected and being changed. For it is
not the case that the progression to actuality of every potentiality [comes about] through affection and change; for 'potentially understanding' is said in two ways, and similarly with   20
everything else. For what possesses a nature [such as] to
receive understanding is potentially understanding; however
what already possesses understanding and has received it, but
is not active[211] in regard to it, is also said to be potentially
understanding. And [Aristotle] showed that these* are not [so]
described in the same way. Having said that the person who

already possesses understanding, but is not active[ly exercis-
25   ing it], is also himself said to be potentially understanding, he
added that the person who is now contemplating and active[ly
exercising his understanding] is the one who is said to be
understanding in the proper sense, no longer being [so] potentially.[212] After this, stating the difference in those who are said
to understand potentially,[213] he showed (417a30) that the first
one said [to have understanding] potentially, the one [so de-
scribed] in respect of his nature, does not make the transition[214]
and become [understanding] in actuality in any other way than
through being affected and altered by learning; while the one
30   who already possesses [understanding] does not also make the
transition to active[ly exercising it] through being affected and
altered.

Having shown that it is not the case that the transition of
everything that is potential to being actual [comes about]
through being affected and altered, he next (417b2) made a
distinction in relation to being altered and affected, and noted
that one [type] is destruction by the opposite and departure
from the [state] the thing was in, which is the way in which all
things that make the transition to [their] opposites are af-
35   fected; the other [type] of being affected he said is not by being
84,1   destroyed, but by being preserved and made to progress in
respect of the way in which a thing [already] is, by that which
is in actuality and like [it]. For activity[215] in respect of [a
thing's] disposition and [its] potentiality of this sort, being the
completion of the disposition, does not come about in respect of
transition to the opposite, but [in respect of transition] of the
same thing from inactivity to activity; what possesses under-
5   standing becomes active in respect of it, which is progression
towards what is the same[216] and alike. And similarly, having
stated how potentiality is related to actuality, he showed how
[this is so], and what sort of potentiality, and related to what
sort of actuality, adding* 'what possesses understanding comes
to be [actually] contemplating' (417b5-6), and this transition is
not an alteration, if alteration is transition from one thing to
another and from an opposite, but [transition] from what is
10   potentially in this way to activity is progression. For this is
[transition] to the very thing it possesses and in the respect in
which it possesses [it].[217] Or rather, if one must call this too

alteration, it will be a second kind and another sort of alteration,[218] – That he took being affected as equivalent to being
altered he showed by saying 'which is not being altered'
(417b6); for he says* this as equivalent to 'which is not being
affected'.

Having shown this he added (417b8) that one must not say
that the person who thinks of something and exercises intellect   15
concerning it is altered, and if not altered, then not changed
either. For if it is not alteration, it is clear that it is not
transition in place or quantity, either. And the progression and
transition of that which is potentially sensing to actually sensing is like this, too. And for this reason sensation is alteration
in the broader sense.

Having said these things he explains after this what sort of
transition from the potential to the actual is alteration, and   20
what not (417b9). That from the disposition to the activity that
is on account of it, as with exercising intellect and thinking*,[219]
since it does not come about through teaching, is not alteration
or change, but a different kind of transition; such a transition
would [fall] under coming-to-be, if [that to which] being completed, and progression towards this, apply [is] in some way a
thing that comes to be.[220] But transition from the material
potentiality to the disposition,[221] which comes about in respect   25
of some teaching and learning, either should not even itself be
said to come about through being affected,[222] if it too is coming
to possess the disposition and completion in actuality, from
[being in] the material potentiality (for in a way such a transition, too, is coming-to-be); or, if someone should call such a
transition, too, alteration, because it is not the taking on of
some natural form, one must say that there are two types of   30
alteration, both that which is towards [possessing] dispositions[223] and towards [a thing's] nature and what is natural [for
it] – at any rate, the better part of the things for which that
which has potential has potential is what is natural for it – and
also a certain [type of alteration] from the better dispositions
themselves to states of privation.[224]

Having said this and drawn [these] distinctions he went on
to sensation, and shows (417b16) what the first potentiality is,
and how, and by the agency of what, the potentiality of this sort   35
makes the transition to the disposition, and how and by the

agency of what the second [potentiality makes the transition]
to activity; and he says that the transition from the material
potentiality to that in accordance with the disposition is
brought about 'by the begetter'[225] – clearly, that is, [what
begets] the living creature; for what is being begotten does not
85,1   yet possess the disposition that is able to sense, but is still [only]
capable of receiving the potential disposition; but when it has
been begotten it at once possesses the disposition that is able
to sense, like that which has received understanding.[226]

Having shown how each of the potentialities applies to
sensation, he added that having sensation 'in actuality is said
in a similar way to contemplating' and exercising intellect
5   (417b18-19). For the activities of sensation and of intellect
differ in this way only: what is heard and what is seen by the
one who senses are outside and not within him, and similarly
with each of the other [objects of sense]. [Aristotle] gave as the
reason for this that sensation apprehends particulars, which*
are not able to be in what senses [them], but have their own
proper existence, while understanding and intellect contem-
10   plate universals, which as universals do not have their own
proper existence, but 'are in a way in the understanding itself'
(417b23)[227] – adding 'in a way', because for these too their
existence and the cause of their being is in the particulars, but
as common[228] they have their being in being thought of, and,
as common, their being is in the intellect which thinks them.[229]
And for this reason exercising intellect is up to us, but sensation
15   is not up to us; for sensation relates to what is present and is
of what is present, but the presence of the things that are
sensed is not up to us so that we can have them when we wish
to.[230] And as sensations are, so are those arts that are concerned
with things that are sensed; for it is not up to those who possess
these [arts] to act when they wish to, for the objects of their
activity need to be present for them.

Passing over saying* more for the moment about the differ-
20   ence between objects of sensation and objects of intellect, he
says that thought depends on us but sensation does not, and,
fitting what has been stated and shown to sensation, he gave
a general account of sensation. He showed first (417b29) that,
since potentiality is said in two senses (for it is in one way that
a child is said to be able to be a general and in another that the

complete[ly grown adult] is; for the latter[231] is not [able to do so] in a similar way to the one who possesses the disposition but is not yet active[ly exercising it]),[232] it is in the second 25 meaning of potentiality that 'potentially perceiving' and 'potential sensation' are meant. He said 'the difference between these potentialities has not been named, but has become clear from [our] account; so it is necessary to use both being affected and being altered as names proper[ly applied]'[233] (418a1-3) to the transition from potential sensation to the actuality, since we do not have any other proper names for them; and so he went 30 on to give an account of sensation, and said that 'what possesses sensation potentially' is 'like what the thing sensed already is in actuality' (418a3-4), because [what possesses sensation potentially] 'is affected' by the thing sensed, not yet 'being like' it, and having been affected 'It has been made alike and is like it' (418a4-5); and he said 'what is affected' as if it were* equivalent to 'what is altered'. And having given this account, not as an account of sensation strictly,[234] but with regard to the lack of 35 proper terms (for it has been shown, that the transition to 86,1 actuality of what is potential in this way is not being affected or alteration or change), he went on to speak individually about each [type of] sensation.

The chief points of what has been said. First [Aristotle] noted (416b33) that sensation is [a matter of] being changed and 5 being affected. After this he enquired (416b35), being affected in what way, whether it is possible for something also to be affected by what is like [it]. After this he raised (417a2) the difficulty why there is not sensation in a similar way of the sense organs themselves, since they are able to be sensed; and to resolve the difficulty he noted that sensation is then* potential, and that on account of this it needs, for actuality, the presence of the things sensed which are able to act [upon it].[235] After this he noted that 'sensation [is spoken of] in two ways, 10 one sort potential, the other actual' (417a9); and after this he said that one must still say, if the distinction has not yet been made, how being changed and being affected differ from being actual, if being changed and being affected apply to what is changed, seeing that change too is said to be a sort of actuality.[236] After this he noted (417a7) the point that everything that is affected is affected* and changed by what acts and is in

15 actuality what the thing that is affected is able to become; and
for this reason when it is being affected it is unlike, since
everything that is affected is unlike, but when it has been
affected it is alike, since sensation [includes] both the potentiality and the actuality. And he showed (417a21) that what is
potential is twofold, and that the transition to actuality for
what is potential is not in every case through alteration.[237]

After this he made a distinction [between ways] of being
altered; this is [what is] indicated by 'being affected' (417b2).
20 For one [type][238] of being affected comes about in the course of
destruction, which is brought about by what is opposite; the
other [type] of being affected is said of what is preserved and
progresses to its own completion by [the agency of] what is like
it. For the activity [which comes] from the disposition is in a
way like the disposition from which it comes, and being affected
thus will not be alteration.[239] After this he showed that the
transition, in accordance with the potentiality for sensation, to
25 actual [sensation] is not the same as that which comes about
through alteration. Nor is what senses affected in the same way
as things that are being destroyed, but rather as what is
progressing towards its [own full realisation].[240] And, having
defined the completion, he said (418a1) that one must use
common terms in the account of sensation, since we do not have
proper [terms] for what is meant.[241] He [then] gave an account
of it and said (418a3) that what is able to sense is potentially
30 what the thing sensed is in actuality, and that it is [by the
sense-organ being] affected by [the thing sensed]* and through
something else, not indeed* in the way in which he previously
said, that sensation in actuality comes about; he had already
said how one must understand being affected and being
altered in the case of the transition from potential sensation
to the actuality.[242] The account of sensation that has been
given is that what is able to sense is potentially like what the
35 thing sensed already is in actuality; when it is being affected
by it, it is not yet like [it], but when it has been affected it is
like [it].

3.4. How it is not the case that both the approach and the   87,1
receding of the sun are alike causes of coming-to-be and
passing away. For the coming-to-be of one thing is the
passing away of another.[243]

If there is coming-to-be when the sun approaches near, and
passing-away when it recedes further away,[244] and the passing
away of one thing is the coming-to-be of another, how is it not   5
the cause of coming-to-be and of passing away simultaneously,
both as it approaches and as it recedes, if it must be both that
things that come to be do so from the passing away of some
other things, and that things that pass away change into the
coming-to-be of other things? But in this way its approach
would in no way differ any longer from its receding.

<Or rather>: of things that come to be some are primary,
others secondary and subordinate contraries to those that come
to be primarily. So the coming-to-be of the primary things in   10
the proper sense will be that which* comes about when the sun
approaches each [region];[245] and since the coming-to-be of some
things is the passing away of others, the things that are
opposite to those that primarily come to be will [then] pass
away. The passing away of the primary things, which is also
passing away in the proper sense, and coming-to-be of the
things opposed to these, which is not coming-to-be in the proper
sense, [will come about when the sun] recedes further away –
if, that is, the comings-to-be and passings away come about in   15
accordance with nature, [with] no cause opposing and resisting
[them]; but in such anomalous [situations] they might sometimes come to be in the reverse way, too.[246]

For coming-to-be and passing away are applied in the proper
sense to the things that come to be primarily, that is the better
of the things that come to be from each other in respect of a
contrast.[247] And the comings-to-be and passings away of these
things, coming about in accordance with the yearly cycle of the   20
sun, clearly come about for the things which it approaches
when it approaches them; but when it recedes they pass away
and die.

3.5. That coming to be of necessity without qualification, and not conditionally, is in the things that come to be always, in a cycle.[248]

25   Aristotle taught in *On Coming-to-Be and Passing Away* 2[.11, 338a4-b5] that the coming to be of some things of necessity without qualification is true only in the case of those things that come to be in a cycle and follow the revolution of the divine [i.e. heavenly] bodies. For since what is of necessity is always (for 'of necessity' indicates what is everlasting), those things will also be of necessity which, coming to be, do so necessarily and always. If those things come to be <always>* that come to be again and again, and these are those which come round in
30   a cycle, these then will also come to be of necessity.

For that none of the things which come to be in a straight line – and these are those which do not come to be again and again, – that none of the things that come to be in this way does so of necessity, he showed as follows. Either [1a] some one of
88,1   the things that come to be in a straight line comes to be to infinity, so that some addition to it is always coming to be, and it never ceases from coming to be, having been completed; or [1b] it comes to be to infinity in this way, that one thing comes to be from another and this never stops; or [2] it reaches a limit and at some time ceases from coming to be. But neither in the
5   case of those of the things that come to be in a straight line that come to be to infinity [1a and 1b] is it possible for <anything>* to come to be of necessity without qualification, nor in those [2] which have a limit; because* what comes to be of necessity comes to be in this way either [i] because* having come to be* it remains everlasting thereafter,[249] or [ii] because it is always coming to be. But none of the things that come to be is either [i] able to remain everlasting when it has come to be, or [ii] comes to be to infinity. For all coming-to-be is limited, and after,
10   having come to be, it has passed away, [a thing] no longer returns or comes to be again. For this was the sort of thing that was [meant by] 'in a straight line'; so that it is not possible to say that any of the things that come to be in a straight line in a limited way comes to be of necessity.

For the things that come to be are the individuals, Socrates, Plato, this horse; and it is not possible for <any>* of them to return again and come to be again. For if any of them did come to be of necessity, 'if what is first, [then] what is later', too,[250] would be true of them; but as it is it is not so.[251] For such things remain everlasting as regards the species, which is not a thing that came to be, but the enquiry was about things which do come to be. And even if human beings do come to be always and do not cease, and the coming-to-be of these too is in a cycle, they will come to be of necessity *qua* human beings, <not>*[252] *qua*, in this case, Plato, in that, Socrates. – Or rather, their coming-to-be is in a straight line to infinity, different [individuals] coming to be at different times, and never still the same one.

And for this reason in this case <*this*>* consequence is sound, 'if what is later, of necessity also what is first'; <but> even if coming-to-be in a straight line [goes on] to infinity, it is not possible for anything to come to be of necessity [in such a case, and this Aristotle] showed through the fact that, in the case of things that come to be of necessity, not only [i] the consequence 'if what is later, [then] also what is first' is true (for *this* is true also in the case of the things that come to be contingently); but [ii], in the case of those things where one of the things that are later comes to be of necessity without qualification, in the case of these 'if what is first, [then] what is later' is true also.

For, from the facts [A] that what is later comes to be of necessity, and [B] that 'if what is later, [then] it is necessary also that what is first come to be' is true of *all* the things that come to be, it follows that [C] it is necessary that, in the case of those things of which the later comes to be of necessity, the first too comes to be of necessity. But in the case of that which comes to be to infinity there is nothing that is later* of which it is true that it will be of necessity without qualification; and, in the case of those things where what is later is not of necessity without qualification, it is not possible to say that what precedes what is later, either, will be of necessity without qualification. For the things that precede what is later derive their necessity from what is later, when that comes to be of necessity; but if there is nothing that is later[253] in the case of things that come to be in this way*, neither will any of the things that come to be first among them come to be of necessity. But conditional necessity will be true of them, that 'if what is later, [then] of necessity what is first as compared to it* will also be'.

Someone might raise the difficulty whether the consequence 'if what is first, [then] also what is later' is true of the things that come to be in a cycle and return again. Well, this conse-
5 quence *is* true of the things that are brought about in a determinate fashion by the [bodies] that move in a circle.[254] If the winter solstice, [then] also the [spring] equinox, and if the [spring] equinox, [then] also the summer solstice, and if the summer solstice, [then] also the [autumn] equinox, and if this, the winter solstice; and <also>, if winter, [then] also spring, and if spring, summer, and if summer, autumn, and if autumn, winter again*. And* in the case of the things mentioned first [i.e. the solstices and equinoxes] the ordered-sequence is deter-
10 minate and permanent and is never retarded or advanced, because the sole cause of the being and ordered-sequence of these things is the movement of the primary [i.e. heavenly] bodies, nothing else contributing towards it; and for this reason it is possible in the case of these things to determine the time, too, and say [not only that they will be of necessity, but] *when* they will be of necessity. But* summers and autumns and winters no longer possess determinacy in a similar way, although they come to be in a cycle and they too themselves follow
15 on the motion of the eternal [bodies], because matter too contributes to their coming to be, being affected by the movements of [the eternal bodies]; and since [matter] does not in every respect, in the way in which it is affected, follow the movements and revolutions of [the eternal bodies] in a similar way, [for this reason the seasons] are not determined in the individual [details of the way in which and time at which they come to be] in the same way [as are the solstices and equinoxes].[255]

And indeterminacy is still more [present] in those things that need more things to contribute to their being;[256] and
20 among these is the coming-to-be of living creatures. And for this reason it is true of them, [speaking] generally, that each of them is everlasting as regards the species (and the cause of this [eternity] is the revolution of the divine [bodies]);[257] but [as for] the coming-to-be of individuals, in the case of which the cause from the proximate efficient [factors][258] has the greatest influence, of these 'if what is first, [then] of necessity what is later' is not true, but 'if what is later, [then] of necessity what precedes it' is true.

3.6. Explanation of a passage from the third [book] of   25
Aristotle's *On the Soul*, in which he showed that there are
not more than the five senses.[259]

'If we now possess sensation of everything of which the sensation is touch (for all the affections of the tangible *qua* tangible
are sensible to us by touch); and [if] it is necessary that, if some
sense is lacking, then some instrument of sensation[260] is lack-   30
ing to us as well; and as many things as we sense by touching
them ourselves[261] are sensible by touch, which we do as it
happens possess, while all those [that we sense] through intermediaries, and not touching them themselves, [we sense] by
the simple [bodies], I mean, that is,[262] by air and water ...' up
to 'nor is there any other body and affection, which does not   90,1
belong to any of the bodies here;[263] [so] no sense is lacking'.[264]

It seems to me that the point of what is said, if one condenses
it into the principal propositions of the arguments, is like this.
[1] Of all the things for which we possess the instruments of
sensation, we also possess sensation. [2] If there are some   5
things of which we do not possess sensation, it is through not
possessing the instruments of sensation for these that we do
not sense them. [Aristotle] said [1] – from 'Of all the things for
which we possess' up to* 'we also have sensation' (= 90,4-5)[265]
– by 'if we now possess sensation of everything of which the
sensation is touch; for all the affections of the tangible *qua*
tangible are sensible to us by touch' (424b24-6). For having
spoken about touch he omitted to add 'and in the case of the   10
other instruments of sensation and senses'; if these are all
taken [into account], 'if we possess sensation of all the things
for which we possess the instruments of sensation' becomes
universal.

Again, he said [2] 'If there are some things of which we do
not possess sensation, it is through not possessing the instruments of sensation for them that we do not sense them' (=
90,5-6) again through the [continuation of the] same [sentence],
'and it is necessary, if some sense is lacking, for some instrument of sensation to be lacking to us as well' (424b26-7) – since   15
[this] is* a conditional and he potentially takes in addition the
opposite of the consequent in what has been supposed, namely,

'but no instrument of sensation is lacking to us'. [For] when this
has been shown, it follows that no sense is lacking to us either.
    I say 'potentially', because he does not take this in addition
straightaway, but, after considering what instruments of sensation we possess, and showing that it is not possible for there

20   to be more instruments of sensation than these, he [then] shows
that no instrument of sensation is lacking to us. He considers
what senses we possess in the following [remarks]: 'and as
many things as we sense by ourselves touching them are
sensible by touch, which we do as it happens possess, while all
those [that we sense] through intermediaries, and not touching
them themselves, [we sense] by the simple [bodies], I mean,
that is, by air and water' (424b27-30). For by these [remarks]
he noted that we possess the instrument of sensation of touch,

25   and in addition to this that the sensation of the things that we
sense through some intermediary comes about by means of the
simple bodies from which the instruments of sensation [that]
we possess [are composed, that is] from water and air.
    The next point after this is to show that, of the simple bodies,
it is from these two only that instruments of sensation can be
[composed], and that from fire and earth it is not possible for
there to be a instrument of sensation. For when this has been
shown it has come to be shown that no instrument of sensation

30   is lacking to us. But [Aristotle] shows this later; first he notes
in addition that the instruments of sensation are of three
[kinds], touch and those from the simple [bodies], that from
water and that from air; but the kinds of things that can be
sensed are more [in number], if some can be seen, some heard,
some smelled, some tasted and some touched. That the instruments of sensation are not equal in number to the things that

35   can be sensed he shows by: 'and things are such that if through
one [instrument of sensation] several things can be sensed that
are different in kind from one another, it is necessary for what
possesses this type of instrument of sensation to be able to
sense both of them' (424b31-3). For on account of this it is
possible to conclude that, if there are certain things that can
be sensed, differing from one another in kind, that come to be
able to be sensed through some one instrument of sensation,
[then] what possesses this one instrument of sensation senses

91,1   both the [types of] things that can be sensed that are different in kind. For it is not the case that, since there are two things that can be sensed that are different in kind, those that can be heard and those that can be smelled, [for this reason] the instruments through which they can be sensed, too, must be different; for both are apprehended by means of air. So [the one who] possesses this will apprehend both of them through this. Again, suppose there are several instruments of sensation 5 through which it is possible to sense one thing; this seems to be the case with things which can be smelled, for it seems that sensation of these comes about both through water and through air. For it seems that [creatures] that live in water apprehend smell through water, but those that respire [do so] through air. For it is through these that everything that possesses only one of these [instruments of sensation] will sense [things that can be smelled]; there is no need for what is going to sense smell to 10 possess both.[266]

Having made noted these [points] and having removed, through them, the necessity for there to be five instruments of sensation because this is the number of differences by kind of things that can be sensed, he next (425a3ff.) shows that it is not possible for there to be an instrument of sensation [composed] of any other of the simple bodies than of water and air; of these we possess the pupil [of our eye], through which we sense things that can be seen, [composed] of water, our hearing of air, and the sense of smell we and creatures that do not [live] 15 in water [have composed] of air, but creatures that [live] in water, of water. It is not possible for an instrument of sensation to be [composed] of fire, as [Aristotle] will show in *On Sensation and things sensed*,[267] nor of earth alone. But if this is so, it is not possible for there to be any other instrument of sensation besides those which perfect living creatures[268] possess. [So] no instrument of sensation is lacking to [creatures] that possess the five senses; and so no sense [is], either. 20

For it is not possible for there to be any simple body capable of being affected besides the four, so that there could be some instrument of sensation from this. For the instrument of sensation needs to be affected in some way by the thing sensed, and for this reason to be [composed] of a body that can be affected; and it has been shown that the fifth body cannot be affected.[269]

3.7. Explanation of another passage from the third [book]
of [Aristotle's] *On the Soul*, in which he enquires how
self-awareness comes about for us when we sense
[things].[270]

'Since we sense that we see and hear, necessarily it is either by
sight that [a person] senses that he sees, or by another
[sense].'[271]

[Aristotle] enquires how self-awareness comes about for us
when we sense certain things, and by what. We sense that we
ourselves are sensing [things]. For to everyone who senses
something there comes about, in addition to the apprehension
of the thing that he is sensing, also a certain self-awareness of
[the fact] that he *is* sensing. Does this self-awareness come
about for us through the same sense as the apprehension of the
thing sensed, so that it is by sight that we both see the things
we see and sense that we ourselves are seeing, or is it that we
sense the objects of sight by sight, but the [fact of] seeing itself
by some other [sense]?

That it is not by another [sense], [Aristotle] showed (*DA* 3.2,
425b13-17) through the fact that there would be several senses
[relating] to the same thing sensed. For if there is going to be
some other [sense] by which we sense [our] seeing, and not the
same sight by which we see, [then] the [sense] which senses the
seeing will simultaneously also sense colours. For the [sense]
that senses the activity that is concerned with the things
sensed will also sense the things with which the activity of
seeing is concerned, and these are the colours. For seeing is
nothing other than activity with sight concerning the objects of
sight; so the sensation [which senses] the seeing is sensation of
the activity concerning the objects of sight brought about by
the sense of sight. And it is not possible to sense the activity
concerned with certain particular things without also sensing
the things with which the activity is concerned.

But if so, there will be several senses of the things sensed,[272]
those which sense them primarily and those which sense the
activities of the senses concerning the things sensed. It is
absurd however to say that the peculiar things sensed by each
sense are capable of being sensed by several senses. Moreover,
if [the sense] that senses and that according to which we sense

that we are sensing are different, this will go on to infinity. For   15
it is through another sense again that we will have self-awareness also of the sensation that we are seeing, and this again
will have another [sense] sensing that, by sensing which it
[itself] creates self-awareness,[273] and this will go on to infinity;
and this is most absurd. So what is left is that it is by the same
[sense] that we sense both the things sensed and our own
activity concerned with the things sensed.   20

But if seeing is the activity of the power of sight, sight will
apprehend both colours and seeing itself. If however that which
sight is able to sense is necessarily coloured, seeing too, if it is
something that can be seen, will be coloured.

Resolving the first difficulty [Aristotle] first (3.2, 425b20-2)
made use of [the fact] that sight is able to sense not only colours
and coloured things, but also the privation of them. For it was   25
shown that every sense itself also senses the privation of its
objects; at any rate, it is by sight that we sense both light and
darkness. Secondly he noted (425b22-4) that seeing too is in a
way coloured, if seeing comes about when the sense-organ
receives the form of the thing sensed without the matter that
underlies it; as a sign of this he mentions that often, when the   30
things seen have departed, there still remain behind in the
senses certain sensations and images of them.

Having said these things to resolve the difficulties that had
been raised, in what [comes] next he shows that, and how,
[self-awareness] comes about. He says (425b26ff.) that the
actuality[274] of the thing sensed and of the sense are one,
differing only in their account, since the being of sensation in
actuality consists in *possessing* the form of the thing sensed   35
without its matter, while that of the thing that is sensed in   93,1
actuality [consists in] its form *being possessed* without its
matter [by the thing sensing it]. For if the change[275] that is
brought about by what causes change is in the thing that is
changed, and the affection that is brought about by the agent
is in what is acted upon and affected, it is necessary that the
change [brought about] by the object of sense, too, and the
affection brought about by it, produce sensation in actuality   5
when they come to be in what is potentially sensation. For as
the action and the being affected are in the thing affected and
not in the agent (for [in that case] the agent would be affected,

and acting and being affected would be the same, as [Aristotle] showed in the lectures on *Physics*),[276] so too with the [action] of what is sensed and the [being affected] of what is able to sense.

10   [Since] these things are in this way, and sensation in actuality comes about by the reception of sensed forms without their matter, it is reasonable that, simultaneously with sensation of the things sensed, we also come to have self-awareness that we are sensing [them, and do so] in respect of the same sense. For it is by receiving the form from the things sensed, which are outside, that we apprehend them, but it is by the sense having the form of the things sensed in itself, and [its] having sensa-

15   tion on account of this, and in a way *of* this, that self-awareness [comes about].

For if seeing comes about by the reception of the form of the thing sensed, and a similar account also applies to the other senses, it is by receiving the form that [sight][277] sees, and simultaneously comes to see itself seeing. The self-awareness of sensation comes about in sensation's simultaneously sensing both the thing sensed and its own proper activity in relation to

20   the thing sensed. And for this reason it follows necessarily, for everything that has sensation, that it is also self-aware of itself sensing; for it follows, for the sensation that senses some one of the outside things sensed, that simultaneously it also senses itself.

3.8. Whether that which is capable of being sensed by all the senses *per accidens*, is capable of being sensed.[278]

25   That which possesses as an accident of itself some one of the things properly capable of being sensed by a sense is capable of being sensed *per accidens* by [that] single sense; for it is through the apprehension of what can be sensed that there also comes about that of what is [capable of being sensed] *per accidens*. For in this way sight is of what is sweet because it belongs *per accidens* to what is pale yellow to be both sweet and honey.[279] If someone were to say that there is something that is capable of being sensed *per accidens* by all the senses, this

30   person would be saying that that which he says can be sensed *per accidens* by all the senses possesses certain accidents such that one can be sensed *per se* by touch, another by taste, another

by smell, another by hearing, another by sight; so that what
can be sensed by all[280] *per accidens* will be capable of being
sensed by all *per accidens* through there being something in
this same thing being capable of being sensed by each [sense][281]
per se, each itself sensing it through what is properly capable
of being sensed by itself.

For it is not the case that what is capable of being sensed by
all the [senses] *per accidens* is not capable of being sensed at
all, as it might seem to someone who understood the expression
without qualification. For what is not capable of being sensed
by any sense is incapable of being sensed; and what is incapable
of being sensed by all [the senses][282] is not the same as what is
capable of being sensed by all [the senses] *per accidens*, because* what underlies the things that can be sensed by all the
senses is a thing that can be sensed in this way.[283] For it is
because its accidents are capable of being sensed by all [the
senses], while it itself is not, that it comes to be capable of being
sensed *per accidens* by all [the senses].

3.9. Explanation of a passage from the third [book] *On the*   10
Soul, through which Aristotle shows that there is something with which we sense everything simultaneously.[284]

'Is it then the case that what judges is simultaneous, and
indivisible in number and inseparable, but separate in its
being? There is a way in which it is as divisible that it senses
things that are divided, but there is a way in which [it does so]
as indivisible. For it is divisible in its being, but in place and   15
in number it is indivisible. Or is this not possible? For potentially opposites are the same thing and indivisible, but in being
they are not [so]; rather they are divisible by being actualised,
and it is not possible to be white and black simultaneously, and
so not [possible] to be affected [simultaneously] by[285] the forms
of these either, if sensation and intellect are like this; rather,
[what judges] is divisible[286] in the same way as the point which   20
some people call either one or two.[287] So in the respect in which
it is indivisible, what judges is single and simultaneous; in the
respect in which it is divisible, it makes use of the same point
twice simultaneously. So in the respect in which it makes use
of the terminus [as] two*, it judges two [things] that are

separated, [and judges them] in a way by what is separated*;[288] but in the respect in which [it judges] one thing, it judges by one thing and simultaneously' (Aristotle, *DA* 3.2, 427a2-14).

25   [Aristotle] has noted (426b8-15) that each sense is in the sense-organ, being in which it senses, and that it senses the things that can be sensed by itself and judges their differences from one another. For sight [senses and judges] white and black, taste sweet and bitter, and similarly each of the others. Through this he has established that what senses certain things also judges their differences; for it does not belong to one

30   [sense] to sense certain things and to another to judge the differences between them according to which they can be sensed; but the [sense] that senses certain things also judges them, and that which judges their differences also senses them.

95,1   For to judge is the same as to sense; and for this reason sensation, too, seems to be a sort of judging.

          [He then] (426b17-23) discovered something that judges not only the differences between things that can be sensed that are opposite to one another, but also [those] of all things that can be sensed. For we also judge the differences in things that can be seen in relation to those of things that can be tasted, and similarly in relation to those of things that can be heard, and

5   also in relation to those of things that can be smelled and those of things that can be touched. He first noted that we judge these things by sensation (for they can be sensed, and we make our judgement of them as of things that can be sensed); and after this he showed that it is not possible to judge the differences in things that can be sensed if what senses them is not one and the same thing. For it is not possible for what does not sense all [of them] to judge their differences in relation to one an-

10   other; for if one thing senses one thing and another another, it is not possible for either of them to be aware by what it is that the things they sense differ from one another. And judging, for sensation, is not in anything other than in sensing.

          From these [considerations] he inferred that there is one thing which senses all things that can be sensed and judges their differences; and next (426b23-9) he showed too that, if it

15   senses them at the same time and simultaneously, when it judges their differences (if it senses [them] at the time when it judges them, and simultaneously judges their differences in

relation to one another), it will also simultaneously sense the things that are judged; for judgement, for sensation, is in sensing.

Having noted these [points], that there is a single sense by which we sense everything, and that it senses simultaneously those things of which it simultaneously judges the differences, after this he raised the difficulty (426b29-427a1) how, if sens-   20
ing in actuality is receiving the form of the thing that can be sensed, apart from the matter, it is possible for what is one single thing simultaneously to sense several things and things that are opposite [to one another]. For if so, it will have simultaneously to admit opposed forms and affections, white-ness and blackness when it senses and judges these, sweetness and bitterness, and similarly the rest. But it is impossible for   25
the same thing to be changed simultaneously in opposite changes, changing to whiteness and to blackness simultane-ously, and to be admitting things that are opposites.

Having shown these things and raised this difficulty, he resolved the difficulty (427a2-5), noting that what judges judges and senses several things simultaneously, being one and not divided, but separated according to the account [given of each aspect]. For as one single thing it is able to admit of one thing according to one capacity, and what is opposite or differ-   30
ent from this according to another, being indivisible in place and in number, that is in its substrate. For what is indivisible in place is what is a single thing in place, and of this sort is what is continuous and undivided, which is also one in number.

But having said this as if to resolve the difficulty raised he added 'or is this not possible' (427a5-6), showing that the difficulty raised is not resolved by this. For what is one single   35
thing in number can differ in the account [given of it] by having differing capacities, in respect of which it is able to admit of opposites; but not by possessing the capacities for opposites in such a way as to be able to admit them simultaneously. For what possesses capacities for opposites is not able to possess   96,1
them in such a way as also to admit their actualities simulta-neously;[289] it is necessary for it to be divided in respect of the actualities, so that one of them comes to be at one time and the other at another. But sensation [as we saw] judged their differences simultaneously, since it senses them and receives   5

their forms simultaneously, if sensing consists in the reception of the forms of things that can be sensed. And since intellect too seems to come about by the reception of the form of the thing that is the object of intellect, for this reason he says 'if sensation and intellect are like this'.

He said this and showed that the difficulty that was raised still remains, as not being able to be resolved; [then] resolving*
10   it he added, as I said before*, 'but it is divisible in the same way as the point which some people call either one or two' (427a9-11),[290] and the other things that follow these; this passage is expressed very obscurely and concisely, but what it means is like this. It requires that that by which living creatures have sensation of things that can be sensed should be such that it can simultaneously be one and many, in the way that a point, too, [is simultaneously one and many], when it is taken as the
15   terminus of many lines. For the straight (lines) drawn from the circumference of a circle to the centre all have the centre of the circle as their terminus, a single point; and this point, being one, is also in a way many, when it is taken as the terminus of each of the lines drawn from it. For if sensation is something like this, [then] in so far as it is one and indivisible, what judges will be one, though it simultaneously judges what is at the
20   termini of the lines since all the termini are together and are a single thing; but in so far as it is taken as the terminus of this [line], and then this, and it is taken as many times as [there are] straight [lines], [in this respect] it is many. And in this respect, again, in so far as there are many termini and [they belong] to different lines, the things that are judged will be many and separated and different; and in a way what judges* will be
25   separated in the way in which the centre was in a way many, and each of these [things that judge] judges the affection on its own particular line. But in so far as what is [formed] from them all is one and undifferentiated and in every way the same, what judges will itself be one thing and will judge [the different aspects] simultaneously. And what has been said to resolve the difficulties that have been raised is like this.

But what is it possible to grasp that is like this in the case of sensation, so as to be one and many simultaneously, in a
30   similar way to the centre of the circle that is taken as the terminus of the many straight lines, it is not easy to discover.

For the ultimate sense-organ, in which the affections of the sensible things come to be, is a body, and it is not possible for the affections from the five organs of sense to be transmitted to it as along lines and to impinge on the same part of the body. For, again, affections that are opposite and opposite changes would come to be in the same thing, if it is through such a change that sensations in actuality [come about]. For the affections that are transmitted to [the common sense] from a single sense-organ cannot come to be in the same part of it simultaneously*, if the sense-organs for opposites are the same, but it is impossible for affections from opposites to come to be simultaneously in the same part of the same sense-organ. For when we look simultaneously at a white and a black thing, [considering] in which part of the pupil the appearance of each of them comes to be, [then], as we see happening also in the case of mirrors, <they do not appear simultaneously in the same parts>*, nor is it possible for these [impressions] to be transmitted to that to which they are transmitted, which is as I said the ultimate sense-organ, in such a way as not to come to be in separated parts of it. So in the case of body it is impossible to grasp anything similar to the image of the point and the lines of which the point is the terminus.

Perhaps it might be able to fit rather the capacity of that body which we call the ultimate sense-organ, [the body] of which the capacity of sensation is the form; this capacity senses and judges the things that come about in that body, of which it is the form and capacity, according to the transmission from the sense-organs. For this capacity is single and, as it were, the terminus of this body of which it is the capacity, since it is to this that the changes are conveyed as their ultimate [destination]. [The capacity,] being incorporeal and indivisible and similar in every way, as being single, in a way becomes many [capacities], since it senses similarly the changes in each part of the body of which it is the capacity, whether the change comes about in it in some one part or in several. For in the judgement of several [parts] the single [capacity] in a way becomes several capacities, since it is taken as the proper terminus of each part.

For the body was not able simultaneously to admit several affections in the same respect, since it is impossible for oppo-

35

97,1

5

10

15

20

sites to come to be in the same thing simultaneously and in the same respect; and the form of white and that of black are opposites. For this reason it is not possible for any body to admit these simultaneously, but in the case of that sense-organ certain of the things that can be sensed that impinge simultaneously come to be in one part of it, and others of the things that

25 are conveyed to it from the initial sense organs in this* way [come to be] in another [part of it]. But the capacity of sensation is not itself prevented from making judgement of them simultaneously, since judging is not the same as being affected. For it is impossible for the same thing to be affected in opposite ways simultaneously, because it is impossible for anything to admit opposites simultaneously, since opposites cannot exist together; but nothing is unable to *judge* opposites simultaneously, because to judge that what is white is white and [to

30 judge] that what is black is black are not opposites in judgement.[291]

For in being affected the opposite is to be affected in opposite ways in the same part and at the same time, and for this reason this is impossible in being affected. In this way in judgement it is impossible to suppose that what is white is white and black together; and for this reason, again, in judgement what is like this cannot exist together.[292] But to say that black is black and

35 white is white is not impossible, because it is not even opposite.

For if it were necessary that the forms of the things that can be sensed should first come to be also in the capacity that judges

98,1 the things that can be sensed, this too itself* would not judge opposites, because it would not be possible for it to admit opposites simultaneously. But, while the affections come about in the sense-organ, the judgement of the things that come to be in this [takes place] in the capacity; for it is not possible for this too to admit the affections which are corporeal, since it is incorporeal. So the capacity of the entire [sense-organ] is not

5 at all prevented from simultaneously judging the things that come about in different parts of the sense-organ. For sensation is judgement, by the capacity of sensation, of what can be sensed; [it takes place] through the affections brought about in the sense-organ through [the objects of sense], and in this way one and the same capacity in a way becomes many simultaneously, through simultaneously making a judgement of the

affections that can be sensed* that come about in each part of   10
the sense organ. For the capacity that judges the affection that
comes about in some one part of the sense-organ also itself
judges the affections that come about simultaneously in *all*
parts of it; the same [capacity] in a way comes to be both one
and many according to the division of the parts of the sense-
organ as it is affected, in the way in which the point, too, which
was single, came to be many, being divided according to the
plurality of the lines of each of which it is the terminus.   15

3.10. About the sea, from the *Meteorology*.[293]

Having proposed in the second [book] of the *Meteorology* to
speak about the sea, 'what its nature is and on account of what
reason there is so great a quantity of salt water' (2.1, 353a32-3),
he first cites the established opinions about it. Of these that of   20
the mythographers stated that the sea possesses its own proper
springs (353a34-b5).[294] Of the natural philosophers, some said
that it came to be from the great amount of moisture that was
drawn up around the earth by the movement and heat from*
the sun, that part being left behind which we call sea (353b5-
11).[295] Others say that when the earth was heated by the
movement of the sun that water which is called sea was   25
separated out as sweat; and on account of this the water is
salty, too, because sweat is (353b11-13).[296] Others make the
earth and its quality the reason for the saltiness. For the water,
flowing through it, takes on such flavours as are possessed by
the earth through which it travels and percolates (353b13-
16).[297]

After this [Aristotle] shows (353b17-354a34) that the sea
does not possess its own proper springs, because all water from
springs, if it [issues forth] spontaneously, flows away from the   30
springs from which it starts and is removed [from them]; as
much as does not flow away is artificial and not itself [298] natural
(for wells are like this), but the sea is neither among artificial
[waters] nor among those that travel and are removed.[299] For
throughout the sea some movements and mutual replacements
come about when the same water flows this way and that; that   35
this comes about in all [parts of] the sea becomes apparent to
us in straits, because in such places its flow this way and that   99,1

becomes apparent, [being] alongside the land. And if any movement of [the sea] comes about in which it travels from the
higher to the more hollow [places], it is not from its own proper
springs but [is caused by] the influx of the rivers which flow
into [it] from the higher [places] whence they have their
5   springs. So a movement of this sort does indeed have its origin
from springs, but not those of the sea, rather those of the rivers
that flow into it.

    After this [Aristotle] showed (2.2, 354b2ff.) that the sea is
not the origin of water [in general] and [so] the fourth element,
as some had supposed who said that the rivers did not only
travel into the sea but also from the sea,[300] and had sweet water
10   because [this water] came from the earth being percolated
[through it].[301] After this he showed that the water which
<percolates*> through the earth is not salty by its own nature,
and gave the reason for the saltiness,[302] since (2.3, 357a5-15)
it does not come about through*[303] the finest and sweetest part
of the water which surrounds and is extended around the earth
being drawn up in an exhalation each day by the movement of
15   the sun, being vaporised because, being lighter and more pure,
it is on the surface; and, this being continuously drawn up, and
in turn changing and being carried down [as rain], the salty
[part] being left behind, on account of its heaviness, in the
proper place of water.

    After this he raised the difficulty, whence is the origin and
reason for the saltiness that there is in the water of* the sea,
and he showed that all water that comes to be salty from what
is not like this[304] does so by the admixture of something (358a3-
20   14). For it is on account of this* that what collects in the bladder
of living creatures is like this [i.e. salty] in flavour; for it seems
that something earthy is mixed with it, which becomes clear
when it settles out in it. Sweat, too, has [something] like this
mixed in it, which the water that is drunk collects from the
body, percolating through it and as it were washing and puri-
fying it. And [water] that has percolated through ash, too, is
25   like this. What is mixed with these and is the cause of the
same[305] property [in each case] is as much as remains unconcocted in the bodies and has not been able to be changed by the
heat which concocts it. For this is what sweat is like, and urine,
and what percolates through ash; for ash too is the [part] of

earth that has not been able to be overcome by fire and to change into it, but has remained as the unconcocted part of the burned timber.   30

Having established these [points] he inferred (358a14-27) that there must be something like this which, being mixed with water, makes sea from it. He says that there must be some unconcocted residue, the mixture of which with the water* comes to be the cause of its saltiness; and showing what this is, he noted that, as in the case of the bodies of living creatures certain unconcocted residues come about in the course of nour-   35 ishment and the conversion [of nourishment], and by the mix- ture of these with water certain salty and bitter excrements come to be in them, just so in the whole [world] too one must suppose that from all the things that grow and come to be some such unconcocted excrement comes to be, and that the earth is   100,1 full of such a dry and unconcocted residue mixed in [with it] similarly to ash. This is mixed in with the exhalations brought about from earth and water by the sun, since it is lighter, and [so] is mixed in with the clouds [when they] condense and change to water; and being carried down continuously with [the   5 rain] it is the origin and reason for the quality of the water of the sea; [but] of this residue, in [the case of] the exhalations from the sea, the greatest part remains behind.[306] For there is also some that is carried up with the water and changes into what is sweet in the concoction and the change [by which water is produced] from the clouds. <But since this is less by as much as there is less that is salty than is sweet in [water] that is rained down>,[307] for this reason* what remains behind is the cause of the saltiness of the water of the sea.   10

That some such residue is carried down with the rain-water he showed (358a27-b6) from the fact that rain brought by the south wind is most brackish, because the south wind has its origin from those regions in which more of the dry exhalation comes about; and the first of the autumn rains are the more brackish, because it is necessary for what is heaviest to be carried down first, and those that have the most of what is   15 earthy in themselves are the heaviest.

[To show] that there is a great deal of this sort of residue in the sea he also appeals (358b6-12) to its being hot. For all things that have been burned possess some power of heat in them-

selves, like lye and ash and the excrement of living creatures, and the excrement of living creatures which are hotter in their
20   gut is hotter. [To show] that it becomes salty by the admixture of some such residue he also appeals (359a16-b4) to recorded observations,[308] citing harbours and rivers which are salty where it happened that the water was denser and more earthy, so as not to allow, on account of [its] density, things to sink in it which have such a nature as to be carried downwards when placed in water,[309] and so that, when heated, on account of their density they produced salt.[310]

25   **3.11.** An attempt to show that names [are] by [our] laying [them] down.[311]

If we are by nature such as to lay down names [to things], and we derive from nature our being able to name and to lay down names for things, it is clear that names are by laying down; for it is by laying down that we lay them down. For it [would] not [be] possible, if the name of each thing existed by nature, for
30   us to lay them down for them.[312] We are by nature capable of receiving knowledge, but we do not possess [the branches of] knowledge by nature; we derive from it our being able to receive knowledge, but not also [the branches of] knowledge; for [if so] we would not be *capable of receiving* [the branches of] knowledge, but in possession of them and knowledgeable. Just so we derive from [nature] our being able to lay down names, too, but
35   not the names as well; for we would no longer be[313] in control of laying them down. For it is not in accordance with nature for those things, for which it is natural to be laid down [already],
101,1 to be laid down by us. If it was not natural for things that the names for them should be laid down by us, it would not be natural for us to lay down names for them; for it is not the same thing to lay down a name and to utter what is [already] laid down. And if names were laid down by nature, it would have to be that all those who speak would say the same things.
5   But if names are by nature, the letters in terms of which they are drawn up have to be by nature; for there is no other <cause> of the difference of <names>* that differ between nations, applied to the same things, besides the combination of letters and syllables in a certain way.[314] And identity of names [for

different things], and plurality of names [for a single thing], and changes of name are also sufficient to establish this.[315]

3.12. That reality is not unlimited.[316]

[I]

[Consider] the argument [A] that* wishes to show that reality   10
is unlimited, through the [claim] that the person who is supposed to be at the limit of the world (*kosmos*) will either stretch
out his hand beyond the world, or be prevented [from doing so]
by whatever it might be [that is outside], and that either way
there will be something outside the world; for either what
prevents, or else that in which there will be what is stretched
out, is outside.[317] [This argument] derives its plausibility from
the image and from sense[-experience], as does also the [argu-
ment] [B] that says that everything that is limited is limited   15
by being up against something*.[318] For both [derive] their
plausibility from sense[-experience]. For the plausibility of the
argument [is due to] the fact that we, having no image of the
opposite of what is [presupposed in] the question,[319] cannot
provide any counter-example to these from our sense-[experi-
ence].

For we have not encountered a limited thing of a sort that
has nothing beyond it; for all things that are limited as parts   20
[i.e. by other parts of a greater whole] are like this, and these
are the only ones of which we have sense-experience); nor does
anything* come to our attention of such a sort that there can
be nothing* outside it; for outside all the things of which we
have sense[-experience] there is something. And for this reason
those who resist such arguments ought not to try to bring
evidence from the senses, [since] the things being enquired into
are outside [the scope] of these; rather, they should try to derive
their objections from the being of the things [in question],
noting in addition as clear in itself[320] that all the same [prop-   25
erties] cannot belong to the part and to the whole, and to the
totality and to each of its parts. And for this reason they ought*
not to seek to transfer the evidence from the senses about the
parts, with which they are familiar, to the totality, which is
outside all sense[-experience] and, in addition to not being

30   supported by any sensory image, is in conflict with many of
them. For the totality would not differ at all from the part, if,
just as there is something outside each of them, in a similar
way [there was something outside] it too.

<If the nature of [the totality] is such>* that by a reasoned
account it is some totality of which all other things are parts,
but sense[-experience] cannot apprehend anything like this, we
should not on account of sense[-experience] abandon any of the
things laid down by reason. For we do not do so in the case of
35   other things either, for we do not say that only things that can
be sensed exist; nor, [just] because in many cases we use the
evidence of the senses to establish [the truth concerning] the
102,1   things we are enquiring after, on account of our being familiar
with and accustomed to them, must we just for this reason use
only this [evidence] as a measure of the truth. For we would
[then] be no different, with regard to coming to know the truth,
from the irrational [creatures]; for the truth in their own proper
objects of sensation is sufficient for them. But it is absurd to
5   say that truth in matters which are not the peculiar [preserve]
of the senses entirely depends on the evidence of the senses.

Well, that it is reasonable that there should be some totality
of which all* the things we perceive by the senses are parts, as
are also all the principles and causes of these, is sufficiently
established by the fact that whole and part are spoken of
correlatively to one another. For the part is a part of some
whole, and the whole is for the parts, if indeed it is a whole, a
10   thing of such a sort that none of the parts is absent from it. So
if individual sensible things are parts, and the whole is that of
which these are parts (for the parts are parts of *some* whole),
[then] it itself is a whole* because everything that is spoken of
as a part is referred to some* whole. And for this reason, even
if the things that are taken first are spoken of as parts of a *part*,
even so it is not necessary for that too, in the respect in which
it is a part, to be a part of some *other* <part>*; and if there is
not *some* whole*, these things' being parts will also be done
away with.[321]

15   But if it is necessary for there to be some whole, to which [as]
a totality what is and is spoken of as a part is referred, and a
whole and a totality are the same (for each of them is defined
by none of its parts being absent), something which is like this

will be limited, if what is limited is that of which no part is absent.[322] And the totality is like this; for neither will there be anything else outside [it] that limits [it] and is limited [by it],   20
nor will anyone be able to stretch out into anything beyond it what is controlled by himself*. For that, outside which there is something that is, will no longer *be* totality and the whole. There is however something outside what is limited [by being] up against something else and what leaves something beyond itself into which* somebody will be able to shoot or stretch out some one of his own parts or of the things under his control.[323]

[II]

This same [point] is also sufficiently established by the fact that   25
the principles of the things that are are limited. For if they are unlimited there will be no knowledge of them;[324] and if not of them, neither of any of the things that come to be from them, if all understanding proceeds from the knowledge of the prin- ciples of the thing that is understood.

And it follows from the principles being unlimited that none of the things that come to be does so in an ordered way. For what order could there be in things that are unlimited? What   30
could be the cause of order among things that are unlimited? For nature would have no place among them, [since] it is characteristic of [nature] that all the things that come about in accordance with it do so for the sake of something [and] for the most part, and it is not possible for this* to come about in things   103,1
that do not admit of order.[325] For why, among unlimited things, should this rather be before that [than vice versa], and one thing first and another later[326] – without which it is not possible for that to come to be which comes to be for the sake of something? For how could a human being or a horse or any other of the things that come to be by nature do so, if one does away with [the fact that] one of the things that contribute to it   5
is first and another second, and that a human being comes from a human being and a horse from a horse in accordance with nature? [How could this be so] if the principles are unlimited and do not admit of any order? For what will order things that are unlimited [in number]? If it is necessary for what is unlim- ited to be organised by luck and chance, and the things that

come to be[327] are seen not to do so in this way (for the things that come to be either in a similar way always or [in a similar way] for the most part are far removed from the afore-
10 mentioned causes, but it is in this way that the things that come to be in accordance with nature are seen [to do so]); then unlimitedness both of the principles and of the things that are[328] will be excluded.

[III]

What?[329] If it is impossible for what is unlimited to be greater than [something else that is] unlimited, but according to the opinions of those who postulate that the principles are unlim-ited[330] it follows that they say not only this but also that there are and there come to be many unlimited things, or rather an
15 unlimited [number] of unlimited things – how could[331] anyone not suppose this opinion to be most absurd? For it is not possible to say that there is something unlimited greater than what is unlimited, if it is necessary to say that what is unlimited is everywhere and occupies all place; for what is not everywhere is no longer unlimited. To leave some space for something else is [characteristic] of what is limited, but it is not possible for anything else to exceed what is like this [i.e. unlimited] nor be
20 up against it, not only not what is limited, but not even what is unlimited. For in this case it would no longer be everywhere. So, for those according to whom there is a plurality of unlimited things, there will be nothing that is unlimited without qualifi-cation. For if there is a plurality of unlimited things, what is unlimited will no longer be everywhere, and there will be something unlimited greater than what is unlimited, if it is necessary for the two unlimited things [together] to exceed the one, and what is composed of the two unlimited things together,
25 too, is unlimited. Again, the three[332] will be greater than the two; and by adding them in this way the increase in what is unlimited will go on without limit. For either they will say that the two unlimited things are not greater and more in number than the one, and in this way it will result that they are saying that what is unlimited is without parts (for it is only in the case of the combination of things like this [i.e. without parts] that what is composed of all the things is no greater than each of

the things that [enter] into the combination; and this is a
property of points alone). Or else, if this is most unreasonable,   30
and it is necessary for equal things that are combined to
produce a result that is double, [then] what is composed of the
two unlimited things will be double; and in this way there will
be something unlimited that is equal to [something else which
is] unlimited, and another [unlimited thing which] will be
double another and also half, and in this way also treble, and
increasing without limit; and what could be more unreasonable
than this?

Moreover, if* it is necessary for the combination even of
things that possess any magnitude whatsoever*, but are un-   35
limited in number, to produce some unlimited magnitude,[333]
and it is not possible for anything to be greater than this
magnitude, [then] it is necessary for the person who supposes   104,1
that the principles are unlimited [in number] to say straight
away that these are in contact with one another and that there
is nothing [else] between them. <For if there were something
left between [them]>*, what is composed of the unlimited
principles and of what is* between them would in this case be
greater than the unlimited [magnitude] produced by the combination of the unlimited [principles, only].[334]

[IV]

That there is a plurality of unlimited things according to those   5
who say that the principles are unlimited is clear also from
what follows. They say that the worlds, too, are unlimited [in
number]. If each of these too is composed out of unlimited
principles, it is necessary for the unlimited things to be unlimited an unlimited number of times over;[335] for each principle
individually, of those in the unlimited worlds, will produce an
unlimited magnitude up against each [other] in their combination with one another one by one*, if it is necessary for what is   10
composed of unlimited things which possess some magnitude
to be unlimited.[336] If on the other hand [each world] is formed
from [principles] limited [in number], [then] the things that are
will be unlimited as many times over as the limited number of
elements of which each world is [composed]. And if the void in
between is reckoned in too, the result will be much greater

still*. If these things are irrational and surpass all absurdity,
15 it is clear how absurd the supposition of unlimitedness is; and
since this follows both for those who say that everything that
is limited is limited up against what is outside it, and for those
who claim the person who is at the limit should be able to
stretch out something beyond and outside the limit, it is clear
that these [claims] too will be liable to the afore-mentioned
absurdities.

[V]

And for this reason one must try to resolve them taking one's
starting-point from the real being (*ousia*) of [the things in
20 question], not from sense-perception which contributes nothing
to our knowledge of them. If the being limited of what is limited
consisted in being considered [as] up against something else,[337]
then our opponents would have a point when they claim that
outside every limited thing there has to be something up
against which it is seen to be limited – *if* it is in this that being
(*einai*), for what is limited, consists;[338] but if what is limited is
what has a limit and what is able to be divided into equal parts
25 and what is composed of limited parts, none of which has its
being in having something outside itself*,[339] those who suppose
that everything limited is limited up against something will
not be supposing any of the things included in the being of what
is limited, but a certain accident of the things to which the
property of being limited belongs <as>* parts of the totality.[340]
It is to these that there belongs the property of being seen up
30 against something else, not because they are limited, but
because they are parts of the totality; [but the person who
argues thus][341] thinks it right to transfer this also to what is
limited as a totality, when it can only apply to the things that
are limited as parts, and not in that they are limited, but
105,1 because they are parts. For if it is in its own nature that what
is limited possesses [the property of] being limited, but what is
limited* against something is like this through its relation to
something else, [then the property of] <being>* limited will not
consist in being limited against something outside it.

The person who introduces, through verbal arguments, a
kind of thing[342] which is as absurd and as much at odds with

the things that are and come to be as we have shown, must not 5
establish it and convince [people] of it on the basis of some brief
persuasion, and not make assumptions* about the nature of
what is limited on the basis of something that is an accident of
some limited things. For this does not follow any longer* for
the person who says that the totality is limited, and they cannot
say anything like this about it on the basis of sense-perception.
The [notion of] juxtaposition [derived] from things that are
limited [and fall] under perception is not like [what applies in 10
the case of the totality], if it is admitted that these, in addition
to being limited, are also parts of the totality, but it is not
possible for the totality itself to be a part of anything. And that
one should not make use of sense-perception in the case of
everything is shown by the very people against whom [our]
argument [is directed], since they suppose [that there are]
indivisible magnitudes which fall outside [the range of things
with a] nature perceptible by sensation, and say that there is
a void, and introduce certain bodies*[343] and movements and
times that have no parts. 15

[VI]

This attempted dialectical argument is based on an accident of
things that are limited, not on the real being of what is limited,
and on accustomed sense-experience rather than on what follows logically. It is just so in the case of the second [argument]
too, which claims that the person who is at the limit of the
totality [of things, the universe] either stretches something* 20
out beyond the limit or will be prevented, and that either way
there will be something outside the totality. For this [argu-
ment] too transfers its dialectical attempt from limited parts
to the totality, and claims the right to use [considerations]
derived from our sense-perception of these things and the
impression (*phantasia*) derived from them as if this applied in
this way to all things. This however is not so; for not everything* that appears (*phainomenon*) is true. For it is not the case 25
that, if someone imagines[344] himself being in a certain region
in which he was once or in which he has never been in the first
place, for that reason he actually *is* there. Sufficient evidence
that not everything that appears is true is also provided by the

empty imaginings that occur to those who are asleep and those who are awake;[345] and it is like these [empty imaginings] to suppose that there is [someone] at the limit of the totality able*

30 to stretch out beyond the limit something that is in [his] control. For what is the difference between this image and supposition and supposing that one was in what is non-existent, and enquiring whether, if one went forward into it, it would admit one or not, and whether, when one came to be in it, one will stand or have nothing to support one, and be able to stretch out one's hand or be impeded by something[346] – for indeed it is

35 from* these that one must make suppositions as to what the non-existent is?

For this reason it is better to refute images like these which are empty, and to follow demonstrations by means of argu-

106,1 ments and make use of the points that have been shown through a plurality of [arguments]; that is, that it is not possible for any body to be unlimited whether simple or composite, nor for any void [to exist]. For in general it is impossible for an extension without body to exist. For neither is it possible for any length to exist by itself separated from any body, nor

5 [any] breadth, nor yet [any] depth. The extensions spoken of by the geometricians in one, two and three [dimensions] are not spoken of by them as having their own proper existence; for by the very thinking of them they are separated from natural bodies, which are bodies in the proper sense, and they consider them apart from bodies and produce their arguments about them enquiring and showing what are the things that can be

10 properties and accidents of them as such [i.e. as abstracted from bodies]. But those who suppose that the void exists are doing nothing other than considering three extensions[347] in real existence apart from matter;[348] [so], when they say that [the void]* is able to receive bodies, they are doing nothing other than saying that an extension is able to receiving an extension. For neither is body in place in respect of anything other than the three extensions in it. It is not inasmuch as body possesses

15 some colour or some flavour or some other one of its accidents that it is in place, but in respect of the extensions in it;[349] and if what is able to receive these is a void of equal [size]*, then an extension will come to be in an extension. If on the other hand the body's own extension is not sufficient for its existence,

but it needs another extension equal to that* in it, then why
will the void too not be in some other extension, if extensions   20
need other extensions* for their being? And yet it is reasonable
that, as it is not possible for a length to exist as something by
itself apart from matter, and similarly neither for surface, so
neither for that which in addition to this* has taken on the third
extension which we name depth – and this is the sort of thing
that they say the void is. So, for this reason, what is outside the
totality will not be void.[350]

But it has also been shown through a plurality [of argu-   25
ments] that it is not possible for any body to be unlimited. For
it is not possible for the simple bodies to be more [in number]
than the five, four that possess matter[351] and the fifth the body
that is divine and moves in a circle;[352] and neither can any of
these be unlimited.[353] And it has also been shown that, the
simple [bodies] being limited both in number and in magnitude, it is necessary that those that have their being as a result
of the juxtaposition and mixture and blending of these should   30
also themselves be limited.[354] And it has also been shown that
it is not possible for there to be a plurality of worlds, but that
it is necessary for all corporeal nature to be within [the one]
world.[355] These things being so, there will not be *anything*
outside this world, which is also the totality, [since] there is*
no other body besides these, nor any empty extension outside
the extension of bodies. To do away with all these things,   35
surrendering to some brief persuasion, is absurd. Those who
are confident must answer[356] those who examine whether a
person who is at the limit of the totality [of things, the universe]
reaches out his hand, or whether he will be prevented, by
saying that he will not stretch it out; he will be prevented; but
<he will be prevented>[357] not in the way they themselves say,
by something which resists him, surrounding the totality from
outside, but much more by there being nothing [there].[358] For   107,1
how could anyone stretch anything out into nothing, or how
could it come to be in what altogether does not exist? For in
nothing he would not even get the impulse to stretch out one of
his limbs in the first place; for this is what the nature of the
non-existent is like.

5   **3.13.** Some points concerning that which depends on
us.[359]

That which depends on us is [located] in rational assent; it is
on account of this that it is in a human being alone that what
depends on us [is found], because a human being is also, alone
of living creatures, rational and capable of deliberation. The
irrational living creatures assent too, but they follow the ap-
10   pearances that come to be in them through their senses from
things sensed, and the affection that comes to be in them from
these, and make their assents being led by these wheresoever
they lead. But a human being, when he makes his assents *qua*
human being, needs reason in addition to the appearances; it
is [by] having this from nature for the judgement of such things
that he is a human being,[360] and through this reason he judges
15   the appearances. And for this reason if, when he deliberates
about the appearance that impinged upon him, it does not seem
of the sort it appeared [to be] in the first place, he does not
assent to it, [though] he would have assented as far as the
affection [that results] from the appearance is concerned*; and
it is this sort of assent which is choice, being a deliberative
appetition. For it is the decision, resulting from deliberation,
about that which [comes] from what is sensed and before
oneself that is choice.
20   If then even when we deliberated it followed that we [al-
ways][361] assented to the appearance, not even assent accompanied by deliberation would depend on us; but since having
deliberated often makes our assent [that follows] on the appearance different from [that which would be produced by] the
affection [that results] from it, it would no longer be reasonable
to say that we 'assent to appearances'. Since we do not assent
25   to appearances, and [our doing so] would do away with what
depends on us,[362] neither will there being something that
depends on us be done away with.
If indeed [it followed] without qualification on every appearance [that] we deliberated upon [it], perhaps it would seem that
[deliberating] itself did not depend on us but was some accompaniment of the appearance brought about by it; and if [the
deliberating] had derived its being from [the appearance] it
would have seemed that the assent [that follows] on [the

deliberating], too, came about in accordance with [the appear-
ance], in accordance with which the deliberating too, on which   30
the assent [followed], [came about]. But if the appearance is
not in control of a human being's deliberating, but deliberating
and not [doing so] depend on him (for we do at any rate assent
to many appearances without having deliberated, in a similar
way to the irrational living creatures),[363] not even such assent
[sc. that *not* preceded by deliberation] will be the product of the
appearance, since [assent] resists [the appearance] in many
cases and in many ways.

That we are in control of deliberating about the appearances   35
is clear from what has already been said, that we have the
power of deliberating or not, and that the appearance is not in
control of this. For if it were not the appearance, what else could
be supposed as in control of this besides ourselves? It is not the   108,1
case that, [just] because we say in a more general way that
what is discovered and approved in accordance with reason,
too, 'appears' to us, therefore we must say that such assent is
'an appearance' and 'to an appearance', if at least an 'appearance' in the proper sense is a change brought about by the
actual sensation.[364]

Moreover, the fact that those who deliberate are praised and   5
those who do not are blamed is a sign that deliberating depends
on us and is not [merely] the product of the appearance. For
praise and blame are for the things that depend on us, and it
is for this reason that we are neither praised nor blamed for
the appearances [that we experience], unless we are for ourselves the causes for some of them; but each of these [praise
and blame] do indeed apply to the assents that follow on [the
appearances]. We are blamed for as many appearances as come   10
to be of such a sort for us on account of our failure to practise
[virtue, where] the practice is [something] of which we are in
control.[365]

[And] since to call in advisers, or these* rather than or
instead of those, depends on us, it is clear that deliberating in
the first place, too, depends on us. For if it depends on us to
make use of these advisers, through whom such an assent
[comes about], deliberating too depends on us.[366] [And] since
the punishments for misdeeds resulting from forethought are   15
greater, on the grounds that [the agents] did [them] in accord-

ance with [deliberate] choice, it is clear that everything that comes about as a result of forethought, too, depends on us.

3.14. Summary of the contents of the fourth book of the *Meteorology,* unfinished.[367]

Having spoken in the second book [of] *On Coming-to-be and Passing-Away* about the four elements, fire, air, water and
20   earth, [and] what their specific being and cause is, and having shown that their coming-to-be from one another, too, is according to the change into one another of the differences that give [the elements] their form, in this [book] which is entitled the fourth [book] of the *Meteorology*, but is more proper to the enquiry concerning coming-to-be and passing-away, he first mentioned (4.1, 378b10-12) the differences that give form to the four elements; and these are two, the first of the simple
25   oppositions, heat and coldness, moisture and dryness. For it is by these being paired with each other in four ways that each of the [four elements] is given its form. After this he showed (378b12-25) that of these four differences two are active, heat and coldness,[368] and two passive, dryness and moisture, and each of the elements [has] one [member] from each of the
30   oppositions, so that all things have* in themselves the power for acting and being affected.

After this he proposed to speak about the effects brought about by the active powers, which are, as he will say, concoction and inconcoction, and the kinds of each of these, and also [about] the kinds and differences of the things that are affected by these, that is the dry and the moist. Having first said (378b28-31) that the things in which a change of this sort is
35   and comes about are things that have grown naturally [i.e. plants] and animals and the parts of [both of] these, since these things, those which primarily come to be in accordance with
109,1   nature, are composed out of the coming-together of the four [elemental] bodies, after this he stated (378b31-379a1) what 'simple and natural coming-to-be' is, that it is 'the change, by the active powers' heat and coldness, of the matter underlying [them] in each nature according to the passive powers, dryness
5   and moisture, when they are proportioned to one another, so that the one [pair] can act and change, the other be changed

and be affected*.[369] For 'the hot and the cold produce' the things
that they produce by these [changes] when they 'prevail over
the matter', and their matter is the second opposition, that is
the dry and the moist.

'When none' of these 'prevails' because they are not proportioned to the matter that is subject to them*, [then] if in certain   10
parts they do not prevail over the matter subject [to them],
'simmering[370] and inconcoction occur' (379a2-3), but if such
weakness of the active [elements] occurs generally in the [proc-
ess of] coming-to-be, there is a change to decay. For 'all natural
passing-away is a path' to decay, and the natural path to
passing-away is through old age and withering (379a4-5); of
these dryness and withering will more properly be spoken of as   15
applied to plants and old age to animals, if it is <reasonable>*
for simmering and inconcoction to come about by weakness of
the active powers in the parts, but of these simmering will more
properly <be applied to> the parts of animals, <inconcoction to
their nourishment>*. But when all things come about in accordance with nature the natural 'end is rottenness' and decay
(379a5-6). For passing-away due to violence is not in accordance with nature. For this reason the things that pass away in   20
accordance with nature first change to being moist because the
heat in them no longer prevails over the moist so as to be able
to concoct it, but finally, when the same moist has evaporated
and been separated out, being separated out and dispersed by
the heat, what is left behind is dry. For the end of things that
decay is to be dissolved into the things out of which they came   25
to be and were constituted when the active [powers], which
were the hot and cold, determined and mixed the moist with
the dry. 'Such passing-away', that is that which is according to
nature, 'comes about when on account of the surroundings
there prevails over what determines' (which was primarily the
hot) 'that which is made determinate by it', (which was moist
and dry) (379a11-12), [and] when, the hot in the things that
pass away and decay being exhausted by the greater heat in   30
the surroundings, the passive [powers] come to prevail. In
general the decaying of things that decay comes about because
of the separation of their nature from them, and the nature in
each thing is the principle of movement[371] in it, and in all the

things which are constituted by nature it is primarily the hot that is like this.

After this he gave an account of decay (379a16-26), saying that it is the destruction of the <heat> in each thing <by that

35   in the>* surroundings. Since decay 'is through lack of the hot, and everything that lacks such a power is cold', both the hot

110,1 and the cold in a way produce decay. For it is brought about by an abundance both of the cold and of the hot, but of the cold that is proper, the hot that is alien. It is through change that is of this sort and comes about in this way that 'things that decay become drier and in the end [become] earth and dung'.

5   This comes about because when 'the proper heat departs' from each of the things that decay the proper 'moist' in them, too, evaporates along with it, and this is the cause of the dryness [coming to be], because there is no longer present in them that which attracts and draws in the moist, which was the innate[372] heat in each thing.

He also added (379a26-9), following on what has been said before, the reason for certain things not decaying in a similar

10   way in the cold. For since in winter the hot in the surroundings is less, the proper hot in each thing is not so weakened and overpowered. Nor (379a29-31) do things that are solidified through coldness decay in a similar way, because on account of their greater coldness the heat in the surrounding air does not prevail over them; for if it was going to influence and change them, it would do so by prevailing.[373] Nor (379a31-3) do things

15   that are fermenting decay, because the heat in the surrounding air is less than the heat in them. And (379a33-b1) the hot in the surroundings does not prevail over things that are in movement and flowing in a similar way [to that it does] over those that are unmoving and at rest; for in this way too the heat in the air is weaker than that in the thing that is moving. For movement increases the hot in each thing by fanning and

20   kindling it. He also gave (379b2-6) the same reason for 'the greater amount' changing and 'decaying less than the lesser'. For there is more hot and cold in the greater amount, and for this reason these prevail over the powers in the surroundings. This is the reason why 'the sea' and other water 'decays' when divided [into small amounts]. He also stated (379b6-8) the reason for certain living creatures being produced from decaying things. For

the heat which is separated out from the decaying things, being   25
natural, produces certain things and constitutes [them out of]
'the things that have been separated out', in the cases where
they happen to have come to be [so as to] be well blended.

Having spoken universally about coming-to-be in general,
and similarly about passing-away, he went on to the account
concerning what he had proposed, and this was to say through
what [means] the 'powers' mentioned beforehand, heat and
coldness, 'produce' the coming-to-be of the things that come to   30
be, and their passing-away, from the things that underlie them;
and in natural bodies these were the dry and moist. For these
are their matter.[374] For since all coming-to-be and change [are
brought about] by the active powers, of which one is heat <and
the other cold, heat>* is properly the cause of coming-to-be;[375]
for it is when the hot prevails over and combines the dry and
the moist, concocting [them] and making them determinate,   35
that coming-to-be [occurs]. If it does not prevail because the
cold is greater, the cold overpowers [it] and is the cause of the
opposites, passing-away and decay.

But since both concoction and inconcoction are [spoken of] in   111,1
several ways, he reasonably proposed to speak about these; and
first he says through what [means] the hot produces the
changes that it brings about in what is subject [to it]. He says
(3.2, 379b12-17) that the proper function of the hot is concoction, and that the kinds and differentiations of concoction are
ripening, roasting and boiling. The proper function of cold is   5
inconcoction, and of this again the kinds and differentiations
are rawness, simmering and scorching. After this he says that
these are not the proper names for the things to which they are
applied, but that because a proper name has not been laid down
for each of these it is necessary to transfer the names from the
things that have been named, and [apply] them to things
similar to those that have been named, and for this reason 'one   10
must not think that the things spoken of *are* these, but such
[as these]'. [He then] says and defines what each of the things
spoken of is, and first (379b18-380a6) he says what concoction
is, and after this (380a6-10) what inconcoction is, which is
opposite to concoction in general. After this he speaks (3.3,
380a11-27) about ripening, which falls under concoction, and
after his account of this he speaks about rawness (380a27-b11),

15   which falls under inconcoction and is opposite to <ripening.
      After this he speaks (380b12-381a12) about boiling, which falls
      under concoction, and after speaking about this he speaks
      (381a12-23) about simmering, which falls under inconcoction
      and is opposite to>*[376] boiling. After this, having said (381a23-
      b13) what roasting is – and this is itself a sort of concoction –
      he speaks (381b13-20) about scorching, which falls under in-
      concoction and is opposite to roasting. Of these he said concoc-
      tion is 'perfection (*teleiôsis*), by the natural and proper hot, of [377]
      the opposed passive [powers]' (3.2, 379b18-19) (for in every
      matter dryness and moisture are opposed to each other and are
20   passive; it is these that are concocted and made determinate
      by the hot), while 'inconcoction is imperfection (*ateleia*) through
      lack of the proper heat' (380a6-7), which is coldness. For the
      things that have concoction as their end (*telos*) have inconcoc-
      tion as failure to achieve the end (*ateleia*).
      Again, he said that ripening (3.3, 380a11-27) is concoction
      and perfection of the nourishment in the body that surrounds
      the seed,[378] and that perfection for these [i.e. for fruits] is for
25   another like this to be able to come to be from it (and he says
      that other things too are called ripe by reference to these), while
      'rawness' (380a27-33) is inconcoction and 'imperfection' of the
      nourishment in the body that surrounds the seed. After this he
      showed (380a33-4), that everything that ripens must necessar-
      ily possess not only moisture but also dryness. After this he
      defined boiling (380b12-381a12) as 'concoction by the heat' in
      the surrounding water of the 'indeterminate moist' present in
30   the thing itself, which is either some breath [*pneuma*] or water.
      And he added the things of which boiling is predicated, these
      being said to be boiled in a more general way.[379] He also defined
      simmering (381a12-23) as the inconcoction opposite to boiling;
      and since boiling is [spoken of] in several ways, simmering [is
      spoken of] in as many ways, with a proper type of simmering
      opposed to each differentiation of boiling. After this he said
      what 'roasting' is, namely that it is 'concoction by heat that is
35   dry and alien' (381a23-4). He said it is brought about 'by dry
      heat, whenever' what is concocted in this way 'becomes drier'
112,1 (381a27-8).[380] The inconcoction which is opposite to the concoc-
      tion called roasting does not, he said (381b13-20), have any
      name very much, but is similar to scorching, when what is

being roasted changes but is not also roasted; this comes about either through lack of heat changing what is being roasted, or because of abundance of moisture in what is being roasted.

Having spoken about these things he went on to the account of the passive powers, which were dryness and moisture, and showing what differentiations there are of these again, and which and how many kinds [of thing][381] come to be out of them, he first reminded [us] that (4.4, 381b23-8) the 'principles of bodies', insofar as they are passive, 'are the moist and the dry', and the other things, as many as are not principles but are and have come to be out of the principles, are mixed out of 'these' (for what is mixed is ranked with 'whichever' it has more of, the things with a preponderance of the dry with the dry, those with [a preponderance of] the moist with the moist); and that* of all the moist and dry things 'some' are said to be so 'in actuality', others in potentiality. After this he noted (381b29-382a8) that the mixture of the moist and the dry is the reason for the things mixed out of them being determinate (for each of them is indeterminate when by itself), and noted that the moist passive element is water, the dry [passive element] earth; the cold is present in these, and seems in itself to be more passive than active.[382] He noted in addition (382a8-14) that every determinate passive body is either soft or hard, and said what the soft and the hard are; hard is what resists and does not yield at its surface, soft is what yields at its surface by yielding, [but] not by division and mutual replacement.[383] Next, since every determinate body is hard or soft, and what is determinate is *ipso facto* solidified, he went on to speak about solidification (4.5, 382a22-382b1); he reminded [us] of the causes besides the matter, that they are the origin of the movement[384] and the form, and noting that these are the causes of all the things that come to be by nature (for [they are the causes] 'of solidification and melting, of becoming dry and becoming moist'), he noted which are the active [causes] and which the affections and kinds of the things that come to be, saying that it is heat and coldness that are active, the things which happen to bodies through these [that are] the affections, the hot and the cold. After this he went back to the account of solidification, and (382b1-2) noting that 'to be solidified is in a way to become dry', he said that one must speak 'about this first'; and first he noted

(382b10-16) which things become dry – namely, water, and all
the kinds of water [there are], and all the things that have
water either in their nature or added to them. After this he
enquired (382b16-27) by which things drying is brought about,
and noting that all things that become dry do so either when
35   heated or when cooled, he added that 'both things that are
heated and those that are cooled are dried by the hot' either
113,1 internal or external: <by external>,[385] those that are dried by
the surrounding heat, by internal [hot], those [that are dried]
by cold. For when the hot present in the things that are
becoming dry is exhausted by the cold and scattered it causes
to evaporate along with [itself] also the moist in them, and
when this occurs they become dry.

5   Having said which things are dried and by which things and
through what – namely, through the hot, either internal or
external – he went on to speak (4.6, 382b28-31) about things
which become moist, and undergo the opposite affection to
those that become dry. He noted that there are differentiations
in becoming moist, for of things that become moist some are
made moist by condensation, as* the air is made moist, that is
10   to say changes to water, which is passive moist. For when the
breath (*pneuma*) is cooled and condensed and thickened and
becomes <cloud>* it produces the change to water. <But others
[are made moist] by the melting of what has solidified>*. [So
speaking] about melting and this sort of change to water, he
said that it would simultaneously become clear also concerning
solidification, for it seems that it is things that have solidified
that melt. To this he added (382b31-383a4), what the things
are that solidify. All the things that solidify do so being either
15   water or kinds of water or of earth and water only. To this he
added by what they are solidified: either by the hot, or by the
cold, or by the moist. And for this reason it is by the opposites
that 'they are dissolved. For the things that have been solidified
by dry hot', i.e. fire, 'are dissolved by water, which is moist and
cold, the things which have been solidified by cold are dissolved
by' the hot, for [they are dissolved by] 'fire'.
20   To this he added (383a6-13), that as many of the things that
are solidified as are 'of water, are not solidified by fire, for' they
are dissolved 'by it'. And if these things are solidified by the
separation of the hot in them, they will reasonably be dissolved

by the presence of these.[386] But it is cold that causes the solidification of these things. And for this reason such things are not thickened, for 'thickening comes about when the moist departs and the dry is condensed', and water, alone of moist   25
things, cannot be thickened because it has no dryness in it. But* (383a13-19) what is a mixture out of water and earth is solidified by both, by the hot and the cold. Since however the solidification of such things is through their being thickened, he said that they are thickened by both, the hot and the cold, 'but not in the same way, but by the hot' when it evaporates   30
the moist, 'by the cold when it squeezes out the hot' in them, with which the moist in them is also evaporated. To this he added (383a19-23) which of the things that are mixed are thickened [by drying], and which are not thickened but solidi-fied.[387]

Having said which things are solidified, and how, and by which, next he spoke (383a26-b17) about things which are dissolved and melted. Of mixed things, those that are solidified by cold are those in which there is a preponderance of earth,   35
'as many as are solidified by the departure of the hot are' dissolved and 'melted by the hot, when the hot enters' into them 'again', as happens in the case of* clay that is solidified on   114,1
account of coldness. 'But as many things as' are solidified 'on account of cooling', but not in this way, that the hot alone is separated from them, but with the moist being evaporated from them along with it as well, these are not dissolved, except by excessive heat, 'but are softened' and beaten out 'like iron and horn'. But he says that these things too are 'melted', which is   5
why he added which other things too are melted. 'As many things as are solidified by dry hot', that is by fire, 'some of them' remain 'insoluble, others are dissolved' by moist. Earthenware is insoluble, as are certain stones, which come to be when 'earth is thoroughly burned by fire' and unified,[388] 'but soda and salt can be dissolved by moist' cold, as he says, meaning by what has the cold in its own proper nature and being, such as is   10
water. Oil does not also have the cold in its own nature and being, and for this reason he did not include it among the kinds of water; it does not have the cold in its own nature, because it contains much air.

As many of the things that are mixed as 'contain more water

15 than earth are thickened by fire, but as many as' [contain] more 'earth are solidified'. And through this he showed (4.7, 383b18-20) that 'soda and salt are more [of the nature of] earth'; for they are solidified by heat, and of this [type] are also stone and earthenware. Next (383b20-6) he raised a difficulty about oil; for it is not solidified by cold, as happens to things [composed] out of water, nor is it solidified by the hot, as happens to things that contain more earth; but it is solidified by neither and

20 thickened by both. He gave as the reason the fact that it is 'full of air', as a sign of which he cited its floating on water, as do air and as many things as have much air in themselves, like timbers. After this (383b26-32) he said how oil is thickened by the cold, and how by the hot. The 'cold thickens' it by changing the air in it into water by cooling (for the mixing* of water with

25 oil makes [the oil] thicker), 'but by fire and by time it is thickened and made whiter, made whiter when [they] evaporate' the remaining watery [substance] in it, and 'thickened' because the air in it is changed into water when it is weakened by the hot. For the lesser heat is weakened by the greater.

After this he noted generally (384a11-20), as [something already] shown, that 'as many of the things that are mixed as

30 are not thickened by the cold, but solidified', are more of [the nature of] water, and of this sort are 'wine, vinegar, lye, urine and whey, while as many as are thickened by fire', the moist in them not being evaporated, 'some are of [the nature of] earth, others share in water and air, honey [being of the nature] of earth', oil sharing [in water and air]. He says that as honey

35 'shares in water and earth', so too do milk and blood. He cited as an indication that milk, being [composed of] both, contains

115,1 more earth the fact that, if the whey is separated from the milk as the milk boils [the milk] is burned,[389] as in the case of other things boiled which contain a preponderance of earth.

After this he gave (384a33-b17) the reasons for some of the things that have been solidified being soluble, others insoluble. 'Soluble are soda' and salt, insoluble is 'earthenware', and

5 'some things can be softened, like horn, others cannot be softened, like earthenware and stone'. The reason [is] that, since there are two things that solidify, as has been said, the hot and the cold, it is necessary that they should be 'dissolved' by the cold and 'the hot', those solidified by the hot [being

dissolved] by the cold, those by the cold by the hot. And for this reason as many things are dissolved by fire as were solidified by water, and 'by water' as many as were solidified by fire. So by water will be dissolved as many things as have been solidified by fire alone, and by fire, on the contrary, as many things as have water as the cause of their solidification. But if certain things have been solidified by both, 'these' will be 'most insoluble'; and solidified by both are as many things as have been heated first and then solidified by cold; and he gave the reason for this. For when, in the case of things solidified by both, the moist in what is being solidified is evaporated by the hot, after this the cold compresses [the thing] and makes it so dense 'that it does not even provide any passage for moist', and for this reason things solidified in this way are indissoluble by both. He says that iron, too, is solidified by both, first having been melted by fire (for it is through this that it comes into being), and after this it is solidified by cold; and this is why a little before he says that it does not melt, but is beaten out and softened. And he says that timbers, too, cannot be melted but burned, because they are composed of earth and air but not water; and as a sign of this he cited, again, the fact that they float on water; for air is like this.

There are missing from the summary, as he wrote before, some of the things stated in the fourth book of Aristotle's *Meteorology*.[390]

3.15. About what is as it were without parts.[391]   25

Things that are as it were without parts are like what is without parts, but are not [in fact] without parts; for neither is anything else which is like something the same as that thing which it is like. Moreover, if* what is like what is without parts* is what appears to be without parts, it is not without parts, as what appears to be a syllogism is not a syllogism. But if it is not without parts, it is clear that it will have parts; and in this way nothing will be without parts. For every part of it that is taken will itself be [only] as it were without parts, since being, for what is said to be without parts,[392] consists in being as it were without parts, if at any rate[393] it is through this that they resolve [the difficulty] that a magnitude is not put together from what has no parts. If however someone were to say that it is *as it were* a magnitude, [then], conversely,[394] it will not [actually] *be* a magnitude. [For] if every magnitude is divisible into parts, what is *as it were* a magnitude will be without parts

35   by its own nature.[395] And if it is without parts, magnitudes will be [formed] from the putting together of things without parts.

116,1   If however someone says that 'as it were' has equivalent force to 'potentially', what is as it were without parts will be potentially without parts. If so, there will be nothing in actuality which will be without parts, if none of the things which are something potentially is in actuality what it is potentially, so that not even what is as it were without parts is without parts. But, if what is as it were without parts is without parts not in

5   actuality but potentially, it will be this potentially while being something else [actually]. Being what, then, is it potentially without parts? And if what is as it were without parts is a magnitude, and it is from these that magnitude is [put together] (for it is [put together] from things that are as it were without parts), every magnitude will be put together from magnitudes and divided into magnitudes, and in this way division will go on even to infinity.

Moreover, if what is as it were without parts is the matter for what is [actually] without parts, and everything that is matter for something <comes to be that thing itself> by some change, <it is by some change*> that what is as it were without

10   parts will be without parts; <and*> since what is as it were without parts is matter for what is without parts, it will be [something] other than what is without parts.[396] But if so, it will create what is without parts either when it is put together or when it is divided; and again it follows, [if one] says that it is divided into things without parts, that magnitudes come to be from the putting together of things without parts.

Alexander of Aphrodisias
Fragments 1 and 2 Vitelli

These two fragments were noted by Vitelli (1895), and published by Vitelli (1902), Bruns having died before he could publish
them as intended. They are preserved in a fourteenth-century
MS in Florence, Cod. Riccard. 63 (on which cf. Montanari
[1971]). This MS contains a sequence of short texts, as follows:

(1) 25r-26r = Alexander *DA* 29,1-33,7
(2) 26r-29v = Alexander *Mixt.* 228,13-238,23
(3) 29v-30v   fr. 1 below, without attribution
(4) 30v   = Alexander *Quaest.* 2.7, 52,20-53,30
(5) 30v-31r   fr. 2 below, explicitly attributed to Alexander
(6) 31r-32r = Alexander *DA* 33,13-38,11
(7) 32r-36v = Alexander *DA* 40,20-59,24
(8) 36v-38v = Alexander *DA* 68,4-73,16
(9) 38v-40v = Alexander *DA* 94,7-100,17

We thus have a sequence of excerpts from Alexander's *DA*,
leaving out most of the general metaphysical discussion of soul,
the *general* discussion of sensation and the whole of the treatment of intellect, with material from elsewhere sandwiched in
between the general account of soul-faculties and the discussion of the nutritive faculty. The excerpt from *Mixt.* is on the
details of blending and of growth; *Quaestio* 2.7 on the nature
of matter. Fr. 1 may have been included because of its reference
to growth, and fr. 2 because of its reference to the incorporeality
of the soul. The existence of such an *ad hoc* compilation raises
questions, as does the transmission of only some of the *Quaestiones* into Arabic, about the date and process by which these
collections reached their present form. Cf. on this Zimmermann
(1994), and below, Additional Note on *Quaest.* 1.1-2.15. Other
examples of the excerpting of groups of Alexander-texts on

related topics are found (cf. Bruns [1892.2] xxvi and n. 1), but these are collections of items all preserved in the main Greek tradition.

While the text of the *DA* in the Florence MS derives, according to Vitelli, from V, supposed by Bruns to be the ultimate source of all the extant MSS of the *DA* and *Quaestiones*, Vitelli points out that the Florence MS has superior readings to V in *Quaestio* 2.7, and superior to Ven. Marc. gr. 257 in the excerpt from *Mixt.* which it also contains. He suspected conjectural emendation, but Montanari (especially 35-43 and 50) showed that the Florence MS is independent of all other MSS of *Mixt.* and is a direct copy of their common source. (Cf. Todd [1976,2] 94-5.) Whatever the provenance of the texts, the identification of all the others as Alexander gives a strong but not conclusive case for supposing that fr. 1 too is from the corpus of material associated with Alexander; though none of texts (1)-(3) has any attribution in the MS (I am grateful for this information to Professor Jonathan Barnes, who has examined the MS; I am also grateful to him for several suggestions relating to text and translation).

Fr. 1 Vitelli (pp. 90-2: Cod. Riccard. 63 ff. 29v-30v)

The question was asked whether the argument that the Stoics call the *sorites* is a sophism or not, and whether it is [an example] of what is called intractable material or not, and, if it is a sophism, to which of the types [of sophism] it is possible to refer it. After attending to the things that seem to me to have been discovered by others, having formed my judgement I am writing[397] to you briefly.

91,1 To say that it is [an example] of intractable material, and then to seek an account and a resolution of an argument that is in its own nature intractable, if indeed they are going to say that any [argument] is intractable – it will result by this argument that most or even all things are intractable of which the knowledgeable possess understanding while the ignorant do not.[398]

5 But I think that the argument is a sophism because it seems to be a syllogism, not being one in reality. For the questioner requires that if something does not belong to a part, neither

should it belong to the whole; and this is false. For it does not
[follow], if being a threesome does not belong to each of the
units, [that] this does not belong to the three taken together,
either; nor, if each of the individual houses is not a city, [that]
the plurality made up of these taken together is not. And the 10
same argument applies to stones worn down by drops of
water[399] and to people hauling ships up on land[400] and to things
heated by fire and to the heap[401] and to the hairy man and the
bald man[402] and the wealthy man and the poor man and the
like. For it is not necessary that what belongs to a certain
number of things taken together should also belong to each of
the things of which the whole collection is [composed]; nor
conversely that what [belongs] to the parts should also [belong] 15
to the whole.

[The argument] possesses its plausibility from [being] grad-
ual. What is worth buying for a hundred drachmas,[403] they say,
is also [worth] buying with the addition or subtraction of a
copper [coin][404] – for the same argument applies both to addition and to subtraction. And by gradually increasing or reduc-
ing [the amount] they lead the argument to the absurdity*. It
is possible to put the question universally: if two are not many,
they will not be[come] many by the addition of one; and if this 20
is so, when one is repeatedly added it seems reasonable that
the things that are already agreed to be many are not many.
And in the same way with subtraction: if a thousand are not
few, they will not become few by the removal of one; and by
[repeatedly] subtracting one they lead the argument into absurdity.

The absurdities mentioned are the result of seeking to get
an exact delineation of things which are by nature such as to 25
be determined with a certain latitude,[405] by sense-perception
rather than by reason. For reason and knowledge[406] are concerned with things that are always the same. And it is for this
reason that in the case of a determinate quantity the sophism
is unconvincing, if someone should ask*, for example, 'if the
unit is not a pair, then are the two taken together not a pair
either?'* The argument commits the fallacy of composition.[407]
For it is not the case that, if sight does not see each part of some 30
gold, it does not see what is composed from them either; nor
that, if a small body is not seen, what is composed of them* is

not seen either. Nor, if a man who possesses one drachma is not wealthy, <is the man who has many drachmas not wealthy either>.[408]

92,1 'When then, with the addition coming about gradually, did he become wealthy instead of being not wealthy?' We will say to the person who asks this: You are demanding an exact determination of what is by nature such as to be determined with [a certain] latitude. The limits of all such things are in a way determined, but the intermediate [stages] are indefinite. The reason for this is that none of the things that are coming to be is without qualification what it is coming to be, and the man who is coming to be wealthy or poor is not, when he is

5 coming to be [so], already wealthy or poor in actuality. So all the things that are coming to be are [subject to] a certain incompleteness in the respect in which they are coming to be, and things that are incomplete are, insofar as they are incomplete, indeterminate and undelineable; and it is in this respect that the argument behaves with contempt [of the facts].

In the case of all things that are coming to be there is something by the addition of which what is potentially a definite something becomes [so] actually – for example, houses. So it is necessary that in the case of all the things mentioned

10 too there should be some final thing by the accession of which one is moved, another seen, another increases, another grows [hair].[409] So, does the confirmation entirely depend on the final [part] and is it this which creates the form and defines the nature [of the thing in question]? Or do both the first and the final [parts possess] the same power, while the power of the whole[410] is not the same? For all the other things too that acquire their proper form gradually do not have their confir-

15 mation entirely depending on the final [part], but in addition with this also on* those that preceded it.[411] The runner does not win by running the final foot [of the course], but by adding one [foot] along with the other [preceding ones]. And the same argument applies to filling things up and to health.[412]

Fragment 2 Vitelli (pp. 92-3; Cod. Riccard. 63, ff. 30v-31r)

(By the same Alexander, from the argument against Heraclides;[413] a consideration of what was said by Aristotle about the fifth substance. In this he argues against a certain Stoic philosopher who criticised Aristotle [by saying] that Aristotle differs from Plato in his opinion about the gods and about the immortality of the soul. In [the course of] this [discussion] Alexander speaks as follows, word-for-word:) 92,5

These things, indeed, in order that they may attack those who [they say] have altogether abandoned the [doctrines] of Plato![414] For if any other of the arguments put forward by Aristotle is opposed to the position of Plato, [certainly] his argument about these things [is], and about the gods and about the soul, as will be shown in the case of these things too at the appropriate time. For if he had not made his name known 10 through the heading of the book, and if the writer did not clearly say* to what sect he belonged, perhaps he could have escaped notice and have seemed to be satisfied with Plato's [doctrines] in writing these things. Since however he proclaims his name through the heading, it is deserving of wonder how it is that, saying he is a philosopher, he is not ashamed when he criticises Aristotle as being most opposed to the opinion of Plato in his 15 doctrine concerning the gods and the soul. For if he criticises 93,1 [Aristotle] for not arguing plausibly against what Plato said about these things, [he himself] being persuaded that what Plato says is true, how will he not much sooner blame the Stoics, whose leader[415] he is, for speaking against Plato on these matters? He *would* [indeed] have blamed them if, when he observed the falsity of their arguments, he had followed [the 5 arguments] which he believed were well stated; for this is [the mark] of a true philosopher, neither oneself to champion things that one is persuaded are stated falsely, nor to become the cause of false opinions in others by inviting them to [accept] these things.

That there is more disagreement in respect of these matters between the Stoics and Plato than between Aristotle [and Plato] is easy for everyone, I suppose, to recognise. For Plato 10 thinks that the first god is incorporeal, and says that he remains in his own place of observation and [his own] intellection, while there are certain secondary gods who oversee the coming-to-be and being of other things; and what Aristotle says is in harmony with this.*[416] And [Plato] says that the soul is a certain incorporeal and imperishable substance, one of which

points is shown [to be true] about it by Aristotle too.[417] [The
15 Stoics] however make god a body, and they think it right for
him, a body, to pass through all things;[418] and they say that the
soul too is a body, and they also say that it is perishable, and
that some souls perish at once along with their possessors when
they perish, while others are preserved until the most absurd
conflagration.[419]

Additional Note on *Quaestiones* 1.1-2.15.

The origin and development of the corpus of Arabic translations of texts attributed to Alexander has been extensively studied by Zimmermann (1994), who has clarified the relation between some of these texts and those that survive in Greek.[420] These include *Quaest.* 1.5 and Dietrich (1964) 19 (cf. Sharples [1992] 36 n. 85), *Quaest.* 1.12 and Dietrich 5 (ibid. 55 n. 150) and *Quaest.* 2.15 and Dietrich 6 (ibid. 116 n. 386). Zimmermann also shows that the versions of *Quaest.* 2.11 (cf. Sharples [1992] 107 n. 351) which are included in Dietrich 7 and Dietrich 27d are different, and that the former is based on the latter; that Dietrich 8, or rather 8a (i.e. the Alexander text listed by Dietrich (1964) 95, as opposed to its sequel from Proclus) is a version of *Quaest.* 1.21 earlier than Dietrich 2b (so too Hasnawi [1994] 53, 55-68; for Dietrich 2b cf. Sharples [1992] 74 n. 220 and references there). Hasnawi (1994) 56-9 and 93-4 gives Arabic texts and French translations of both Dietrich 8a and Dietrich 2b.

Dietrich 8a lacks the introductory references of *Quaest.* 1.21 to quantity and relation (as does also Dietrich 2; see Hasnawi [1994] 61), and indicates that light is introduced (at 35,9 in the Greek text) as raising a possible difficulty for the foregoing claim that actuality is form, since it is actuality and yet is affection – and so quality due to relation – rather than form. (True, it has already been argued that the forms of artefacts fall under the category of quality.) There is thus no need to postulate a lacuna after 35,8 with Bruns. The reference to quantity at the start of *Quaest.* 1.21 is purely introductory, and that to relation is taken up again in the discussion of light at the end of the *Quaestio* (for which cf. now also Accattino [1993] 52 n. 45; for light as a relation Alexander *in De sensu* 134.11ff. with Accattino [1992] 54, but with *Quaest.* 1.21 35,10 contrast, with Hasnawi [1994] 66 n. 29, *Quaest.* 1.2 7,3-4). Sharples (1992) 74 nn. 220-1 should be amended accordingly. The structure and theme of the *Quaestio* are discussed by Hasnawi (1994) 66-7, who relates it to the discussion in Aristotle *Phys.* 3.1, 200b32ff. of the categories in which movement or change belongs and to discussion in the ancient commentaries of whether its being in several categories makes it a homonymous term, noting that, while Philoponus *in Phys.* 349,5-6 attributes to Alexander the view that movement is homonymous, according to Simplicius *in Phys.* he held that movement generically is in the category of relation, while the movements or changes in the different categories are related to each other homonymously. Hasnawi further (64-6) connects the title of Dietrich 8a, 'That form is the actuality of movement and its perfection', to the definition of movement or change (*kinêsis*) as the actuality of the potential *qua* potential at Aristotle, *Phys.* 3.1, 201a10-11, and this may be a more accurate expression of the theme of the text, which *couples* a discussion of the category of movement or incomplete activity/actuality, placing it in the category of relation (as in Alexander cited by Simplicius, above) with that of the category of complete activity/actuality, i.e. form (cf. 35,3-4 and Sharples [1992] 74 n. 223).

Hasnawi has also clarified the exact relation between the Arabic versions of *Quaest.* 1.22 and 1.21 in Dietrich 2; I am grateful to Fritz Zimmermann, too, for discussion of this issue. The statements at Sharples (1992) 74 n. 220 that 'three of the Greek *Quaestiones* are presented as a single text' in Dietrich 2 and 3, and at id. 77 n. 231 that the Arabic version of *Quaest.* 1.22 (Dietrich 2a) is 'followed immediately' by the version of *Quaest.* 1.21 (Dietrich 2b) should be modified, for Hasnawi (1994) 62 n. 20 notes that the three texts (Dietrich 2a, 2b and 3) are each separated in the MS by a sign of three dots; and the rest of Sharples (1992) 77 n. 231, on the end of 1.22, should be deleted. The Arabic, when the division between the two texts is correctly placed, is in fact a rendering of the Greek (Hasnawi, ibid.). The version of *Quaest.* 1.21 in Dietrich 2b begins with the words 'Motion is an affection' before continuing with 'For if to be moved is to be affected ...' (cf. Sharples [1992] 74 n. 220). Whether something has been lost from the Arabic text before these initial words of Dietrich 2b is questioned by Hasnawi (1994) 61-2 n. 20.

On the relation between soul and body in Aristotle, the concern of *Quaest.* 1.8, 1.17 and 1.26, see n. 155 to *Quaest.* 2.26 and the discussions cited there; also Ellis (1994). In connection with a related issue, the possible circularity of Aristotle's definition of soul as the actuality of a body potentially possessing life, the paragraph division in *Quaestio* 2.8 in Sharples (1992) is potentially misleading; the argument at 54,11-14, that the definition is not circular because Aristotle has indicated what the nature of the body is like, is to be interpreted as a continuation of the preceding argument that 'organic' and 'potentially possessing life' are defined in terms of the living creature's activities.[421] 'Moreover' thus amounts to something like '*And*, to make it clearer how this provides a solution ...'. The alternative, that 54,11-14 indicates a completely different solution to the initial problem by defining the relevant body independently of the activities for which soul is the potentiality, for example in terms of its physical structure,[422] is hardly acceptable; for (1) there would be no indication in the text of what the actual definition might be, (2) the application of a definition of this type to *organic* body is not very plausible, and (3) 'moreover', *eti*, is used in the texts attributed to Alexander to introduce a further argument for the same point,[423] not to introduce an alternative solution to a problem, for which the *vox propria* is *ê*, 'or rather'.

The citation of Alexander at Simplicius *in Phys.* 19,5-11, to which my attention has been drawn by André Laks (see above, n. 228 on *Quaest.* 3.3, and his forthcoming paper cited there) provides a further parallel to the closing paragraphs of *Quaestio* 1.11. That text argues that the universal is posterior to there being *some* individual (24,8-16) but prior to *any particular* individual (24,16-22), in each case basing the argument on the principle of *sunanaireisthai* – what is, or is not, removed along with what. Simplicius cites Alexander as arguing that the universal is prior 'in nature' on the same basis as in 24,16-22 in the *quaestio* (*in Phys.* 19,5-7) but not prior 'in the strict sense' (*kuriôs*) because it is not a substance (19,8-11; in *Quaestio* 1.11 *ousia* is mentioned rather in connection with what is contained in the being of a thing.) Not surprisingly, Simplicius finds the contrast between priority 'in nature' and priority 'in the strict sense' unacceptable, and, as a Platonist, opts for the priority of the universal – while going on to say that Alexander's argument can be saved if it is the *post rem* universal resulting from abstraction that is posterior, since the particular is not removed along with this (19,12-17; this, ironically enough, is similar to the actual argument of 24,8-16 of the *quaestio*). Whatever the implications of Simplicius' citation, presumably derived from Alexander's *Physics* commentary, for the authenticity of *Quaestio* 1.11 as a whole (on which cf. Sharples [1992] 50 n. 126; the fact that Simplicius gives the argument at 19,12-17 as if it were his own is scarcely an argument against his having in fact found it in Alexander), the attribution of the argument at 19,5-7 to Alexander is a further consideration against regarding 24,16-22 of the *quaestio* as un-Alexandrian (on which issue cf. Sharples [1992] 54 n. 148).

It may further be added that, as Laks op. cit. notes, Simplicius goes on to attribute to Alexander a *different* interpretation of the passage of the *Physics* in question (19,29-33). But Alexander (apparently) introduced this second interpretation with 'it was said that', suggesting that he did not himself endorse it.

Also related to *Quaestio* 1.11, apparently, is a report by Philoponus *in DA* (*CAG* 15 37,32, cf. 38,10) of Alexander's interpretation of the same statement by Aristotle with which the *quaestio* is concerned, 'the living creature that is universal is either nothing or posterior' (*DA* 1.1, 402b7). The argument attributed to Alexander by Philoponus here – that what is common exists only in thought – is perhaps closer to *Quaest.* 1.3 than to 1.11; within 1.11 it is closer to the second argument ([II] of Sharples [1992] 50 n. 126) than the first. And this is the more striking because the opening words of the passage in Philoponus are identical to the *incipit* of a short unpublished text, 'Alexander *On Universals*', in MS Milan, Ambrosianus graecus Q 74 sup., 176v-177r, as cited by Martini and Bassi (1906), vol. 2 p. 770.

Alexander's account of the souls of the heavenly spheres (for which cf. *Quaest.* 1.1 and 1.25, and 2.19 in the present volume) has been analysed by Accattino (1992). The Arabic version of *Quaest.* 2.3 (cf. Sharples [1992] 93 n. 307) has been translated, and the content of the Greek version and the relation of the Arabic text to it discussed, by Fazzo and Wiesner (1993), especially 125-7, 149-52; for *Quaestiones* 1.25 and 2.3 see also Fazzo and Zonta (forthcoming).

Abbreviations

DG = H. Diels, *Doxographi Graeci*, Berlin 1879.

DK = H. Diels and W. Kranz, *Die Fragmente der Vorsokratiker*, Berlin 1952.

FHSG = W.W. Fortenbaugh, P.M. Huby, R.W. Sharples (Greek and Latin) and D. Gutas (Arabic), eds, *Theophrastus of Eresus*, Leiden 1992.

LS = A.A. Long and D.N. Sedley, *The Hellenistic Philosophers*, Cambridge 1987.

SVF = H. von Arnim, *Stoicorum Veterum Fragmenta*, Leipzig 1903-5.

References to 'Bruns' are to his edition (= Bruns [1892,1]; see the Bibliography) unless otherwise indicated.

Textual Emendations

2 and 3, lists of headings, title. Read *skholikôn* for V's *skholiôn*. See n. 37 above. In the list of headings for book 3, transpose and renumber those for 3.6 and 3.7; see n. 50.

2.16, 61,9. Read *proeirêmenon* for *prokeimenon* with *SVF* 3.19.

2.16, 61,10. Delete *mê* and *ou* in 61.10 with *SVF* 3.19. See n. 57.

2.16, 61,16. *SVF* 3.19 proposes *poiousôn* for *poiountôn*, so that the reference is to the arts rather than the agents. This makes the discussion more consistent, the reference being to the arts throughout, but hardly seems necessary.

2.16, 61,21-2. *SVF* 3.19 proposes *dia <to> panta ê dia <to> tina kai allôs … hepesthai*, '… in every way, because all or at any rate some of the things [included] in them follow differently and not as was expected …'. But this does not seem to improve the structure of the argument.

2.17, 62,10. Read *epei <epi> hulêi*; cf. 62.12.

2.18, 62,22. Read *<en> teleiotêti* with Victorius.

2.18, 62,30. Read *aei* for *dein* with Spengel.

2.18, 62,31. Read *<gar> tis* with B², Victorius and Spengel.

2.20, 64,36. Read *en autois* for *an autois*. I owe this suggestion to Richard Sorabji.

2.20, 65,7. Read *ei ek* with Spengel.

2.20, 65,9. Read *autou* (or *autôi?*) with Schwartz; *autôn* codd.

2.20, 65,10. Read *metebanen* (Bruns, fort.) for *metaballein*.

2.20, 65,11. Read *ho* (Bruns, fort.) for *hon*.

2.20, 65,12. Read *tôi tên* with B²S², the Aldine and Spengel.

2.21, 65,23. Read *pronoein kai* for *pronoeisthai* with Apelt (1906) 10.

2.21, 65,24. Omit *kata Aristotelê*. See n. 99.

2.21, 65,25. Omit *ginesthai*. See n. 100.

2.21, 66,19. Read *esti* for *einai* (suggested by Bruns in his apparatus).

2.21, 66,22. Read *pronooumenou* for *prokeimenou* with Diels (in Bruns' apparatus), *prokeimenou* being an anticipation of the next line.

2.21, 66,30. Read *tis* for *tinos*, with Bruns in his apparatus.

2.21, 67,4. Apelt (1906) 10 proposes *exapinaiôs* for *spaniôs*. See n. 106.

2.21, 67,9. Read *diaireisthai* for *diairesin* with Bruns in his apparatus.

2.21, 67,18. Read *oute kath' hauto <estin oute kata sumbebêkos: to gar kath' hauto> pronoein*, with Apelt (1906) 10.

2.21, 67,28. Read *<hôst' oligon> apodein*; cf. Bruns' apparatus.

2.21, 67,28-9. Read *kath' hauto kai proêgoumenôs*, conjectured by Spengel and approved by Bruns in his apparatus.

2.21, 67,32. Read *pronoountas*, conjectured by Spengel and approved by Bruns in his apparatus.

2.21, 68,10. Read *mentoi* with Victorius and Spengel, approved in Bruns' apparatus; perhaps *en toutois mentoi to einai ekhon.*

2.21, 68,17. Read *erôtêsis* for *eis*, conjectured by Spengel and approved by Bruns in his apparatus.

2.21, 68,31. Read *ginomenas* for *ginesthai* (conjectured by Bruns in his apparatus).

2.21, 69,7-8. Read *kataleipomenon, ei tukhoi, khionos, ân aphelêi tis to leukon*, with Apelt (1906) 11.

2.21, 69,24-5. Read *hôi* for *to* in 69,24, conjectured by Bruns in his apparatus, and consequently omit *<ho>* in 69,25.

2.21, 69,29. Read *atelestero<n to>* and *legein* for the second *legousin*. Cf. Bruns' apparatus.

2.21, 70,2. Read *mêti ge* with Schwartz (in Bruns' apparatus).

2.21, 70,4-5. Read *tinos* (interrog.) *<gar> agathou tois anthrôpois kat' autous hoion te ginesthai <aitian> tên theian pronoian*, with Apelt (1894) 71. Von Arnim *SVF* 2.1118 conjectures *aitian agathou ... oukh hoion te, oukh hoion* being the reading of B²S², the Aldine and Spengel; 'It is not possible for divine providence to be the cause of good for human beings.'

2.21, 70,14. Read *kai* for *ê* with B².

2.22. The translation is based on, and the notes refer to, *not* Bruns' text on pp. 71-2 of his (1892,1) (= Bruns¹), but to the revised text included in the Addenda on pp. xlv-xlvi of the same volume (= Bruns²). See above, n. 122.

2.22, 71,11. Read *to auto* with the MSS and Bruns¹, not just *auto* with Bruns².

2.22, 71,12-13. Read *ta metaxu tou teleutaiou* with the MSS and Bruns¹, not *tôn metaxu to teleutaion* with Bruns².

2.22, 71,14. Omit *to* (suspected by Bruns¹'s apparatus but retained by Bruns²).

2.22, 71,26. Read *tou kai to* with the vulgate, not *to kai ta* with Spengel and Bruns.

2.22, 71,30. Read *toutôi* for *touto*.

2.22, 71,31. For *ta kai* Richard Sorabji conjectures *to kai ta*, giving the same sense with rather more natural Greek.

2.22, 72,6. Read *esesthai touto* (conjectured by Spengel): *hepesthai toutôi* ('... that this follows this necessarily simply') Bruns²; *esesthai toutôi* vulg.

2.23, 72,12. Read *tautês* with B²S², the Aldine, Spengel, DK and Radl 79 n. 58, 222 n. 1. The reference must be to the magnet; cf. 72,22-4 below.

2.23, 72,26. Diels, but not Kranz, proposed *allêla* for *allêlas*.

2.23, 72,26-7. Read *enarthmion* for *enarithmion* with Karsten (DK 31B91, vol. 1 p. 344.8, taking *mallon enarthmion, autar elaiôi* as the end of a hexameter). If Alexander was not quoting directly from the text of Empedocles (where the metre would ensure the correct reading) but from some intermediary source, the error may not be his own.

2.23, 72,29. Read *kenon* with Diels (in Bruns' apparatus, and in DK). So Radl 80 n. 60, 222 n. 30.

2.23, 72,31. Read *oietai* for *hoti einai* with Apelt (1906) 11. Diels in DK, followed by Radl 80 n. 61, proposed *ekeinou*; 'and rarer than it'.

2.23, 72,32. Read *eukinêtoter' on<ta ta atoma> thatton* with Diels in DK, followed by Radl loc. cit. Bruns in his apparatus already suggested *eukinêtotera*.

2.23, 73,9. Read *ei de* (Schwartz, in Bruns' apparatus) and *legei* for *legetai* (with the Aldine and Spengel).

2.23, 73,16. Read *kai gar to pur kaiein ha kaiei autôn tôi [de] eisduomenon,* suggested by Bruns in his apparatus. Diels in DK suggested *to <men> gar, to pur, kaiein ha anakêkiei autou, to de ...* (*to de* being the reading of BS[2], the Aldine and Spengel): 'for the one, fire, burns whatever of it gushes forth, while the other, the vinegar, penetrating into each attracts and consumes ... .'

2.23, 73,18. Diels in DK suggests *tou <oun> sidêrou,* 'So the iron ...'.

2.23, 73,22. Diels in DK suggests *apo toutou <hugron> helkein,* making 'the moisture' explicit.

2.23, 74,3. Read *en heautôi <mê katekhein>,* suggested by Schwartz in Bruns' apparatus.

2.23, 74,20. Read *hê trophê* for *tên trophên* with Radt 85-6, following a proposal originally made by G.A. Palm in 1867.

2.24, 75,28. Read *alêthes kai to kath' <ho> hekastêi;* cf. Bruns' apparatus.

2.27, 77,5. Read *<deixas> mê* with Spengel (approved by Bruns in his apparatus).

2.27, 77,29. Read *psukhên, <kata deuteron de to sôma to tên psukhên>* with Schwartz (in Bruns' apparatus).

2.27, 77,29. Read *<hou> houtôs* with Victorius and Spengel.

2.28, 78,26. Read *oute poiotêtes oute posotêtes* suggested by Schwartz and approved by Bruns in his apparatus.

2.28, 78,32-3. Read *en tôi oikeiôi logôi,* conjectured by Spengel, for *en tôi tou oikeiou logôi* of the MSS, accepted by Bruns.

2.28, 79,12-13. Read *tou genous ... lambanomenou,* conjectured by Spengel; cf. the similar use of a genitive absolute at 79,10 above, and Bruns' apparatus.

3.2, 81,8. Read *peri <tês energeias> tês apo tês hexeôs,* as suggested by Bruns in his apparatus.

3.2, 81,19. Read *tôn allôn au kinêseôn* (for the MSS *ou kinêseôn*) with Apelt (1894) 71.

3.2, 81,20. Read *metaballein* for *metaballon*. (V clearly has the latter.)

3.2, 81,28. Read *autai* for *hautai*.

3.2, 81,31. Read *en* for *ou* with Spengel.

3.2, 82,8. Read *tínôn* (interrogative) with Spengel, but retain *kinoumenôn* as less obvious than *kinêseôn* and avoiding repetition. (I am grateful to the anonymous reader for drawing my attention to Spengel's reading. V clearly has the non-interrogative *tinôn* without the accent and with an acute accent on the preceding *dia*, giving the sense 'such coming-to-be would come about through certain things being moved'.)

3.2, 82,10. Read *kata tas tekhnas <energeiai eis tên teleiotêta sunteloien an> tôn tekhnôn*, suggested in Bruns' apparatus.

3.2, 82,19-20. Read, hesitantly, *ti* (Bruns) *empodizoi, <tês> tôn empodizontôn tas energeias* (Bruns) *anaireseôs kai autês ginomenês*. Bruns reports the readings of V accurately; it has a raised point after *anairesis* and no other punctuation between *ei mê* in 19 and *kinêseôs* in 20. This suggests construing *anairesis* and *tis* together; but what is wanted is a statement that movement is involved in making the activity possible, not in preventing it.

3.3, 83,23. Read *<ho> hoti*, conjectured by Bruns in his apparatus. The Arabic omits the clause.

3.3, 84,7. Punctuate with a comma before *prostheis* rather than with a full stop after it. The Arabic omits 84,4-7.

3.3, 84,13. Read *ison eipen auto <tôi>*, suggested by Bruns in his apparatus. The Arabic omits 84,12-14.

3.3, 84,21. Read *ekhei* for *ekhein*, conjectured by Bruns in his apparatus. The Arabic has 'like understanding' (p. 178.87 Ruland), which might seem to confirm this.

3.3, 85,8. Read *ha oukh hoion te [de]*, suggested by Bruns in his apparatus and confirmed by the Arabic (p. 182.118 Ruland).

3.3, 85,20. Read *pleon <legein> nun legei*, suggested by Bruns in his apparatus. The Arabic omits *huperthemonos ... pleon nun*, renders *legei*, and omits everything from *ta eirêmena* in 21 to *kuria autôn* in 85,30.

3.3, 85,33-4. Read *hôs ison an eiê tôi*, suggested by Bruns in his apparatus. The Arabic simply has 'By "being affected" the Philosopher means alteration' (p. 186.143 Ruland).

3.3, 86,8. Read *tote* for *to de*, conjectured by Spengel. The Arabic simply has 'sensation is potential' (p. 188.160 Bruns), not rendering *to de* or *tote*.

3.3, 86,13-14. Read *pan to paskhon paskhei te kai kineitai hupo*, suggested by Bruns in his apparatus. The Arabic supports this, having 'a thing is affected and changed' (p. 188.166 Ruland).

3.3, 86,30. Read *hup' autou*, conjectured by Bruns in his apparatus. The Arabic just has 'affected by what affects it' for *hup' autou kai di' allou*: p. 194.202 Ruland.

3.3, 86,30. Read *ou mên* for *ou men* with Victorius and Spengel, and punctuate also after *proteron* in 31. The Arabic omits *ou mên* and *eipen proteron*.

3.4, 87,10. Read *kuriôs, hê* (relative) *ginetai*; *hê kuriôs ginetai* suggested in Bruns' apparatus, but *kuriôs* is used in this text to modify *genesis* rather than *ginesthai*. I am grateful to the anonymous reader for pointing this out.

3.5, 87,29. Read *d' <aei>* with Diels, cited in Bruns' apparatus. Bruns himself conjectured *tina* for *ta* ('if certain things come to be that come to be again and again').

3.5, 88,5. Read *hoion te <ti>* (Bruns, in apparatus).

3.5, 88,6. Read *dioti* (Bruns, tentatively in apparatus).

3.5, 88,6. Do not add *hôs* ('comes to be in such a way that either [i] having come to be') with Bruns.

3.5, 88,7. Read *genomenon* for *ginomenon*.

3.5, 88,13. Read *<ti>* (Bruns, in apparatus).

3.5, 88,19. Read *<ou> katho* with Spengel (cited in Bruns' apparatus).

3.5, 88,21. Read *<hautê> men hê akolouthia>*.

3.5, 88,31. Omitting Bruns' comma after *husteron*, which could imply that in such a case there is simply nothing that is later; see above, n. 120. There is no punctuation here in V.

3.5, 88,35-6. Punctuate after *tôn houtô ginomenôn* with V, rather than before *epi* with Bruns.

3.5, 89,2. Perhaps we should read *to pro autou* for *to prôton autou*.

3.5, 89,8. Punctuate after *palin*, 'again', with V; Bruns punctuates before it, remarking that for *palin kai* ('And again') one would expect *alla*, 'But', and supposing that something may have fallen out of the text.

3.5, 89,8. Delete *ei* after *kai*.

3.5, 89,13. Read *de* with Victorius and Spengel rather than *te* with the MSS and Bruns.

3.6, 90,6-7. Read, hesitantly, *ex 'hôn ekhomen' <heôs> 'pantôn <kai ais-thêsin ekhomen>' dia tou*; cf. Bruns' suggestion in his apparatus, but also 90,5 above. That so short a sentence as 90,4-5 should be referred back to in this way rather than quoted as a whole is surprising; but *ex* in 90,6 needs to be accounted for somehow.

3.6, 90,15. Read *sunnêmenon <on>*, suggested by the anonymous reader.

3.8, 94,7. Read *kata sumbebêkos <aisthêton, tôi> aisthêton*, suggested by Schwartz and approved by Bruns in his apparatus.

3.9, 94,22-3. Punctuate the Aristotle text as follows, with Ross in his edition of Aristotle *DA*: *hêi men oun dusi* (*dis* Ross after Trendelenburg) *khrêtai tôi perati, duo krinei kai kekhôrismena, estin hôs tôi kekhorismenôi* (*estin hôs kekhôrismenôs* Ross).

3.9, 96,9. Read *luesthai, luôn epênenken, hôs proeipon, all' ...*, with Schwartz (approved by Bruns in his apparatus).

3.9, 96,24. Read *kai tropon tina houtô kekhôrismenon* <*to krinon*>, suggested by Bruns in his apparatus.

3.9, 96,37. Read *hama* for *hoion*, suggested by Bruns in his apparatus.

3.9, 97,4. Read *katoptrôn*, <*oute hama en tois autois emphainetai*> *oute*, suggested by Bruns in his apparatus.

3.9, 97,25. Read <*pathôn*> *ep' auto pheromenôn* <*touton*> *ton tropon*, suggested by Bruns in his apparatus.

3.9, 98,1. Read *autê* for *en hêi*, suggested by Bruns in his apparatus.

3.9, 98,10. Read *aisthêtôn* for *aisthêtên*; Bruns in his apparatus suggests <*tên tôn*> *aisthêtôn*, but while the *tôn* may be right the *tên* seems to require taking *tôn … ginomenôn* in 98,24 as a rather awkward genitive absolute.

3.10, 98,22. Retain *apo*, deleted by Spengel and Bruns.

3.10, 99,11. Read *gês* <*diêthoumenon*>, suggested by Bruns in his apparatus.

3.10, 99,11-12. Read *hôs mê genomenês tôi* (cf. Bruns in app., but he has *to* rather than *tôi*; an error?)

3.10, 99,18. Delete *kai*; so Bruns in his apparatus but not, by an oversight, in the text.

3.10, 99,20. Read *dia touto* for *dia touton*, with Spengel.

3.10, 99,32. Read *hê* for *tês*, as suggested by Bruns in his apparatus.

3.10, 100,9. Read <*tôi de elatton einai touto tosoutôi, hosôi kai en tôi huomenôi to halmuron tou glukeos elatton,*> *toutôi dê to*, as suggested by Bruns in his apparatus. See above, n. 307.

3.11, 101,6. Read *esti* <*onomatôn aitia*> *tês diaphoras*, suggested by Bruns in his apparatus.

3.12, 101,10. Read *ho logos* <*ho*> *deiknunai* with Usener ap. Bruns (1892,1) xlv, Bruns (1893) 6 n. 6; von Arnim *SVF* 2.536.

3.12, 101,15. Read *para ti* for *perati* with von Arnim, *SVF* 2.536, comparing 104,15, and Todd (1984) 186 n. 3, comparing Alexander ap. Simplicius *in Phys.* 467,2-3.

3.12, 101,18. Usener ap. Bruns (1892,1) xlv and Bruns (1893) 6 n. 6 proposed *antimarturoun, enên tôi logôi pithanotês* <*tis*>, 'owing to the fact that … there is in the argument a certain plausibility'. But Todd argues that emendation is unnecessary (in his unpublished translation and commentary; see the Introduction. References in what follows to 'Todd' without further details being specified are to this version).

3.12, 101,20. Read *prospiptei* <*ti*> with Bruns (1893) 6 n. 6.

3.12, 101,21. Read *hou mêden ektos* Usener ap. Bruns (1892,1) xlv.

3.12, 101,22. Usener ap. Bruns (1892,1) deleted *on*.

3.12, 101,25. Todd proposes *prolabontas* 'presupposing' for *proslabontas*.

3.12, 101,27-8. Read *dei* for *dein* with Todd. He also proposes *zêtountas* for *zêtein;* 'one must not, seeking evidence from the senses … familiar, transfer it …'. Usener ap. Bruns (1892,1) xlv and Bruns (1893) 6-7 n. 6 reads *mêde [dein] zêtein … para tôn merôn … metapheront'*, 'and for this reason [one ought not to enquire] by transferring the evidence of the senses from the parts, with which they are cognate, to the totality'.

3.12, 101,31. Read *<ei de toiouton hê phusis ekeinou>* with Bruns (1893) 6-7 n. 6; in his apparatus in *Suppl. Ar.* ad loc. Bruns suggests rather *<ei de toiouton hê tou pantos phusis>*.

3.12, 102,6. Read *hou merê panta hôn* with Bruns (1893) 7.

3.12, 102,11. Read *auto holon tôi* with Bruns in app.; at Bruns (1893) 7 he suggests alternatively *toutôi holon*, and rejects *apo tou* as a possibility. Todd retains the MSS *atopon*, deleting *tôi,* and takes the whole argument as a *reductio*; 'if individual sensible things are parts, *and* the whole of which these things are parts [is itself *only* a part, being externally bounded], ... it is absurd for everything ... to be referred to some totality' (because there would not then be one).

3.12, 102,12. Read *to holon ti* with BS¹F¹ and Todd in his unpublished translation. Cf. 105,20.

3.12, 102,14. Read *<merous> meros; <kai> ei mê holon ti*. Victorius, followed by Bruns (1893) 7 n. 1 and 8, proposed *<merous> meros, <hou> ei mê holon ti*, 'and if there is not some whole of *<this>*' (i.e., of which this is a part); in the apparatus to his edition Bruns proposed rather *<ho> ei mê holou ti*, 'if *<this>* is not some [part] of a whole'. Todd has *<ho> ei mê holon ti*, 'and if *<this>* is not a whole>'; this may be right, but the connecting relative follows awkwardly after the negative in 102,12-14 as construed here.

3.12, 102,18. Todd proposes *<to> peperasmenon*.

3.12, 102,21. Read *huph' hautou* with the Aldine and Spengel.

3.12, 102,23. Read *eis ho*, with MS L (cf. Bruns [1892,1] xlii) and Bruns in his apparatus ad loc.

3.12, 102,32. Read *<ho> oukh hoion te*. Todd keeps the MSS text and understands 'and it is not possible for Nature ...'.

3.12, 103,9. Todd adds *ginomena <kata phusin>*.

3.12, 103,12. Bruns (1893) 9 n. 1 tentatively suggests *sunthetôn* for *ontôn*.

3.12, 103,15. Bruns (1893) 9 n. 1 retains *gar* with an obelus; in (1892,1) he had accepted Schwartz's *an*. See n. 10. Todd treats *ti gar* as part of the following sentence, which he concludes with a question-mark after *legein* in 103,15.

3.12, 103,19. Todd reads *<tou> peperasmenou*.

3.12, 103,34. Read *eti d' <ei>*, suggested by Bruns in his apparatus.

3.12, 103,34. Read *kai tôn tukhon ti megethos ekhontôn* with Usener ap. Bruns (1892,1) xlv.

3.12, 103,35. Todd reads *têi sunthesei*; 'for things ... to produce some unlimited magnitude by their combination'.

3.12, 104,2. Read *<ei gar leipetai ti metaxu>*, suggested by Bruns in his apparatus.

3.12, 104,4. Read *ek tou metaxu* with Usener ap. Bruns (1892,1) xlv.

3.12, 104,9. Read *têi pros allêlous [têi] kata mian sunthesei,* suggested by Bruns in his apparatus.

3.12, 104,13. Read *eti* for *ekhoi* with Spengel, cited in Bruns' apparatus. See n. 14.

3.12, 104,26. Read *hautou* Usener ap. Bruns (1892,1) xlv.

3.12, 104,28. Read *hois* <*hôs*>, suggested in Bruns' apparatus.

3.12, 104,30. Todd reads *axiousi* with Spengel.

3.12, 104,32. Todd deletes *oukh hêi ... hêi merê* as a gloss.

3.12, 105,1-2. Read *to de pros ti perainon.*

3.12, 105,2-3. Read *peperasmenon* <*einai*> *en,* suggested by Bruns in his apparatus.

3.12, 105,7. Read *lambanein* with Usener ap. Bruns (1892,1) xlv.

3.12, 105,7. Read *eti* for *epi,* as suggested by Bruns in his apparatus.

3.12, 105,14. Read *sômata* for *asômata* with Usener ap. Bruns (1892,1) xlv and Bruns (1893) p. 10; rejected however by Todd.

3.12, 105,20. Read *ti* for *te,* suggested by Bruns in his apparatus.

3.12, 105,24-5. Read *ou gar* <*pan*> *to phainomenon* with Todd (1984) 189 n. 20, comparing 105,27 and Aristotle *Metaphysics* 4.5, 1010b1-2.

3.12, 105,28. Todd deletes *kai egrêgorotôn,* comparing Alexander *in Metaph.* 313,1-4, on 1010b10-11.

3.12, 105,29. Read *dunamenon* for *tôn dunamenôn,* with Schwartz (cited in Bruns' apparatus).

3.12, 105,34. Read *apo* for *hoti* with Todd.

3.12, 106,10. Read *hoi* as article rather than relative, with Todd.

3.12, 106,12. Read *ho* for *hoi* (deleted by Bruns) with *SVF* 2.536.

3.12, 106,16. Todd reads *autôi* for *autois,* but see nn. 35 and 349.

3.12, 106,17. Punctuate after *kenon,* as suggested by Bruns in his apparatus, rather than before as in his text.

3.12, 106,18. Read *tôi* for *tou,* as suggested by Bruns in his apparatus.

3.12, 106,20. Read *einai diastêmatôn* with Todd in his unpublished translation.

3.12, 106,22. Read *mêd' ho pros toutôi [to] proeilêphos,* suggested by Bruns in his apparatus; *mêde pros toutôi to* Todd.

3.12, 106,30. Todd deletes *kai kraseôs* as a gloss.

3.12, 106,33. Todd reads *toude* <*tou* (Spengel)> *kosmou, ho kai* <*to*> *pan.*

3.12, 106,34. Read *ontos* for *einai,* as suggested by Bruns in his apparatus.

3.12, 106,35. Todd reads *tôn diastaseôn,* comparing 106,6-10 above.

3.12, 106,38. Todd deletes *de* rather than adding a second *kôluthêsetai* with Spengel and Bruns.

3.13, 107,17. Delete the first *tôi,* as suggested tentatively by Bruns in his apparatus.

3.13, 107,24. Apelt (1894) 71 proposed *eti ei mêde* or *epei* <*ei*> *mêde.* But cf. the similar asyndeton at 108,11.

3.13, 108,11. Read *tousde* for *toude,* as suggested tentatively by Bruns in his apparatus.

3.14, 108,30. Read *panta <ekhein>*, conjectured by Bruns in his apparatus.

3.14, 109,6. Do not postulate a lacuna with Bruns. See n. 369.

3.14, 109,9. Read *mêden toutôn tôi <mê> logon ... ekhein* with Bruns in his apparatus, comparing Alexander *in Meteor.* 182,17 (presumably; for his 127r9 read 127r14?).

3.14, 109,16. Add *<eulogon>* (Bruns in his apparatus).

3.14, 109,18. Read *zôiôn, <legoito, apepsia de epi tês trophês tôn zôiôn>* with Bruns in his apparatus, comparing Alexander *in Meteor.* 182,21. But the sequence of argument in the passage is not clear.

3.14, 109,35. Read *tês en hekastôi <thermotêtos têi en tôi> periekhonti* (Victorius, as corrected by Bruns in his apparatus).

3.14, 110,33. Read *thermotês, <to de psukhrotês, thermotês>* as conjectured by Bruns in his apparatus.

3.14, 111,15. A section appears to have dropped out of the text through homoioteleuton. See n. 376.

3.14, 112,13. Read *legesthai* for *legetai* (so Bruns, conjecturally, in his apparatus).

3.14, 113,9. Read *<hôs> hugrainesthai* with Victorius and Spengel (in Bruns' apparatus). But the corruption of the text is clearly more extensive.

3.14, 113,11. Read *<nephos> ginomenon* (Diels, cited in Bruns' apparatus).

3.14, 113,12. Read *metabolên, <ta de kata to têkesthai to pepêgos>* (Bruns, tentatively in his apparatus).

3.14, 113,26. Read *to de memigmenon* (Spengel) for *to dê memigmenon*.

3.14, 114,1. Read *epi* for *hupo* (Bruns, in his apparatus).

3.14, 114,24. Read *mixis* for *psuxis,* as required by the syntax and by comparison with Aristotle *Meteor.* 4.7, 383b27-8, Alexander *in Meteor.* 208,30 (I am grateful to Eric Lewis for the latter reference). The error in the *Quaestio* is already present in V.

3.15, 115,27. Read *eti ei homoion amerei to phainomenon,* conjectured by Spengel and approved by Bruns in his apparatus.

3.15, 116,9. Read *kata tina metabolên <tout' auto ginetai, kata tina metabolên>* to *hoionei ameres,* conjectured by Schwartz (in Bruns' apparatus).

3.15, 116,10. Read *<kai> epei,* suggested by Bruns in his apparatus.

Fr. 1 Vitelli, 91,18. Read *ei<s t>o adoxon* (Barnes); the MS, he notes, has *ei ho adoxon.* Vitelli prints *eis adoxon.*

Fr. 1 Vitelli, 91,28. Read *ei <de> tis erôtôiê,* suggested by Vitelli in his apparatus *exempli gratia.* The punctuation in the translation follows the MS (reported by Barnes); Vitelli has a full stop after 'unconvincing' and a comma after 'either?'.

Fr. 1 Vitelli, 91,31-2. Read *to ex autôn [êgoun ek tôn mikrôn],* excising the latter phrase as a gloss on the former, with Barnes; Vitelli has *to [ex autôn êgoun] ek tôn mikrôn.*

Fr. 1 Vitelli, 92,15. Read *kan (=kai en) tois prohuparkhousin* (Barnes); *kai tois prohuparkhousin* MS.

Fr. 2 Vitelli, 92,11. Read *legôn* for *logôn*.

Fr. 2 Vitelli, 93,12. Read *hôi* for *hôn*, as suggested by Vitelli in his apparatus.

Notes

1. This Introduction is based, with appropriate modifications, on that to my previous translation of *Quaest.* 1.1-2.15 in this series.

2. cf. Simplicius, *in Phys.* 707,33; 1170,2; 1176,32; Philoponus, *in An. Pr.* 136,20.

3. He was appointed as a public teacher of Aristotelian philosophy, possibly in Athens, between AD 198 and 209. The dates of his teachers, and other evidence for his possible intellectual contacts, suggest that he was already philosophically active in the latter part of the second century, as his appointment would in any case lead one to expect. Cf. Todd (1976,2) 1 n. 3, Sharples (1987,1) 1177-8, (1990,1) 83-4, 92-4, and further references there. (For works cited by author's name and date only, see the Bibliography.)

4. In Greek, the *de Anima libri mantissa* (*Supplement to the Book* On the Soul) and the *Ethical Problems*; other texts survive in Arabic. See further below, and for a general survey cf. Sharples (1987,1) 1189-95. The texts that survive in Greek were edited, along with the more substantial treatises *On the Soul*, *On Fate* and *On Mixture*, by Bruns (1887) and (1892,1), on which the present translation is based.

5. I have endeavoured to say more about the evidence the minor works attributed to Alexander can give us for the functioning of his 'school' in Sharples (1990,1).

6. The Arabic texts are listed by Dietrich (1964), supplemented by Van Ess (1966); cf. Sharples (1987,1) 1187-8 and 1192-4. The Arabic texts are sometimes close to the Greek, sometimes less so; passages are on occasion omitted or transposed, and in some cases even the relation between the texts is disputed. See the notes to individual *quaestiones* in the present volume.

7. So Bruns (1892,1) v. The *Ethical Problems* are thus sometimes cited as '*Quaestiones* book 4', a title that has no MS authority. The *Quaestiones* and *Ethical Problems* should be distinguished from the (definitely spurious) *Medical Puzzles and Physical Problems* also attributed to Alexander and edited by J.L. Ideler, *Physici et Medici Graeci Minores*, Berlin 1841, and H. Usener, *Alexandri Aphrodisiensis quae feruntur Problematorum libri 3 et 4,* Berlin 1859; confusion between the two collections is not unknown. Cf. Sharples (1987,1) 1198, and below n. 54.

8. This collection is translated into English by Sharples (1990,2).

9. Notably the two edited by Vitelli (1902) and included in the present volume.

10. 'Scholia logica' are referred to in what may be a gloss at Alexander, *in An. Pr.* 250,2; and an 'Explanation and summary of certain passages from (Aristotle's) *de Sensu*', which Moraux suggests may have been a similar collection, is referred to by a scholion on *Quaest.* 1.2. Cf. Moraux (1942) 24; Sharples (1987,1) 1196.

11. cf. Sharples (1992) 3 n. 10.

12. cf. Bruns (1892,1) xi; Sharples (1990,2) 25 n. 48, 29 n. 66, 39 n. 111, (1992) 3 n. 11; below, nn. 54, 79, 150, 157, 207, 243. See also below n. 120, on the title to

Quaest. 2.22 – where however Bruns' suspicions seem unjustified at least as far as the reading in the cited text of Aristotle is concerned – and n. 390, on the title and closing comment added to *Quaest.* 3.14.

13. Alexander's commentary on the *de Sensu* cites not only the lost *de Anima* commentary (167,21) but also a section of the *Mantissa* (*in Sens.* 31,29, citing *Mantissa* 127-30; cf. P. Wendland, preface to *CAG* 3.1, v; Moraux [1978] 297 n. 71). Boethius seems to know both Alexander's *On Fate* and the last section of the *Mantissa* (*in Int. editio secunda* 196,19ff. and 236,11-16; Sharples [1978] 257-9). But it is one thing to show that some of these texts were known at a given date, another to show that the collections existed in their present form.

14. Notably in the case of *Mant.* 169-72; cf. Sharples (1975,2). Cf. in general Sharples (1990,1) 101-3.

15. Bruns (1892,1) v-xiv; cf. Moraux (1942) 19-28 and Sharples (1987,1) 1189-95.

16. Whether or not introduced by the common formula *ê* 'Or rather'; see below, at nn. 74, 82, 152 and 171.

17. As Bruns (1892,1) xii-xiii notes, these are characteristic of the *Mantissa* rather than of the *Quaestiones*; they also occur in the *Ethical Problems*. (*Quaest.* 2.28, however, approaches close to the type.)

18. cf. Bruns (1892,1) ix. Different discussions of the same topic sometimes read 'almost like (answers to) exam questions set in successive years' (a description I owe to Richard Sorabji).

19. cf. n. 197, and Sharples (1990,1) 103-10. *Quaest.* 2.21 is actually in the form of a narrated dialogue; but this is likely to be a literary construction rather than the record of an actual discussion, especially given its somewhat tortuous construction (notably at 70,6-24).

20. For example, the last four sections of the *Mantissa* (pp. 169-86) are linked by subject matter with Alexander's treatise *de Fato, On Fate*. Cf. Moraux (1942) 24; and on the exact nature of the relation in the case of two of these sections cf. Sharples (1975,2) and (1980).

21. Moraux (1942) 23; in the present volume, *Quaest.* 2.24-7, 3.2-3, 3.6-9. On the *Quaestiones* as evidence for the text of Aristotle's *de Anima* cf. Ross (1961) 2-3.

22. See Sharples (1987,1) 1195. Notably for the present volume, *Quaest.* 2.17, 2.22, 3.4 and 3.5 are part of a sequence concerned with Aristotle's *de Generatione et Corruptione*; cf. Todd (1976,2) 19 n. 90.

23. See Sharples (1992) 50 n. 126, and the title of *Quaest.* 2.22 with n. 12 above; also below, nn. 270, 284, 316.

24. cf. *GC* 2.10, 336b31ff., 2.11, 338a18ff., and *Quaest.* 3.4. See also Sharples (1992) 93-4 n. 307.

25. cf. *Quaest.* 1.25 41,11ff., 2.19 63,22ff. and 3.5 89,20ff.

26. cf. also fr. 2 Vitelli; both in the present volume.

27. ed. Ruland (1976). See also Fazzo and Zonta (forthcoming).

28. Moraux (1942) 200.

29. On the whole question of divine providence cf. Sharples (1987,1) 1216-18 and references there; also now Fazzo and Wiesner (1993).

30. Bruns (1887) v dates it to the tenth century, Thillet (1982) to the late ninth.

31. cf. Montanari (1971); Sharples (1992) 102 n. 329.

32. Thillet [1982] 31 n. 3, 56.

33. Notably, by translating *energeia* by both 'activity' and 'actuality' within a single text. cf. nn. 67, 198, 211, 215, 274. Another problematic term is *dunamis*; in the physical context of *Quaest.* 3.14 it has been rendered by 'power' (whether active or passive), but elsewhere 'potentiality' or 'capacity' seemed more suitable – though I am aware that the exigencies of translation may thus impose more separation between different areas of philosophical discourse than Alexander, or Aristotle, would have wished. Again, *kinein* and its cognates have generally been rendered by 'change' in psychological ones but 'movement' in physical ones where the reference is clearly to spatial movement – e.g. that of the heavens –, sometimes involving a contrast with *metabolê* as a more general term for all types of change. See nn. 63, 198, 275, 371, 384.

34. cf. Sharples (1992) 8 n. 30, and n. 72 in the present volume.

35. cf. Sharples (1992) 8 n. 31, and nn. 163, 349, 385 in the present volume; also n. 277.

36. The translations of *Quaest.* 2.22 and 3.5 appeared in Sharples (1979), of 3.13 in Sharples (1983,1), and of 2.20 in Sharples (1983,2).

37. Bruns prints the full title only in the heading to book 1; in fact it is present in MS V at the start of the second and third books as well, but with the ungrammatical *scholiôn phusikôn aporiôn* ... replacing book 1's *phusikôn scholikôn aporiôn* (cf. Bruns [1892,1], apparatus to 1,1).

38. For the list of chapter-headings to *Quaest.* 2.1-15 see Sharples (1992) 14-15.

39. Aristotle, *GC*, 2.11, 337b25ff.

40. i.e. the magnet.

41. Aristotle, *DA* 2.1, 412a6ff.

42. ibid. 2.1, 412b15ff.

43. ibid. 2.1, 412b26ff.; entry added to the table of contents by Victorius.

44. ibid. 2.2, 413a20ff.; entry added to the table of contents by Spengel.

45. See n. 1 above. In the MSS the chapter-headings for book 3 appear at the start of that book; in the present volume it seemed more convenient for the reader to place the chapter-headings of the second part of Book Two and of Book Three together at this point.

46. See below, n. 203.

47. Aristotle, *DA* 2.5, 417b5.

48. ibid. 2.5, 416b32.

49. The title of the *quaestio* has 'it is not the case that ... they are'. See below, n. 243.

50. In the MSS *Quaest.* 3.6 and 3.7 are transposed and wrongly numbered in the table of contents. The sequence of passages in *DA* under discussion makes it clear that the body of the book has the correct sequence and the table of contents is incorrect; I have therefore restored the correct order in the table as well.

51. Aristotle, *DA* 3.2, 425b12.

52. ibid. 3.1, 424b24-425a13.

53. ibid. 3.2, 427a2.

54. This *quaestio* is classified by Bruns (1892,1) vi as a problem in the strict sense. It has been discussed by Ierodiakonou (forthcoming), who compares it with the discussion of similar issues at Alexander, *in Top.* 32,26-34,5 and by Galen, and shows that our *quaestio* is trying to reconcile opposed views, both of which can find some support in Aristotle, and is doing so in the context of an on-going debate about the status of medicine as an art. I am most grateful to Dr Ierodiakonou and to Dr Alan Lacey for discussion of the details of this text. 61,4-23 = *SVF* 3.19.

Stochastic arts are those (such as medicine or navigation; Alexander *in Top.* loc. cit.) which cannot lay down procedures, or predict their outcome, with precision (61,10-22), and for which the successful achievement of their objective depends in part upon factors external to the art itself (61,18-19). The perfect practice of the art, in the sense of the practitioner doing everything that could be expected of the most skilled person ('making every effort': more literally, in the Greek here, 'doing everything as far as they themselves are concerned', and so throughout), is still not enough to guarantee success; and in this respect stochastic arts are contrasted, in Alexander *in Top.* loc. cit., with 'productive' arts such as building and weaving. Our text poses a dilemma; *either* (I) the end of the stochastic arts is simply the perfect practice, in which case achieving the *end* will not depend on external factors any more than the achieving of the end of non-stochastic arts does, though achieving the end will not necessarily mean success in achieving the objective – one can be an excellent doctor in one's treatment of this particular patient without necessarily curing him or her. (This, as Ierodiakonou notes, finds some support in *EN* 3.3, 1112b11-15 and *MM* 1.18, 1190a1-28.) Or else (II) the end is to achieve the objective, and in that case the end for stochastic and non-stochastic arts will be the same, achieving the objective, but in the case of the stochastic arts it will depend on external factors while in that of the non-stochastic ones it will not. (This way of putting the point is somewhat artificial, for in the case of the non-stochastic arts achieving the end automatically implies achieving the objective.) (*This* view is supported, as Ierodiakonou again notes, by *Top.* 1.3, 101b5-10 and by *Rhet.* 1.1, 1355b10-15.) As Ierodiakonou explains, our text resolves the dilemma (at 61.23ff.) by accepting view (II) as far as the *end* is concerned, but reformulating the distinction drawn in view (I) between end and objective as a distinction between *task* and end, a distinction which is also made in Alexander, *in Top.* loc. cit.

The status of medicine as an art is also discussed by Galen who, as Ierodiakonou shows, emphasises the certainty of general rules by contrast with the variability of the subject-matter to which they are applied on particular occasions (cf. 61,20-2 here, and, more explicitly taking the Galenic view, [Alexander], *Medical Problems* 2 prologue, p. 52,14-19, 53,5-9 in Ideler. This was referred to by Nicoletto Vernia, *contra perversam Averrois opinionem,* Venice 1505, fol. 5.2 as from Alexander's '*Quaestiones* on nature'; the correct identification is due to Mahoney (1968) 280-1. See above, n. 7). Alexander on the other hand, in his *Prior Analytics* commentary, analyses arts such as medicine in terms of propositions that hold only for the most part (*in An. Pr.* 39,17-40,5; 165,8-15; 300,3-12). Cf. also Alexander's account of the failures of divination at *Fat.* 6, 171,7ff., *Mant.* 186,8 – by contrast with the Stoic account for which the explanation is neither in the subject-matter nor in a necessary limitation in the art itself, but in the imperfect understanding of the practitioners (*SVF* 2.1210, cf. Tacitus, *Annals* 6.22.6). The contrast between practice and success in (I), and the identification of the *former* as the end, is strongly reminiscent of Stoic ethical doctrine; cf. LS 64C, 64F.

The title is doubly awkward (cf. above, n. 12). First, it represents the issue as being one about the other arts rather than, as it is, one about the stochastic arts. But secondly, it is most naturally taken as implying that both types of arts have as their end making every effort towards achieving their objective, but that they have this as their end in different ways. However, the conclusion in 61,23ff. is that making every effort is not the *end* of stochastic arts. To take *oukh* with *hexousi* rather than with *homoiôs*, 'How the other arts will not, in a similar way to the stochastic arts, have as their end making every effort ...', makes the title an assertion of (I) rather than of (III) and confuses the distinction between having different ends and having ends in different ways on which the contrast between (I) and (II) depends. The title seems to be based on an inadequate study of the text.

55. That is to say, in a way that does not depend on any factors external to the art itself.

56. That is, by not achieving their end in the same way, in that their doing so depends – as it does not in the case of the non-stochastic arts – on factors external to the practice of the art itself.

57. i.e.: [if the end of stochastic arts is making every effort, whereas that of non-stochastic arts is succeeding, then], although in both cases *achieving* the end depends on the art alone and not on external factors, the ends are different. But to say that on this view the end is 'achieved in the same way' is not the most perspicuous of claims; and I take it that this explains the addition of *mê* and *ou* in 61,10 – whether the apparent corruption of *ei kai* into *ou kai* earlier in the line reflects a subsequent attempt to mend the damage or an unconnected corruption.

58. More literally, 'when [the agents] do [everything] as far as [the arts] are concerned' (see n. 55 above); or, with von Arnim's emendation, 'when [the arts] do [everything] as far as they themselves are concerned'. See Textual Emendations.

59. Literally *hupekkauma*, the 'fire-sphere' or region of fire immediately below the aetherial heavens in the Aristotelian universe; cf. Wildberg (1988) 126. Our text treats this, rather than the actual burning fires on earth, as one of the four simple bodies or 'elements'; so too Philoponus (Wildberg [1988] 167-8). For Aristotle in *Meteor.* 1.3, 340b23 terrestrial fire, called 'effervescence' (as here) and 'excess of heat' is real fire, the fire-sphere 'what we are accustomed to call fire' (cf. *Meteor.* 1.4, 341b22 and *GC* 2.3, 330b25). Alexander in his commentary on the *Meteorology* (14.25ff.) follows Aristotle in identifying terrestrial fire as real fire, but refers to the fire-sphere as 'the one of the elements which is called fire', implying that it is an element but is not rightly called fire. Simplicius, *in Cael.* 439,14 cites Alexander – presumably in the lost commentary on *Cael.* – as interpreting the 'air' ignited by the movement of the heavens at *Cael.* 2.7, 289a20 as the fire-sphere while saying that elsewhere Aristotle called the fire-sphere both fire and an element. What all three Alexander texts – the *Meteorology* commentary, the *Cael.* commentary reported by Simplicius, and the present *quaestio* agree on is that it is the fire-sphere rather than terrestrial fire which is elemental. Cf. Sharples (1990,1) 98-9.

The present *quaestio* indeed takes this for granted, concerning itself with the consequent problem that, if the fire-sphere is elemental fire but is less hot than the fire that burns on earth, this might suggest that terrestrial fire is more pure than elemental fire. Our text answers this by claiming that it is admixture with matter that gives terrestrial fire its distinctive nature. The fact that terrestrial fire needs matter as its fuel had already caused Theophrastus to call its elemental nature into question (*de Igne* 4-9; cf. Sharples (1985) 580-3, to be read together with Battegazzore [1987-8]).

The present text is counted as an *epidromê* or summary of Aristotelian doctrine by Bruns (1892,1) x; but it is surely a 'problem' in the proper sense in content, even if not in form.

60. 'not' is not in the MSS at this point, but is present in the list of titles at the start of book 2; it is consequently added here by the printed editions.

61. The example of fire and iron is discussed from a different point of view, in a critique of the Stoic doctrine of total blending, at Alexander *Mixt.* 9, 222,35.

62. Or, reading <*oukh*> *houtô*, suggested by Bruns in his apparatus but not printed in his text, 'is not hot in the same way [as terrestrial fire]'.

63. This text is in fact concerned to contrast the limited natural movements of the sublunary elements with the unending natural circular movement of the heavens. The basic contrast is Aristotelian enough, though there are two specific points of contact with other material attributed to Alexander (below, nn. 65 and 67). Bruns (1892,1) viii classes it among the *epidromai* or summaries of Aristotelian doctrine. 'Movement' (*kinêsis*) might also be rendered by 'change', for nature is a source of all sorts of change; but the concern of the present *quaestio* is with locomotion, and the more general term *metabolê* is rendered by 'change' at 62,25 below.

64. The words used for coming-to-be in a place in this clause, and for the coming-to-be in the sense of generation in the previous clause, are cognate (there *hê genesis ... ginetai,* here *genesthai*); I have translated in a way that does not obscure this.

65. cf. Alexander, *DA* 22.7 with Sharples (1987,1) 1215 and references there. Lang (1992) 16, 98 and 107-14 has argued that it is a distortion to interpret as an immanent *principle of movement* nature which in Aristotle himself is rather a principle of *being moved* (*Phys.* 2.1, 192b21); she does not however note that the distortion, if such it is, is already present in Alexander.

66. That is, as the sequel shows, the divine or heavenly body or bodies.

67. *energeia,* rendered by 'activity' two clauses earlier. For the general doctrine here – the regular movement of the heavenly spheres emulates the changelessness of the Unmoved Mover – cf. Alexander, *Quaest.* 1.25 40,18.

68. It is the actuality of the potential, *qua* potential; Aristotle, *Phys.* 3.1, 201b10-13. I use 'are in imitation of' rather than 'imitate' to capture the perfect *memimêtai* (62,34).

69. It is the heavenly body that is most properly body, according to our author.

70. The thought may be: being circular and occupying a circular place, it will never have to cease from movement, either through running out of space in which to move (as would eventually happen in the case of rectilinear movement in an Aristotelian universe), or, perhaps, through having reached its natural place.

71. I have inserted 'the heavens' to mark the fact that the Greek here changes back from singular to plural.

72. The Greek has the optative, but the simple future is more natural English idiom, as often. See above, n. 34.

73. This *quaestio* is classed by Bruns (1892,1) vi as a problem in the strict sense. Like its predecessor, it is concerned with the contrast between the heavens and the sublunary region; but it draws the contrast in a way that is central to Alexander's doctrine of providence, the sublunary region alone being in need of providence, and this consisting in the regular movement of the heavens giving the sublunary region the only sort of permanence it can have, the permanence of kinds or species though not of individuals. The same doctrine is stated both in the last part of *Quaest.* 1.25 and in the treatise *On Providence* surviving in Arabic (33,1ff., 87,5ff. Ruland [1976]); and for the permanence of species cf. also *Quaest.* 3.5 and above n. 25. The way in which the problem is presented in the present text, however, highlights a problem: are the heavens too – and thus the world as a whole – not dependent on the Unmoved Mover for their continued movement, which surely constitutes their 'ordering' if not their being? See further on this Sharples (1983,3) and, in general, Fazzo and Zonta (forthcoming). – The first part of the Arabic text listed by Van Ess (1966) as his 33 is a (pretty free) paraphrase of this *quaestio*; it is translated into English, and its relation to the Greek original discussed, in Fazzo and Wiesner (1993), 138-40 and 152-3. The Arabic text is as yet unpublished.

74. The common formula for introducing a solution to a problem; see above, n. 16.

75. The clear statement that the heavens are ensouled is noteworthy. Cf. Sharples (1982) 208; also Accattino (1992) 42.

76. cf. *Quaest*. 1.25 40,18, and above at n. 67.

77. Above, n. 73.

78. cf. Alexander, *Fat*. 6, 169,26, and *Quaest*. 2.3 50,6.

79. Misleadingly put; the point at issue is not, as this might suggest, whether what has changed from A to B still has the potentiality *for being B* – an issue which does indeed arise in *Quaest*. 1.19 and 2.15; cf. Sharples (1992) 117 n. 389 – but rather, as the first sentence of the discussion shows, whether it retains the potentiality *for becoming A again*. See above, n. 12. The general point is introduced in the context of, and applied at the end of the *quaestio* to, the question of the perishability of the world; see below, nn. 80, 92, 93. – This *quaestio* is classified by Bruns (1892,1) vi as a problem in the strict sense; it was discussed and translated at Sharples (1983,2) 102-5.

80. *Cael*. 1.12, 282b4 asserts that whatever comes to be perishes, but not that it becomes again what it was previously. 283b21 asserts that physical bodies are destroyed *by* (rather than *into*) the things of which they are composed, but Simplicius (*in Cael*. 358,10ff.) interprets this in terms of coming-to-be from the opposite and perishing into the opposite. Bruns refers to *Cael*. 1.10, 279b4, but this seems to be only a general reference to the beginning of the whole discussion of the imperishability of the universe. See below, n. 92.

81. Aristotle, *Metaph*. 8.5, 1044b34ff. makes the point that wine is not the matter of vinegar, or a living man of a corpse; rather, the wine and the vinegar have the same matter, water, the matter of the wine becoming that of the vinegar by corruption. He does not explicitly make the point that the vinegar cannot turn back to wine again (except by becoming water first), but clearly could have done so. His example differs from Alexander's in that it involves corruption rather than coming-to-be proper; but it makes the same point that the change is not directly reversible. Cf. on this Gill (1988) 197-8 and (1989) 94-7; Shields (1993) 17 and n. 34. The reversibility of change is asserted by Plato in *Phaedo* 70-2 (I am grateful to Alan Lacey for drawing this to my attention in the present connection); it is also central to Aristotle's account of the Presocratics' material principles (*Metaph*. 1.3, 983b8ff.), and might seem to follow naturally from the doctrine that change is between opposites (*Phys*. 1.5, 188a30ff., 5.1, 224b28ff.). Hence the need for clarification.

82. See above, n. 16.

83. If 'log' *were* the opposite of 'bench', one *might* expect the bench to turn back into a log again. But neither 'log' nor 'wood' is the opposite of 'bench'. On the relation of coming-to-be to form and privation on the one hand, and the opposites on the other, see *Quaest*. 2.11 with Sharples (1992) 107 n. 351, and Alexander, *Ethical Problems* 30.

84. The two cases envisaged are perhaps (i) that of the bench being physically broken up, so that the bench is no more but the wood survives, and (ii) that of the wood of which the bench is composed rotting away or being burned, so that one is left with neither the bench nor the wood. But even in the first case the bench has not turned back into the original log; and in the sense in which the *wood* survives, the bench did not come to be by change from the wood, but was wood all the time. 'Something like this' might be intended to cover cases like that of a structure collapsing if the fastenings holding it together disintegrated with age, when the cause is not external to the structure as a whole though it *is* external to the surviving material.

85. Schwartz transposed *ginomenon* and *hupokeimenon* in 64,16; 'as the thing which underlies is natural, so is that which comes to be'. And it is true that the preceding paragraph has suggested that the arts or crafts, too, deal with *matter* that is natural; though in fact one art may use as its matter the product of another art. More importantly, the present sentence is misleading in suggesting that the important issue is the contrast between nature and art; for complex natural bodies too come to be from ingredients which do not persist – such as the menses, below at 64,36-7 – and in these cases too the change is not directly reversible. What *is* perhaps true is that, while some natural changes are reversible and some not, no change due to art is reversible in the sense of returning to something that has not been actually present all the time (like the sand of a sandcastle, an example I owe to Alan Lacey, or the bronze of a statue).

86. That is, prime matter, as is shown both by the statement that it never exists in actuality and by the contrast with the reference to the elements which follows.

87. That is, the simple bodies, earth, air, fire and water.

88. Or 'potencies'.

89. The concept of ingredients that are preserved, in potentiality, in a mixture and can be separated from it again is crucial to Alexander's distinction in his *de Mixtione* of mixture or blending from mere juxtaposition on the one hand and from coming-to-be and passing-away on the other (14, 230,14ff., cf. 15, 232,20ff. and Aristotle, *GC* 1.10); bodies that can be blended in this way are those that act on one another, and this applies to the four primary bodies (13 229,30ff.).

90. Or 'capacities', but I have here preserved a single translation for *dunamis* wherever possible. This agrees with Alexander's account, in his *de Anima* (10,14ff., 17,9f., 24,3f., 21ff., 71,14ff.) of the soul as the product of the mixture of the bodily elements, often attacked for un-Aristotelian materialism; see recently Accattino (1988); Robinson (1991) and my reply at *Classical Review* 43 (1993) 87-8, and also below, n. 145.

91. For instance, iron (composed of earth and water, Aristotle, *Meteor.* 4.6, 383a33).

92. 'if' is Spengel's conjecture. The intention of this paragraph is to strengthen the claim that the coming-to-be of the world would imply its perishing (simply) – for which cf. *Quaest.* 1.18 and Sharples [1992] 66 n. 196; Alexander, like Aristotle, himself rejects both – by arguing for the stronger claim that it would imply its perishing into its initial ingredients. But the argument for this is hardly convincing; see the next note.

93. Presumably because it is assumed that, if the world came to be at all, it would have done so from earth, air, fire and water, which clearly are present in it now, in an altered condition (altered in that none of them exists anywhere in the world in an absolutely pure form; otherwise we would have juxtaposition rather than change). But the assumption that these are the things from which the world would have come to be seems arbitrary; why should it not have come from quite other substances, earth, air fire and water being products of these which can only exist in the context of an ordered world, much as flesh can only truly exist in a living body (Aristotle, *Meteor.* 4.12, 390a2 – though he does say that this is less clear in the case of flesh than in that of a hand)?

94. 'World' implies an ordered whole, so that the world could be said no longer to exist, even if the matter of which it was composed survived.

95. The sense requires that this be the reference of *autôn,* even though the preceding *autois* ('in them'), which could in isolation refer to the constituents ('something *among* them gains the upper hand'), must in context refer back to 'the composite bodies'.

96. This *quaestio* in the form of an incomplete dialogue has two main sections: (i) a challenge to the dilemma that divine providence must either be the primary concern of that which exercises it or be purely accidental, which is held to contradict the very nature of providence (65,21-68,19); (ii) objections to the theory that the well-being of mortals is the primary concern of the divine (68,19-70,6). Both the dilemma in (i) and the arguments against primary providence in (ii) have parallels in a treatise (not in dialogue form) by Alexander surviving only in two Arabic versions, Dietrich (1964) nos 15 and (less complete) 18; these are edited and translated into German by Ruland (1976). The Arabic treatise goes on to give Alexander's positive characterisation of divine providence; the present *quaestio* breaks off at the point where this is about to start, and may well never have been completed. Doubts about the attribution of our *quaestio* to Alexander have been signalled by Silvia Fazzo (Fazzo and Wiesner [1993] 123 n. 7). See also Fazzo and Zonta (forthcoming).

Alexander is arguing, as several passages make clear, against Platonist opponents who themselves assert a theory of providence as the primary concern of the divine, and accuse Aristotle of denying providence or making it purely accidental. Their identity is discussed by Merlan (1969) 88-91; see further below. The application to divine providence of the three ways in which providence or forethought can, it is said, be neither primary nor accidental (by being intended and willed, though not a primary intention, 67,10-22; by being ultimately in one's own self-interest, 67,30-68,4; and by being for universals rather than for particulars, 68,5-11) is discussed by Sharples (1982) at 204-8. 68,19-23, 68,28-69,11 and 70,2-6 form *SVF* 2.1118; cf. below, nn. 110, 113, 115.

97. The Greek actually has 'we were', but this may be an editorial 'we'. The following 'I tried to show' is singular in the Greek too.

98. That is, the heavens; cf. Sharples (1992) 18 n. 20. In the present *quaestio* Alexander speaks sometimes of 'the divine' and sometimes of 'the gods'; this is appropriate to his being concerned for the moment less with his own theory of the physical mechanism by which providence operates than with what can be said about divine providence in general.

99. The MSS have 'those who deny that the providence we speak of exists, according to Aristotle' or perhaps 'those who deny that the providence we speak of is in accordance with Aristotle'. But this obscures the connection with the next clause; what is at issue *at this stage* is not a distinction between positions claiming to be Aristotelian, but simply whether there is room in the Peripatetic position for anything that can properly be called providence at all. Our author does indeed promise in due course to give an Aristotelian account (70,8ff. below); but in the present sentence I suspect 'according to Aristotle' has been inserted as the result of a misunderstanding. See the next note.

100. The MSS have 'say that providence is *said to occur* accidentally'. But this is needlessly complicated; all that is needed is an assertion by the opponents that Aristotelian providence is only *called* providence accidentally, and if that is conceded what follows will justify the claim that it is not in fact providence at all. The influence of the heavens on the sublunary region certainly *had* previously been described as accidental in Aristotelian doctrine; cf. 'Aëtius' 2.3.4 (*DG* p. 330) and Adrastus of Aphrodisias (ap. Theon Smyrnaeus, *Expos. rer. math.* 149,14f. Hiller). I suspect *ginesthai* was repeated by mistake from earlier in the line, but was retained in the text together with the correction *legesthai* which was intended to replace it.

101. cf. Aristotle, *Metaph.* 6.2, 1026b13ff. and the use made of it at Alexander(?) *Mant.* 170,12; Sharples (1975,2) 48 and n. 111.

102. *pronoia* and related terms can be applied both to divine providence and to human forethought, and the author uses examples from the latter to make points about the possible types of the former. I have therefore used whichever seems most appropriate at each point.

103. For the example cf. Aristotle, *Metaph.* 5.30, 1025a6; Alexander, *Fat.* 8, 172,25.

104. If Alexander's opponent is the Platonist Atticus (see below), there may be an ironical allusion here to the divine Craftsman of Plato's *Timaeus*. True, Plato's Craftsman there delegates much of his concern for the world to lesser gods (*Timaeus* 41C, 42E); this was emphasised by some contemporary Platonists (cf. Apuleius, *de Platone* 1.12 and [Plutarch], *de Fato* 9, 572F-573A, 573E-574A; Dillon [1977] 323-6), and Alexander was well aware of it (cf. below, n. 416). But Atticus may not have stressed this point; or Alexander may choose to disregard it. Alexander's argument here may in any case be dialectical: Theophrastus had argued that thunderbolts were not due to divine agency at all (*Meteorology* p. 270 Daiber [1992], the source of Lucretius 6.387ff.), and we need not suppose that Alexander disagreed with him in reality. For Alexander's own position on divine knowledge at least of sublunary *species* see below n. 119, and for his denial of divine foreknowledge of contingent events see *de Fato* 30 with Sharples (1983) 27 and 165.

105. Literally just 'contrary to reason'.

106. cf. Aristotle, *Phys.* 2.5, 196b10ff., 2.8, 198b34ff., Alexander, *Fat.* 8, 173,15. Apelt (1906) 11 emends 'infrequent' to 'sudden', on the grounds that chance has nothing to do with infrequency, but this seems wrong. It is noteworthy that, where some modern interpreters (e.g. D. Frede [1984] 282-3) have denied that infrequency is central to the Aristotelian concept of chance, our author apparently finds it necessary to insist that unexpectedness is as relevant as infrequency. (Against Frede see my remarks in Sharples [1987,2] 209-11; and for a discussion which clarifies the whole issue Judson [1991]). The second hands in B and S, the Aldine and Spengel indeed have *ep' elatton*, 'we define it less by its being', which Bruns compares with Simplicius, *in Phys.* 334,6ff.; but the relevance of this to the preceding argument here is less obvious.

107. This paragraph, from 67,22 to 67,29, is rightly bracketed by Bruns as an anticipation of what follows. The introduction here of the second and third ways of forethought being neither *per se* nor accidental disrupts the sequence of the argument; and 67,27-8, stating that the universal is not different from the particulars, flatly contradicts 68,9-10, which says that what is common is different from what falls under it, even though the general point is the same. (There is no terminological distinction between 'common' and 'universal' at issue here; cf. Sharples [1992] 55 n. 149, and on Aristotle's own usage cf. Fine [1993] 42 and n. 69, 245-6.) Alexander's attempt to argue that providence is concerned with the preservation of species, but not with individuals (see above, n. 25) is apparently attacked by Nemesius, *de Nat. hom.* (Morani) 43, p. 130.12-18, on the grounds that

– for an Aristotelian especially – the species exists only in the individuals. Cf. Sharples (1983,4) 152.

108. 'change in the goal'; i.e. if the welfare of the sheep were the primary concern, this would be *per se* concern for the sheep; in fact in such cases the ultimate goal is changed so as to be the benefit of the shepherd, but it is only to this extent that such concern is differentiated from that which is *per se*.

109. It is odd to say what is common depends on the particulars for its being *one* thing; perhaps we should read *en toutois mentoi to einai ekhon,* 'though having its being in these'.

110. With the objection that primary providence makes the gods inferior to mortals cf. Alexander, *On Providence* 21,19ff., 63,7ff. (Ruland, 1976). Damascius, *in Platonis Phaedonem* 1.32.4ff., p. 43 Westerink (= *SVF* 2.1118, there ascribed to Olympiodorus) attributes to the Stoics themselves the point that terrestrial masters care for their slaves in their own (the masters') interest; it is not altogether clear whether the subsequent application of this principle to the gods too is the Stoics' or Olympiodorus' own. Cf. Dragona-Monachou (1976) 156ff. especially 158.

111. There are nevertheless two texts attributed to Alexander in which it seems to be suggested that the preservation of the sublunary world *is* of benefit to the heavens: *Quaest.* 1.25 40,34-41,4, and *On the Principles of the Universe*, pp. 127,42-128,4 in Badawi (1968). Moreover, the context of the present passage is an attack on the idea that providence is a *primary* concern of the gods; relating benefit to oneself was cited at 67,30 above as a reason for regarding forethought or providence as neither primary nor accidental. So perhaps the present context is dialectical, and the sequel would have shown that for the gods to derive benefit from what is mortal is not in fact so absurd after all, though not to be classed as primary providence. Cf. Sharples (1982) pp. 207-8, and n. 113 below.

112. Bruns' emendation; the MSS have 'their own proper ordering'.

113. Merlan (1969) suggests that this may be the Platonist Atticus, and 69,7-10 of the present text are printed as fr. 3 bis (?) of Atticus by E. des Places, *Atticus*, Paris: Budé 1977, 50. Cf. below, n. 118. Von Arnim in *SVF* 2.1118 however suggested that the quotation was from the Stoic Posidonius. Alexander, *de Prov.* 7,21ff. (Ruland, 1976) attributes the theory of primary divine concern for sublunary individuals to Plato, in the opinion of some, and to the Stoics. Surprisingly enough, the idea that to be providential is as essential to god as heat is to fire re-appears in Alexander, *de Prov.* 69,3ff. (Ruland, 1976), but there in the exposition of Alexander's own positive theory. Perhaps the intention in our *quaestio* too was to reintroduce the example later, showing that what is objectionable is not the example but the way in which the supporters of primary providence use it. For dialectical argument in this opening part of the *quaestio* see n. 111 above, and for irony at the opponents' expense n. 118 below.

114. With the objection that some details are not worthy of divine concern cf. Alexander, *Mixt.* 11, 226,24ff.; *Mant.* 113,14; *de Prov.* 25,1ff. (Ruland, 1976); and for the existence of evil as evidence for not all being brought about by providence, *de Prov.* 9,20ff. (Ruland, 1976), Alexander fr. 36 Freudenthal (1884), and the next note.

115. This argument is developed at greater length in *Quaest.* 1.14. It is particularly apt against the Stoics, for it is they who said that virtue alone was good and that it depended on us. More generally, for the problem for the Stoics of reconciling a belief in divine providence with (as they claimed) the wickedness of the vast majority of people, cf. Alexander, *Fat.* 28, 199,14ff., *de Prov.* 25,18ff. (Ruland, 1976).

116. In fact Aristotle does *not* speak explicitly of divine providence; Alexander in this and other texts is constructing a theory of providence from Aristotelian materials.

117. It is detailed study of the development of Aristotle's thought by earlier writers that our author is disclaiming, not study of the issue of divine providence itself. Bruns approves Schwartz's addition of *skepsamenon*; the sense may be clear enough, in what is after all a parenthetical comment, without it.

118. Merlan (1969) 90 and n. 3 points out that Atticus' work was probably entitled 'Against those who profess the [position] of Plato by means of the [statements] of Aristotle' (Eusebius, *Praep. Ev.* (Mras) 11, p. 6.19-22); our author may be alluding ironically to this.

119. The text breaks off here, just as the positive exposition is about to start. But other texts suggest that *all three* ways of being neither *per se* nor accidental apply to divine providence in Alexander's view; it is concerned with species rather than with individuals (cf. 68,5-11 above and n. 25); the souls of the spheres, if not the supreme Unmoved Mover(s), are aware of their effect on the sublunary (cf. 67,10-22 above and Sharples [1982] 206-7); and the divine heavens benefit from the preservation of the sublunary (cf. 67,30-68,4 and above, n. 111). That the divine should be aware of the sublunary conflicts with traditional interpretations of Aristotle, *Metaph.* 12.9. In recent years, indeed, several scholars have argued that Aristotle allows the Unmoved Mover some degree of knowledge of the sublunary world (cf. Norman [1969], Sorabji [1983] ch.10, Lear [1988] 295-309 and George [1989]; however, George [1989] 67-8 points out that Alexander, as reported by Averroes, argued for a contrast rather than a parallelism between production by the crafts and that by the Unmoved Mover in *Metaph.* 12.4, 1070b33-5).

120. Some MSS of Aristotle, and Philoponus' commentary (*in GC* 304,23f., 309,15f.) have 'but not even conditionally' here. Bruns in his second thoughts (cf. n. 122 below) supposed that Alexander – unlike the editor who supplied the title – also had this reading, and that he understands the point in the same way as does Philoponus, that there cannot even be conditional necessity in an *infinite* series because of the principle that such a series allows no ordering of earlier and later terms (Philoponus, *in GC* 309,17-31; cf. Alexander, *in Metaph.* 152,6ff., and below at n. 326). But it is clear that Alexander *does* hold that there can be conditional necessity even where there is no absolute necessity (cf. 71,12 here, and *Quaest.* 3.5 88,25f., 28f.) and that there can be conditional necessity in an infinite sequence (71,15f., 3.5 89,1f.) See also Praechter (1894).

121. Understanding *einai;* so apparently Forster.

122. Aristotle, *GC* 2.11, 337b25-8. – This *quaestio* is translated and discussed, together with 3.5 below, in Sharples (1979). Divergences are noted, not from Bruns' text on pp. 71-2 of his (1892,1), henceforth referred to as Bruns[1], but to the revised text reflecting his second thoughts in his (1892,2) and partly included as Addenda at p. xlvi of his (1892,1) (henceforth Bruns[2]). Bruns' revised interpretation was in turn discussed by Praechter (1894).

Aristotle's argument in *GC* 2.11 is concerned to make two points which concern us here. The first is that the fact that x is conditionally necessary given y will only make x necessary 'without qualification', if y itself possesses such necessity – or derives it from a further principle z; more generally, absolute or unqualified necessity can only be present where a thing either possesses it in itself or derives it from a principle which does so (in *GC* 2.11, and in *Quaest.* 3.5 below, the regular motion of the heavens). It may indeed seem odd to describe a *derived* necessity as 'absolute' or 'unqualified' at all, and strictly speaking such derived unconditional necessity is a complex notion – 'x is necessary' in this sense being short for 'x is necessary given y, and y is necessary *per se*'. But it is still a usage that serves a purpose in an Aristotelian perspective – in a system that admits *de re* necessities in the natural world at all, it matters considerably whether that given which something is necessary is itself necessary or not. Cf. further Sharples (1979) 36 and Joachim (1922) 272-3.

Aristotle's second and less defensible point in *GC* 2.11 is that there is an asymmetry between *a fronte* and *a tergo* necessity, between the necessitation of what is earlier (in time) by what is later and the reverse. Alexander and Philoponus both attribute to Aristotle, rightly or wrongly, the view that 'if what is earlier, then what is later' cannot even be true except in cases where what is later is independently necessary (71.27-32 here, *Quaest.* 3.5 88,26f.; Philoponus, *in GC* 308,3-25, with criticism of the supposed Aristotelian position). Cf. Aristotle, *An. Post.* 2.12, 95a27ff.; Balme (1939) 4; White (1985) 45, 50ff., 147, 153-60, 221; reservations are expressed by Huby at *Classical Review* 38 (1988) 287. See also the discussion at Sorabji (1980) 143-54, especially 144 n. 3 and 152 n. 24.

123. This could be taken either as denying that what is later can derive absolute necessity from what is earlier, or as denying that it can derive even conditional necessity; the latter claim, at least, is highly questionable. See preceding note.

124. Regularity (wrongly understood here as identity of *tokens*?) being a necessary, even if not a sufficient, condition for necessity. Bruns[2] deleted *to,* giving 'it does not even come to be', since he took the point to be that there is no earlier or later in an infinite series. But see above, n. 120.

125. Assuming *per impossibile,* for the sake of the argument, that there is a last member in an infinite series. Cf. Bruns (1892,2) 21f.

126. Reading *ta metaxu tou teleutaiou* with Bruns[1]. Bruns[2] has *tôn metaxu to teleutaion* ('the last of the intermediate [members of the series] only derives ...'. But the point of mentioning the penultimate member is only that it will in turn impart what it derives from the final member to those that precede it; and, for the use of *metaxu* in Bruns[1], Praechter (1894) compares Aristotle, *Cael.* 293a32, *Sens.* 440a18 (cf. also 447a9).

127. Premiss [i] is redundant; [ii] and [iv] alone are sufficient to give [iii]. It is all the more striking, therefore, that Alexander introduces the dubious principle [i].

128. Aristotle, *GC* 2.11, 337b28-9.

129. This is surely correct as an interpretation of Aristotle's meaning at *GC* 2.11, 337b28. It is accepted by Praechter (1894) and by Joachim (1922); Bruns (1892,2) 22-5 rejected it, but his arguments are unconvincing. See Sharples (1979) 37 and 44. It follows that 'first' has the sense of 'primary in the order of derivation of necessity', *not* of 'first in time'.

130. The intended meaning is clearly 'true in such a case', i.e. in that of a series with no primary member that is necessary unconditionally. Compressed expression has led our author to say that the consequence cannot be true of something that does not even exist; an unintended truism.

131. Aristotle, *GC* 2.11, 338a6-9. In the last clause the MSS of Aristotle are here divided between 'are coming to be' and 'have come to be', which seems the more natural reading; Philoponus in his commentary supposes the latter (311,14f.).

132. That is, the magnet. This *quaestio* is classed by Bruns (1892,1) viii as a 'problem' in the proper sense in content though not in form. It is translated into

German and discussed by Radl (1988) 78-87; a Greek text is printed at Radl (1988) 222-4. Simplicius, *in Phys.* 1055,24ff., on the reference to types of pulling at Aristotle, *Phys.* 7.2, 244a11, reports Alexander as discussing, presumably in his *Physics* commentary, how the magnet moves without contact, and arguing that even if the magnet does not touch the thing attracted the power (*dunamis*) from it does so; according to Simplicius (op. cit. 1056,1) Alexander then referred to the theory of effluences (cf. 72,10-74,4 here) before suggesting, and earning Simplicius' approval by doing so, that attraction by the magnet is not the sort of case Aristotle had in mind at this point. There is no hint in Simplicius' report, however, of anything like the solution to the problem of action at a distance eventually advanced in our *quaestio,* in terms of the iron's desire for something it lacks.

133. 72,9-26 = Empedocles, 31A89 DK. Diels suggested (DK vol. 1 p. 306.9) that the source used for Empedocles by our *quaestio* was probably Theophrastus' *Physical Opinions.*

134. This is the required sense; the Greek in fact has the converse, 'the magnet will not be moved towards the iron any more than the iron towards the magnet'. But for a similarly reversed emphasis cf. Alexander, *Fat.* 9, 175,17 with Sharples (1983,1) 242. 'No more x than y' is equivalent to 'as much y as x', and 'as much x as y' can be substituted for 'as much y as x'. Indeed Radl (1988) 80 renders our present passage 'the stone will be moved to the iron as much as the iron to the stone'. – The argument is in any case based on a misapprehension; a magnet *will* move towards iron just as much as iron to a magnet.

135. 72,26-7 = Empedocles, 31B91 DK.

136. 72,28-73.11 = Democritus, 68A165 DK. Gottschalk (1965) 131-3 suggests that it is this Atomist theory that is referred to by Strato ap. Simplicium, *in Phys.* 652,21-5 and 663,3-8.

137. 73,11-25 = Diogenes of Apollonia, 64A33 DK.

138. The magnet is discriminating in what it attracts where amber is not; if there was sawdust on the surface of the iron, it would fly to the amber straight away, but in the case of the magnet it does not do so, only being carried to it as the iron is. Radl (1988) 84 notes that Plato, *Timaeus* 79E-80C explains magnetic attraction, the action of amber and that of cupping-glasses all alike by the process of mutual displacement; cf. Plutarch, *Platonic Questions* 1004DE, 1005BD.

139. 'seems' presumably qualifies the assertion that the attraction does not take place in the same way, although the sequence of ideas in the Greek makes that point more remote from the word 'seems' than I have made it in my translation. It could be that 'seems' qualifies just the claim that the sun attracts moisture, given that it is only *per accidens* that the natural direction of movement of evaporated water is towards where the sun happens to be, and that in any case the sun, being in the heavens and composed of the fifth element, is not itself hot, and affects the water only indirectly by heating the fire-sphere below it (cf. Aristotle, *Meteor.* 1.3, and above *Quaest.* 2.17). But this may be over-ingenious; our author is probably assuming the everyday non-technical notion of the sun drawing up vapour.

140. If it were nourishment, it would (in due course) be made like the living creature.

141. *sidêritis* 'iron-like' is in fact, with 'stone' expressed or understood, a regular name for the lodestone.

142. For the analogy between living creatures and inanimate objects cf. Alexander, *DA* 22,7ff. It is not however made clear what the quality is that the magnet possesses and the iron lacks, unless it is simply dryness.

143. Alexander's text (unlike Aristotle's) has 'one kind of the other things that there are'. Such a seemingly illogical use of 'other' to mean 'all', i.e. '*itself and* the rest', is possible Greek idiom in such a context, but not natural in English.

144. I use this phrase to translate *tode ti*; and so repeatedly in this *quaestio*.

145. Aristotle, *DA* 2.1, 412a6-9. The present *quaestio* is classed by Bruns (1892,1) viii as an *exêgêsis* or commentary (I take it that at Bruns [1892,1] x 'II,2.24.26 III,7.9' has been repeated in error from viii). It is discussed by Moraux (1942) 44-7, who notes its use of Aristotelian texts and its emphasis on form, together with the un-Aristotelian idea that the form has come to be in the mixture of the underlying materials (75,12-13). See above, n. 90.

146. i.e. earth, air, fire and water.

147. That is, substances compounded of form and matter.

148. i.e. plants, which for Aristotle possess nutritive soul but are not *zôia*, 'living creatures' (i.e. human beings and other animals).

149. Aristotle has 'of a natural body of this particular sort (*tioudi*), that possesses ...'.

150. Aristotle, *DA* 2.1, 412b15. Although this *quaestio* is described in the title as an *exêgêsis* or commentary, it is in effect a problem in the strict sense; cf. Bruns (1892,1) viii-ix. Though it forms part of the sequence relating to the *DA* (see above, n. 21), it is concerned, like *Quaest.* 2.18 and 2.19, with the contrast between the heavens and the sublunary region. For 'principle of *movement*' (*kinêsis*) see above, nn. 33, 63.

151. That is, the heavens; cf. Sharples (1992) 18 n. 20.

152. *ê*, the standard formula for introducing the solution to a problem; cf. above, n. 16.

153. This seems an odd suggestion, given that Alexander generally supposes that the heavenly spheres do have souls; cf. above, n. 75. The anonymous reader suggests we should emphasise *comes to be*; the souls of the heavenly spheres do not come to be in them, but are present in them eternally. But the alternative solution at 76,21-3, as the anonymous reader also notes, will still suggest that the heavenly spheres are without souls.

154. Aristotle, *DA* 2.1, 412b26. This text is treated by Bruns (1892,1) xi as a 'fragment', contrasting the much fuller treatment of the same point in *Quaest.* 1.26 and *Mant.* 119-22.

155. The argument is that if the seed is only potentially, not actually an organic, functioning body, it is only when soul is actually present that the body is organic. But in that case the soul is not present in an organic body as if that were something that could exist in itself, independently of soul. For the thesis that soul is not in a substrate in this way cf. *Quaest.* 1.8; also 1.17, 1.26, *Mant.* 119-22, and the Additional Note on *Quaest.* 1.1-2.15, below. There has been much discussion in recent years of the problems such a view creates for Aristotle in terms of his being able to distinguish between soul and body at all; in addition to the seminal paper of Ackrill (1972-3) cf. Williams (1986), Whiting (1992), Cohen (1992) and Shields (1993), and for Alexander himself cf. *Quaest.* 2.8 and 2.9, and n. 90 to *Quaest.* 2.20 above.

156. This text is classed by Bruns (1892,1) ix among the *epidromai* or summaries of Aristotelian doctrine; as he notes (cf. xi), the titles of *Quaest.* 2.25, 26 and 27 show no recognition of the differences in character between them. The argument is largely an explanatory paraphrase of Aristotle, *DA* 2.2.

157. Aristotle, *DA* 2.2, 413a20.

158. ibid. 2.1, 412b5-6.

159. I have simplified the sentence-structure: the Greek in fact has a string of past participles, 'having shown', 'having enquired', 'having said', with the main verb at 'after this he showed' in 77,22.

160. That is, nutritive soul can exist without sensory (e.g.), but not vice versa. Cf. Aristotle, *DA* 2.3, 415a1-3.

161. i.e. an animal (including human beings) rather than a plant. Cf. n. 153 above.

162. Or perhaps 'sensory souls'; cf. 77,17-18 below.

163. The Greek has 'from those before it'. Spengel proposed reading the plural; but these texts are often careless about pronouns. Cf. above n. 35.

164. Literally, 'that of each part of soul there is soul or [only] a part of soul'. The phraseology is odd, but the reference must be to Aristotle's question at *DA* 2.2, 413b13 whether each faculty is a (separate) soul or a part of soul. Has our author been misled by a text of the *DA* that there had, or that he took to have, *toutôn hekastou* rather than *toutôn hekaston*?

165. So the text, but it seems to be corrupt (so Bruns). It is not clear either in what respect the soul is similar to the body or why this should be a reason for its being separable from it. The possibility of some part at least of the soul being separable from the body is raised by Aristotle at *DA* 1.1, 403a10, 2.1, 413a6; the reference to the soul being something *of* the body apparently derives from *DA* 2.2, 414a21 – and for soul as being 'of' the body but existing in its own right cf. *Quaest.* 2.9 54,26ff., 29ff., with Sharples (1992) 106 n. 346 – but Aristotle's point in *DA* 2.2, 414a19ff. is precisely that the soul is not itself an (independent) body. Spengel here conjectured *akhôristos*, 'inseparable', for *khôristê* 'can be separated'. (I am grateful to the anonymous reader for comments on this passage.)

166. The phraseology is again odd; matter is often enough said to *possess* (*ekhein*) form, but here it is said to *sunekhein* the form, which implies more than 'contain'. I have translated by 'comprise', because the arranged matter can in a sense for Alexander be said to constitute the form (though see above, n. 90); if anything the implications of *sunekhein,* literally 'hold together', are even stronger than this. Aristotle, as one might expect, speaks rather of form as 'holding together' the body; *DA* 1.5, 410b12 and 411b7-8.

167. This naturally suggests the question: *of what* is the body the matter? Hardly of the body, unless 'body' is an ambiguous term (for which see the discussions of Williams, Cohen and Shields cited in n. 156 above); either therefore of the person as a whole (in which case the soul too should be the form of the *person*), or of the soul. The reference to the body possessing the soul should not in any case be taken to suggest that the body could exist *as a body* in the absence of soul. Cf. above n. 156 and the references there.

168. An (incomplete) Arabic version of this *quaestio* (no. 24 Dietrich) was edited by Badawi (1971) no. 10; cf. Gätje (1966) 276-8. The text is discussed by Lloyd (1980) 59-61. Its form is to some extent like that of a 'problem' in the strict sense, arguments for the identification of matter and genus (77,32-78,6) being followed by arguments against this (78,6-79,18), although in a problem in the strict sense one would have first arguments for a conclusion, then the statement that the conclusion was problematic, and then refutation of the arguments that apparently led to it. Bruns (1892) vi indeed suggests that such a statement of the difficulty may have fallen out of the text. However, this *quaestio* is also akin to the collections of arguments that form the fifth group of texts recognised by Bruns (1892) xii-xiii, even though here the successive arguments start with 'also' (*kai*) rather than 'moreover' (*eti*).

169. *eidos* means both 'form' and 'species'; the former is more appropriate to the contrast with matter, the latter to that with genus. The ambiguity is not a chance one, since it is precisely of species that there are forms. I have translated by 'form', 'species' or (as here) 'species or form', depending on the context.

170. *diaphorai* is the technical term for the differentiae of genera; but for consistency's sake it has been translated by 'difference' throughout this *quaestio*.

171. The standard formula for the solution to a problem, though it has not actually been stated that the conclusion reached in the first paragraph is problematic. See above, nn. 16, 168.

172. cf. *Quaestiones* 1.19, 2.15.

173. For this paragraph the Arabic (above n. 1) has 'And a second distinction consists in that the part of the matter is like its whole, while on the contrary the part of the genus is not like its whole. For man is in no way a beast, I mean, that the "living creature" that belongs to Socrates cannot be in Plato or another man. And I say further that "living creature" (*sic*; "matter" 78,16) is a thing ...' (after Gätje). The text then breaks off. If 'beast' indicates 'a living creature other than man' the point that the living creature in Socrates cannot be in a creature of another species, and the point that it cannot be in another man, are two valid but *different* points, which the Greek does not distinguish.

174. Literally 'in number'. The point is presumably that, while an individual human being may perish, his or her matter does not; though to speak of matter as such, rather than of matter as qualified by some form, as individual or numerable seems problematic. The generic element in an individual human being does not survive him or her in the same way; rather the genus, like the species, survives only through the succession of its individual instances (the instances of a genus not in any case being different from the instances of its species; just as there is no universal human being apart from Socrates, Callias and the rest, so there is no universal living creature apart from Socrates, Callias, Fido, Achilles' horse Xanthos ...).

175. cf. above n. 25.

176. That is, the being composed of matter and form.

177. As the sequel shows, this must mean 'forms treated in isolation from their matter'. The reference to 'genera of species and accidents' makes it unlikely that it is *just* those forms which by their very nature are not found in matter, such as the Unmoved Movers, that are meant.

178. See Textual Emendations. 'Genera of substances' presumably refers to the genera of beings compounded of matter and form, *as opposed to* the genera of forms considered in the abstract. Cf., perhaps, Aristotle, *Metaph.* 7.10, 1035b27-30.

179. The Greek has 'it was not', presumably as a reference to a general established principle; Spengel conjectured the present tense.

180. The intended sense is 'genus, i.e. the genus of enmattered beings, cannot be separated from matter and exist independently in a similar way to that in which (proximate) matter *can* be separated from form' (cf. 78,22-3). But the expression 'separated from matter in the same way' is awkward, since in the case of matter and form it is the separation of the former from the latter that is in question, not vice versa. Spengel emended to 'is not separated in a similar way to matter', i.e. 'to that in which matter is separated from form'.

181. The thought seems to be that the genera of compound beings are defined in a way that involves reference to both matter and form, and that therefore while the matter can survive the ceasing-to-be of the form or species the genus cannot. However, as the text goes on to say, while the living creature in Socrates cannot survive the death of Socrates, and living creature in general could not survive the disappearance of all individual living things, living creature in general certainly can survive the death of any one particular man. Cf. *Quaest.* 1.11 ad fin.

182. cf. *Quaest.* 1.26 42,9.

183. A table, for example, comes to be in wood, and the existence of the wood does not depend on the form of *table*; it exists in advance, independently of the form of table, though it may of course be further analysed itself into matter and some *other* form.

184. 'Living creature' cannot be considered separately from its species in the way that 'wood' can from 'table', because 'living creature' is a part of the being of each of the species, with the appropriate differentiae in each case.

185. The thought is: it might be suggested that species come to be in the genus as their matter in the same way as tables come to be in wood as their matter; but this is not so, since the form of the species is composed of a differentia and an element shared with other members of the genus (see the next clause), and the latter is the whole nature of the genus, while no account of tables, as such, can include the whole nature of wood. For the use of *sumplêroun* 'complete' cf. Ellis (1994).

186. Literally 'in accordance with its proper account'.

187. It is to form that *individuality* is owed, but that does not mean that matter may not be the cause of there being a number, or even a particular number, of individuals each of the type defined by form. (Cf. Aristotle, *GA* 4.4, 772a21, a35.)

188. Matter is prior to the particular individuals that come to be by the combination of matter and form; but the genus depends for its existence on the separation by thought of the common element in the genus from the differentiae with which it is combined in each actual case. (On the other hand, the existence of the genus is not dependent on that of any *particular* species; cf. Sharples [1987,1] 1201f. and references there, and in particular Alexander's *Refutation of the assertion of Xenocrates that the species is prior to the genus* [= Dietrich no. 4] discussed by Pines [1961] 27.)

189. cf. the previous note; also Alexander, *DA* 90,2-14, and Boethius, *Second commentary on Porphyry's* Eisagoge, 164,3ff.

190. Bruns (1892,1) xi suggests that this definition was included in the *Quaestiones* by accident. The compiler presumably found it among materials in some way deriving from Alexander and relating to Aristotle, *DA,* and was reluctant to lose it. At *DA* 69,19 Alexander refers to a discussion elsewhere of the difference between memory and recollection, for which cf. Aristotle, *de Memoria* 2, 453a6ff., arguing that recollection is a deliberate searching. Cf. Sorabji (1972) 111, and the next note.

191. For the statement that an impression (*phantasma*) occurs in the *body* cf. Aristotle *de Memoria* 2, 453a14-16, 'the experience is something bodily, and recollection is searching for an impression in something like this', where Sorabji (1972) loc. cit. argues that the body in question is the heart; also Alexander, *DA* 69,10 and *Mant.* 145,10-13.

192. See below, n. 196.

193. Aristotle, *DA* 2.5, 417b5. Bruns (1892,1) viii-ix notes that, though an explanation of an Aristotelian passage, this text takes the form of a problem and, like 2.25 above, shows the affinity between the *exêgêsis* and the problem proper.

194. The first potentiality is the state of someone who has not yet learned; the second potentiality, first actuality, or disposition (*hexis*) that of someone who has learned, and hence is in a position to exercise his understanding whenever he wishes, but is not doing so at the moment; the second actuality is the condition of someone who is currently exercising understanding. Cf. Aristotle, *DA* 2.1, 412a22-8, 2.5, 417a21ff.

195. Aristotle's text has '*either* this is not alteration ... or [if it is alteration] it is another kind of alteration'.

196. Ross (1961) 236-7 argues that Alexander here has a false reading, and that the correct reading would give simply 'that leading to actuality from potentiality that which exercises intellect and thinks', the MSS of Aristotle having a mixture of this and Alexander's reading.

197. 'by' is Bruns' emendation; the MSS have 'from'. 'The commentary' (*exêgêsis,* the word translated 'explanation' in the title above) could refer to one particular commentary-text, or to the general tradition of commentary; and 'it was enquired' could refer either, with 'from', to a specific occasion in discussion (cf. Sharples [1990,1] 104-6) when the need to consult the commentary was felt, or, with ('by'), to a general tradition of discussing the issue at this point in Aristotle's *DA*. Cf. Sharples (1990,1) 105 n. 153. (I am grateful to the anonymous reader for discussion of this matter.)

198. 'actuality' represents *energeia,* above rendered by 'activity'; 'change' represents *kinêsis,* since this rendering seems more appropriate than 'movement' in psychological contexts; and the more general term *metabolê* has therefore been rendered 'transition'. Cf. above, nn. 33, 63, 67.

199. Literally 'much more will it not be', but that is clumsy in English.

200. i.e. locomotion, growth and diminution, coming-to-be and passing away. Cf. Aristotle, *Phys.* 3.1, 201a9-15.

201. *noêtikê hexis*; cf. the doctrine of *nous en hexei* in Alexander, *DA* 85,11-86,6 and *Mantissa* 107,21-8.

202. Literally 'exercising intellect and being active/actual' (*noein te kai energein*).

203. The (second) actuality is 'the same' as the (first) actuality, in the sense that the former is the potentiality for the latter, or that they are the same thing, in one case potentially and the other actually. When cited at 81,6 and 81,12 above, however, Aristotle's text had not *tauton* 'the same' but *auto,* 'this very thing'. Most MSS of Aristotle's *DA* itself and ancient sources for the text have *auto,* but one MS (X, Ambrosianus 435, 12th-13th cent.), and Sophonias' and Philoponus' paraphrases (but not the actual citation in Philoponus) have *h(e)auto* 'itself ' – as does the *table of contents* to Alexander, *Quaest.* 3 (above, at n. 46). Cf. Ross (1961) on Aristotle, *DA* 2.5, 417b6, and below n. 240.

204. See n. 199 above.

205. That is, a builder's activity of actually building involves bodily movements – handling the bricks, and so on – but the builder's starting actually to build on a particular occasion, as opposed to just being experienced and able to, is not itself a change or movement in him or his condition.

206. Aristotle, *DA* 2.5, 416b32. In spite of the title given to it, this *quaestio* is a summary (*epidromê*) rather than an interpretation (*exêgêsis*); Bruns (1892,1) ix. It also exists in an Arabic version (Dietrich no. 14), entitled simply 'Treatise by Alexander of Aphrodisias concerning sense-perception and how it comes about, according to the teaching of Aristotle'. The rendering is sometimes close but sometimes amounts to a simplified paraphrase rather than a translation. It has been edited and translated into German by Ruland (1978). I have not below noted all the passages of the Greek text that the Arabic omits, or all its explanatory additions, only those that seem important for the argument of the treatise. From the Arabic the text was translated into Latin by Gerard of Cremona; the Latin version was edited by Théry (1926) 86-91, and, following Théry, by Ruland (1978) as an appendix to his edition of the Arabic. It is to be distinguished from the medieval Latin translation (from the extant Greek) of Alexander's *commentary* on Aristotle's *de Sensu*, edited by Thurot (1875). A scholion on *Quaest.* 1.2 refers to an 'Explanation and summary of certain passages from Aristotle's *de Sensu et sensato*' (see Sharples [1992] 24 and n. 39); Dietrich (1964) 96f. suggested that the Arabic text which is in fact a version of our present *quaestio* might have formed part of this work. Against this suggestion, however, is the fact that *Quaest.* 3.3 is closely linked not to Aristotle's *de Sensu* at all, but to *DA* 2.5.

It is strange that this turgid and repetitive summary of Aristotle's argument, which it is difficult to believe can have been written by Alexander himself, enjoyed such subsequent popularity.

207. The general discussion of sensation is in *DA* 2.5; those of the particular senses in 2.7-11.

208. 'something' (*ti*) is a variant reading in the passage of Aristotle Alexander is citing; Ross and Hamlyn both prefer *te* there, giving simply 'in the course of being both changed and affected'. For 'change' rendering *kinêsis* and its cognates see above, nn. 33, 198.

209. Aristotle's text has rather 'what is affected is what is unlike'.

210. My translation attempts to capture the vagueness of the original, for it is not just a question of distinguishing the potential *from* the actual. Indeed the Arabic not unreasonably interprets this passage as implying the drawing of *two separate* distinctions, rendering 'potentiality and actuality both fall into two sub-species' (p. 172,42-3 Ruland); this influences its rendering of subsequent passages (cf. nn. 212-13 and 237 below).

211. *energoun*, cognate with *energeia* which has been translated by 'actuality' or 'activity'. See above, n. 33.

212. For 'for "potentially understanding" is said in two ways ... no longer potentially' (83,19-26) the Arabic has: 'all potentiality exists in two forms, of which one is like the person who has it in his power and nature to acquire understanding, even when he does not yet have understanding. The other is like the person who has acquired understanding and wisdom; even when he, on a particular occasion, does not understand [i.e. is not engaged in actual understanding], nevertheless he has understanding. In the same way actual understanding too exists in two forms; the one is the person with understanding who, on a particular occasion, is not [engaged in] understanding, the other the person with understanding who, on a particular occasion, is engaged in understanding' (p. 172,46-50 Ruland). See above, n. 210.

213. For 'After this ... understanding potentially' (83,26-7) the Arabic has: 'When the Philosopher has enquired into potentiality and actuality, and shown that each of the two exists in two forms ...' (p. 174,51-52 Ruland). See above, n. 210.

214. Throughout this *quaestio* 'transition' renders *metabolê*, which includes progression to full actuality on the one hand and change (*kinêsis*) and alteration on the other. Cf. *Quaest.* 3.2 at nn. 192 and 195.

215. *energeia*, translated by 'actuality' in the previous sentence; but cf. the contrast with 'inactivity' below. Cf. above, n. 211.

216. The actuality is 'the same' as the potentiality in that both are F – the one actually F and the other potentially F. Cf. above, n. 203.

217. For 'For activity in respect of a thing's disposition ... in which it possesses [it]' (84,1-9) the Arabic has rather: 'But the first alteration, that is the first type, is destructive alteration, which only comes about through the destruction of something and its departure from its condition. Alteration of the second type however comes about without the destruction of anything; rather, it is completed and perfected and lets its perfection become apparent; as with the person with understanding who is inactive, for he is perfected in understanding without being destroyed in [respect of] his own condition. ... (lacuna). ... This type is not rightly called alteration, for real alteration is from something to something else and from one opposite to the other' (p. 176,69-75 Ruland).

218. Literally 'another nature (*phusis*) of alteration'. In the recapitulation at the end of the *quaestio* it is simply asserted that this type of transition is indeed *not* alteration; cf. below, nn. 237 and 239; also *Quaest.* 3.2 at n. 195.

219. Accepting Bruns' emendation (see Appendix I); without it the sense would be 'as being able to exercise intellect and thought' (I am grateful to the anonymous reader for pointing this out).

220. Normally coming-to-be is a more radical form of change than alteration; here the point is that what passes from (second) potentiality, while not being *altered*, does 'become' in an attenuated sense. But the point is an aside.

221. *hexis*. One may compare Alexander's doctrine of the material intellect and intellect *en hexei*; cf. above, n. 201.

222. For 'either should not ... through being affected' (84,26) the Arabic has 'comes about not without change and alteration' (p. 178,91-2 Ruland); 'if it too ... the taking on of some natural form' (84,26-30 Bruns) is omitted in the Arabic.

223. Coming-to-be (in the strong sense, not that of n. 220) involves taking on a natural form, so a change that does not involve the taking on of a new form must therefore be classified as something less than coming-to-be or generation, hence as alteration. Things that exist by nature have, before they develop fully, potential both for realising their nature and for failing to do so; the natures which they realise are thus, in the sequel, 'the better part of the things for which that which has potential has potential' and 'the better dispositions'. See nn. 81, 246.

224. For 'both that which is to possessing ... states of privation' (84,30-3) the Arabic has 'one is from the potentiality to the readiness [arrangement, form, disposition; i.e. *hexis*], that is the readiness for the actuality, the other from the arrangement to the actuality' (p. 178,94-5 Ruland).

225. In the case of sensation (as opposed to intellect), the living creature has the *hexis* (as opposed to the full activity, the second actuality) as soon as it is produced.

226. For 'but when it has been begotten ... has received understanding' (85,1-2) the Arabic has: 'but when it is fully created, it possesses the readiness (cf. n. 224 above) [relating to] sense-perception, that is, it is readied for sense-perception; and when something perceptible is present, it at once perceives it, as the person with understanding who is readied for understanding (i.e. possesses the *hexis*); for he thinks of a thing as soon as he wishes. [So also with the living creature (i.e. non-rational creatures?); if it is readied for sense-perception and something perceptible is present, it at once perceives it.]' (p. 180,103-7 Ruland). Ruland brackets

the last sentence as a repetition; it may be noted that in elaborating the comparison, already present in the Greek, between sensation and thought, the Arabic risks
obscuring the difference that sensation is not up to us in the same way as thought
since the former requires an external object and the latter does not (cf. n. 85,14-16
below).

227. Aristotle however has 'in the *soul* itself'.

228. 'Common' and 'universal' are here equivalent terms; cf. n. 107 to *Quaest.*
2.21, and Sharples (1992) 55 n. 149; also Simplicius, *in Phys.* 19,1, where *katholou*
of Aristotle, *Phys.* 1.1, 184a23-4 is rendered by *koina,* and ibid. 19,5-6, where
Alexander is cited, suggesting that the usage derives from him. (I am grateful to
Professor André Laks for drawing my attention to this group of passages, which
he discusses in a paper forthcoming in vol. 7 of *Rutgers University Studies in
Classical Humanities.*)

229. cf. Sharples (1992) 6 and n. 24. 'which thinks them' reflects Bruns'
emendation *auta* for the MSS *autôi,* 'in the intellect itself which thinks'. The
anonymous reader points out that the MSS reading would give an acceptable sense
and emphasis; but Bruns' emendation is supported by comparison with Alexander,
DA 88,8 and 90,8.

230. For 'And for this reason … when we wish to' (85,14-16) the Arabic has: 'and
the ability to think of [the universals] rests with the thinker; for the intelligibles
are subject to our will, that is to say, the universals are present with us when we
wish; therefore the cause of thinking is internal to us. But the ability to perceive
objects of sensation does not rest with us, that is, [it is not the case] that, if we wish
it, they are present to us and we can perceive them' (p. 184,126-9 Ruland).

231. Comparison with Aristotle suggests that the contrast in the previous clause
is between the child and the adult (rather than between the child and the
completely trained general); it is then natural to take 'the latter' here as referring
to the adult, and the present clause as introducing a *further* contrast between
adults who have not studied military strategy and those who have but are not
currently on campaign (see the next note). It must be admitted, however, that this
complicates the issue by introducing a *third* sense of potentiality, and hardly gives
a natural sense to the connecting 'for'. I am grateful to the anonymous reader for
discussion of this passage.

232. One might rather expect 'is not at the moment exercising it'.

233. Or 'as current names for'.

234. With Bruns' emendation the text could mean 'having given this account of
sensation, not as a strict [account]'. Something like this is in any case what is
meant.

235. The Arabic has 'which are able to actualise sensation' (p. 188,160-1
Ruland).

236. See above, n. 68. For 'and after this he says that … sort of actuality'
(86,11-13) the Arabic has: 'then he distinguishes affecting and being affected, in
that he says: affecting is the movement that proceeds from what affects, but being
affected is the movement in what is affected [caused] through what influences [it]'
(p. 188,164-5 Ruland).

237. See above, n. 218. Before 'And he shows that potentiality is twofold … is
not in every case through alteration' (86,17-18) the Arabic adds: 'Then he makes a
distinction concerning potentiality in the following way: there are two kinds of
potentiality. Of these one is the potentiality which comprises susceptibility of
<readiness for> actuality, [that is], material potentiality; the other kind is poten-

tiality that is readied for the actuality. Then he also makes a distinction concerning actuality, in that he says: there are two kinds of actuality. Of these one is the actual that is readied for actuality, even when (on a particular occasion) it is inactive and not actualised; the second kind is busied and active, that is, not inactive' (p. 190,173-8 Ruland). See above, n. 210.

238. For 'After this he makes a distinction … "being affected" ' (86,18-19) the Arabic has: 'Then he also makes a distinction concerning alteration, in that he says: there are two kinds of alteration; of these one comes about through being affected, the other without being affected and changed. Then he also makes a distinction concerning being affected, as follows: there are two ways of being affected' (p. 190,181-3 Ruland). In what follows the two types (86,19-20 and 20-2 Bruns) are stated in reversed order, with the added comment 'the first kind [i.e. the second in the Greek] is [being] affected without anything departing from its condition, as we established just now, but rather through its progression to its own completion and perfection under the influence of what is like it' (p. 192,187-9 Ruland).

239. See above, n. 218.

240. Literally 'towards itself'; cf. above, n. 203.

241. For 'And, having … what is meant' (86,26-8), the Arabic has: 'Then the Philosopher returns once more to sensation and says: this is not rightly called alteration, for it is not affected and influenced through [any] destruction; but we indicate it by this word [alteration], for through the shortage of words and phrases we have no appropriate expression for it' (p. 192,196-9 Ruland).

242. For 'He [then] gave an account … to the actuality' (86,28-33) the Arabic has: 'When the Philosopher has dealt with these things, he defines sensation in the following way: sensation is a matter of potentiality of the second type; it is like what is actually capable of being sensed. But when sensation is affected by what affects it [i.e. the object of sensation] it is actually like it and is actual sensation. The Philosopher however here means "being affected" only in the second sense, that is a change which comes about without alteration, movement, and passing from one condition to another, but preserves [a thing's] own nature and ascends and advances to its own fulfilment and perfection' (p. 195,201-6 Ruland).

243. This text is counted by Bruns (1892,1) vi as a problem in the strict sense of the term. The theme of the effect of the seasonal movements of the sun on sublunary coming-to-be is shared with the following *quaestio*, 3.5, and with other texts in the collection; but our text is concerned to answer a logical problem it creates. Whereas the title of the *quaestio* asserts that the approach and the receding of the sun are *not* alike causes of coming-to-be, the list of chapter-headings for book 3 of the *Quaestiones* asserts that they *are* (above, n. 49); since the solution given is that the approach of the sun produces coming-to-be *in the primary sense*, the title is correct; approach and receding *are* both causes – and it is this that constitutes the problem – but they are not causes *in the same way*.

244. So Aristotle, *GC* 2.10, 336b17. Our problem is generated by the combination of this with the claim that the passing away of one thing is the coming to be of another; cf. above, nn. 81, 83. The same problem is discussed by Philoponus, *in GC* 289,27-290,7, but without Alexander being named, even though his own lost commentary on *GC* is frequently cited in Philoponus'; cf. also ibid. 293,6-8 and Joachim (1922) 260.

245. Literally, 'each [group of] things'. Cf. 87,20 below. 'Subordinate contraries' is explained by the context (and see the next note); not here in the logical sense of an inclusive disjunction.

246. i.e. in abnormal situations the primary things will pass away with the approach of the sun and come to be with its withdrawal.

247. For this 'polarisation', as it were, in coming-to-be see above, n. 81, and Gill cited there; also n. 223.

248. This *quaestio* is classed by Bruns (1892,1) as a problem in the strict sense; but this seems inappropriate, the characteristic 'or rather' at 88,19 relating to a minor point which does not affect the general contrast between the continuity of the species and the non-recurrence of the individual. The text might better be regarded as a summary of Aristotelian doctrine. It is translated and discussed, along with *Quaest*. 2.22 to which it is closely related, in Sharples (1979); see also White (1985), cited in n. 122 above.

249. Apparently an interpretation of 'it should always be by coming-to-be' at *GC* 2.11, 337b34. But Aristotle probably there intended continuous coming-to-be rather than remaining in perpetuity after having come-to-be; the words in any case look forward to the one case of absolutely necessary coming-to-be that Aristotle admits, that of things that come to be always because their coming to be is cyclical.

250. i.e. as well as 'if what is later, [then] also what is earlier', which is true in every case (below, 88,24-6). See above, nn. 122-3.

251. All children have adult parents, but not all adults become parents of children: Aristotle, *GC* 2.11, 338b10, Alexander, *Fat*. 24, 194,8ff. The present text clearly takes Aristotle to be claiming that there is no *a tergo* necessity where there is only specific, not individual recurrence (so too 88,22ff. below, and Philoponus, *in GC* 313,13-15); but while this is true in the case of adults and children (not all adults are necessarily parents; cf. Alexander, *Fat*. 24 194,8-15), it is not clear that it is so in every case. The cycle of rain following cloud, and cloud rain, involves *a tergo* necessity (*An. Post*. 2.12, 96a3ff.), while the earlier and the later rain are only identical in species, not as individuals (*GC* 2.11, 338b17f., unless indeed we press the concession at 338b18f.; cf. also the successive winters at 89,7f. below). Alexander's connection between absence of individual recurrence and absence of *a tergo* necessity reflects Aristotle's somewhat compressed remarks at *GC* 2.11, 338a10-13 together with Alexander's connection of the infinite rectilinear sequence, discussed by Aristotle at *GC* 2.11, 337b25-9 and 338a6ff., with the non-recurrence of human beings as individuals (88,19ff.).

252. Added conjecturally by Spengel.

253. To be interpreted as meaning 'nothing later that is absolutely necessary'. Bruns indeed initially proposed reading *husteron <ex anankês>* here, before revising his interpretation of *Quaest*. 2.22 to suppose that in an infinite sequence there is no ordering at all. See above, n. 120.

254. That is, the heavenly bodies; 'circle' here renders *kuklos*, translated in what has preceded by 'cycle'.

255. Interpreting 'seasons' in terms of changes of climate rather than of periods of the calendar, which *are* regular. In the last section of the *Mantissa* (186,13-20) Aristotle's reference at *Meteorology* 1.14, 352a28 to *khronoi heimarmenoi*, in connection with the seasons of the ordinary year and the corresponding periods of the great year, is cited in support of the doctrine, also put forward in Alexander's *Fat.*, that fate applies for the most part but admits of exceptions. It is striking that the point that fate admits of exceptions is *not* made in Alexander's commentary on the *Meteorology, ad loc*. But the point that the seasons admit of variation is so commonplace that it would be rash to draw any conclusions from it concerning the authenticity or the relative date of composition of the present *quaestio*.

256. cf. Aristotle, *GA* 4.10, 778a4ff. and White (1985) 27.

257. cf. above, nn. 24-5.

258. The father and the motion of the sun are both causes of the generation of an individual, but the father is the proximate cause; cf. Aristotle, *Physics* 2.2, 194b13, *Metaphysics* 12.5, 1071a14-16.

259. This text is rightly described in its title as an interpretation or *exêgêsis* (cf. Bruns [1892,1] ix) of an argument in Aristotle, *DA* 3.1 of which Ross (1961) 269 is led to say 'I have tried in my summary to show the articulation of the enormous sentence which extends from 424b24 to 425a13'. Maudlin (1986), indeed, has argued that commentators in general, and among them both Ross and Alexander here, have misinterpreted as Aristotle's own single argument what is in fact a dialectical debate, 424b22-30 and 425a7-13 expressing not Aristotle's own views but those of an opponent.

260. One might expect *aisthêtêrion* to mean 'sense-organ'; but as the sequel shows, Alexander takes the *aisthêtêria* to be not ears, eyes, etc., but the *three* means or instruments through which the senses operate, air, water, and touch, the organs of the *five* senses being composed of these. Cf. 90,30ff., 90,34, and Aristotle, *DA* 3.1, 424b32-3.

261. So Alexander (and at p. 90,21 below) and two MSS of Aristotle; the majority of the Aristotle MSS have 'by touching them themselves' (cf. Aristotle 424b29-30, and 90,23 below).

262. *hoion,* which often means 'for example'; but not here, since air and water are the only media through which remote sensation operates (cf. 91,16 below).

263. i.e. the sublunary elements, earth, air, fire and water, as opposed to the heavenly aether (cf. 91,23 below).

264. Aristotle, *DA* 3.1, 424b24-425a13.

265. Our author's procedure here and at 90,12ff. is to quote from his own previous formulation of the argument – here, from 90,4-5 – and then to identify what in the text of Aristotle corresponds to his own formulation.

266. The consequent to 'if ' in 91,5 (rendered above 'suppose there are several instruments') never appears; it should be of the form 'what possesses just one of them will sense what can be sensed through both' (cf. Aristotle 425a2-3). Bruns marks a lacuna; it may rather be that Alexander's parenthesis ('this seems to be the case with things that can be smelled … it is not necessary for what is going to sense smell to possess both') has in effect already supplied what is required and so caused an anacoluthon. Aristotle himself uses the example of *sight* through air and water (425a1-2).

267. Aristotle, *Sens.* 2, 436a22ff.

268. That is, as opposed to the imperfect ones which are not capable of locomotion and possess only touch among the senses; cf. Aristotle, *DA* 3.11, 433b31ff.

269. The heavenly aether can only undergo locomotion, not change in quality or quantity; Aristotle, *Cael.* 1.3.

270. This text is an explanation (*exêgêsis*) of Aristotle, *DA* 3.2, 425b12-426a2, following Aristotle's exposition pretty closely. Bruns (1892,1) viii notes it as one of the few (along with 2.2, 2.24, 2.26 and 3.9) which are of such a form that they could have been parts of a continuous commentary. See the Introduction at n. 23.

271. Aristotle, *DA* 3.2, 425b12.

272. If, for example, awareness of seeing is by a different sense from sight itself, then, as the previous paragraph has shown, this different sense *too* will have to have the objects of sight as its objects; so they will be the objects of two senses, of this different sense and of sight itself.

273. It is by sight that we see, but (on the present hypothesis) by sense[2] that we are aware that we are seeing, and (we may suppose) by sense[3] that we are aware that we are aware that we are seeing.

274. *energeia,* previously here rendered 'activity'; see above, n. 33.

275. *kinêsis;* here the wider sense of 'change' rather than 'motion' in the sense of locomotion seems appropriate.

276. Aristotle, *Phys.* 3.3, 202a21ff.

277. Bruns in his apparatus considers adding here the explicit reference to sight which is grammatically required by the feminine participle *labousa;* but the original author may have carelessly left it to be understood. The *Quaestiones* often seem careless over the gender or number of pronouns (see above, n. 35); the present passage may be a rather similar case.

278. Bruns (1892,1) x counts this text as a summary (*epidromê*) of Aristotelian doctrine; it is concerned with one specific point, that what is not a proper object of any sense can still be sensed accidentally. Aristotle, *DA* 3.1, 425a30ff. describes the case where two senses perceive each other's proper objects accidentally because these objects are accidents of the same thing; see the next note.

279. Not because this honey might equally well have been some other colour, but because not everything that is pale yellow is sweet or honey, and it is *qua* pale yellow that we actually see it. Aristotle has the example of yellow (*xanthos,* rather than *ôkhros* 'pale yellow') and bitterness both belonging to bile (*DA* 3.1, 425b1-2).

280. I do not know why here, and here only in this *quaestio,* the dative plural of 'all', elsewhere feminine to agree with 'senses' expressed or understood, appears in the masculine.

281. The Greek has 'capable of being sensed by all the senses', but I have translated in this way to show that this is meant distributively; there is a different property in the thing for each of the five senses, not *one* property sensed *per se* by them all.

282. In the sense that it cannot be sensed by any of them, not in the sense that it can be sensed by some but not all; I have translated literally to bring out the parallel with what follows.

283. Literally 'a thing-that-can-be-sensed of this sort'.

284. This *quaestio* is classed by Bruns (1892,1) viii among the *exêgêseis* or interpretations of Aristotelian texts. He argues that its character is such that it could have formed part of a commentary; but in fact a relatively rapid summary of the earlier part of the Aristotelian chapter is followed by a detailed discussion of 427a9-14, and this would hardly be appropriate in a continuous commentary. Cf. the Introduction, at n. 23.

Aristotle resolves the problem of how the common sense (not so named in this passage) can judge the objects of different senses simultaneously by invoking the analogy of a point which can be regarded as one or as many. Our author objects that simultaneously being affected in different ways cannot apply to the physical sense-organ, but can apply to the capacity of judgement. The analogy is also employed in the same context at Alexander, *in Sens.* 164,13-16, 165,17-20, and, with an explicit reference to 'the common sense', at Alexander, *DA* 63,8-13; cf. Thurot (1875) 383 and Bréhier (1924-38) vol. 4 195 n. 2 and 196 n. 1. As Henry (1960) 436-8 notes discussing our text in the context of its suggested use by Plotinus 4.7, 6.11-14, Alexander in all three contexts speaks of the centre of a circle with many radii, whereas Aristotle speaks only of a single point that can be treated as two, apparently when it divides a line. Themistius, *in DA* 86,18-23, gives Aristotle's comparison to the point and then adds 'or rather, the centre of a circle'; I owe this reference to Robert B. Todd, who describes this (private communication) as one of several instances of Themistius' use of Alexander's *DA* as a source. Against Henry, Moraux argued (*Gnomon* 50 [1978] 532 n. 1) that the comparison is traditional.

285. Literally, 'undergo the forms'.

286. Ross here supplies '<both indivisible> and divisible' from Themistius *in DA* 86,23 and Simplicius *in DA* 201,6-7.

287. Some MSS of Aristotle have 'which some people speak of *qua* both one and two' (cf. Ross's apparatus ad loc.)

288. See Textual Emendations. In the text of Aristotle Trendelenburg proposed 'In the respect in which it uses the terminus twice' (*dis* for *dusi*); and for 'in a way by what is separated' the MSS of Aristotle have 'in a way separately' among other variant readings. Cf. Ross ad loc.

289. cf. *Quaest.* 1.16 29,21-3; 1.19 32,21-3; 2.15 60,18-20.24-5.

290. See above, n. 286.

291. cf. Aristotle *Int.* 14, 23b4. (I owe this and the reference in the following note to the anonymous reader.)

292. cf. Aristotle *Metaph.* 4.3, 1005b26-8.

293. This *quaestio* is an analysis – but a selective one, see below – of the discussion of the saltness of the sea in Aristotle, *Meteorologica* 2.1-3, 353a32-359b26, classed by Bruns (1892,1) x as an *epidromê* or summary. It may also be compared with Alexander's surviving commentary on those chapters (Alexander, *in Meteor.* 66,1-89,20).

294. Hesiod, *Theogony* 282, 785-92 (Lee [1952], 123 n.).

295. Anaximander and Diogenes of Apollonia; cf. Alexander, *in Meteor.* 67,3-14 = Theophrastus fr. 221 FHSG, and DK 12A27, 64A9, 64A17 (Lee [1952], 124 n.).

296. Empedocles (Aristotle, *Meteor.* 2.3, 357a24, Alexander, *in Meteor.* 67,14-17) and Antiphon (DK 87B32). Cf. Lee [1952], 125 n., but also the next note.

297. Xenophanes (DK 21A33), Metrodorus (DK 70A19), Anaxagoras (DK 59A90). Lee [1952], loc. cit. But Xenophanes is reported only as speaking of an admixture of earth flowing into the sea, where Anaxagoras and Metrodorus spoke of the water being filtered through earth. Cf. Alexander, *in Meteor.* 67,22-7, and nn. 9,11 below. The theories cited in nn. 3-5 appear also in a probable fragment of Theophrastus, *P.Hibeh* 16 = Democritus DK68A99a = Theophrastus vol. 1 p. 463 FHSG); Democritus there seems to be associated with the third view rather than, as Lee loc. cit. suggests, the second.

298. Bruns conjectures 'not naturally stationary'. But Aristotle (2.1, 353b23ff.) classifies well-water with stationary water.

299. Bruns adds here 'He gives the reason for the apparent flowing of the sea', to supply a main verb to the participle *deixas* in 98,29 (rendered by 'After this [Aristotle] shows' above). It is perhaps as likely that there is an anacoluthon.

300. Xenophanes (DK 21B30; cf. Lee [1952] 133 n.). But see the next note.

301. The summary here of 2.2, which is not primarily concerned with saltiness, is extremely compressed by contrast with those of 2.1 and 2.3. The immediate point, that some had suggested that the freshness of rivers is to be explained by the naturally salt water having been strained through earth, is made by Aristotle at 2.2, 354b17-18; it is to be contrasted with the theory that it is filtering through earth that makes water *salty* (see n. 5 above and n. 11 below; also Aristotle, *Sens.* 4, 441b1ff., Theophrastus, *CP* 6.3.1, Alexander, *in Sens.* 71,24-72,4 = Theophrastus fr.212 FHSG, and Eichholz [1949] 145).

302. i.e. as reported at 99,18-100,10 below.

303. Rendering Bruns' conjecture, which at first sight seems odd because what follows seems to resemble Aristotle's own explanation. But in the account rejected here there is no reference to the dry exhalation *from the land*; and Aristotle rejects the view criticised here at *Meteor.* 2.3, 357a11ff., the essential point of which is that a closed cycle of evaporation from the sea can not explain the sea becoming *more* salty, since the evaporated water returns to the sea again; the contribution from the land is needed too. The theory here rejected is the more unacceptable to Aristotle because it is advanced in the context of the view that the world and the sea had a beginning and that the sea became progressively more salty; but our summariser has concentrated on the question of saltiness rather than on the more general issue of the sea's origins. Aristotle goes on (357a15-24) to reject the view that it is an admixture of earth carried down by the rivers that makes the sea salty (cf. 98,26-8 above); but our summariser includes neither this nor the subsequent criticism of Empedocles (357a24-b21).

304. The Greek actually has 'not from what is like that', but the sense seems the same.

305. For 'the same' Schwartz (in Bruns' apparatus) suggested 'of this sort'.

306. The theory combines two points; [i] in the case of exhalation from the land, the salty constituent is carried up and, falling down again in the rain, contributes to the saltness of the sea; [ii] in the case of exhalation from the sea, the salty constituent is for the most part left behind. Aristotle himself makes point [i] at 358a15-27, then goes on to note the brackishness of some rain as evidence for this (358a27-b6; 100,10-15 here) and only then goes on to make point [ii] (358b12-16) before combining them both at 358b23-34.

307. Added by Bruns on the basis of Alexander, *in Meteor.* 86,4-5; cf. Aristotle, *Meteor.* 2.3, 358b12ff. Aristotle's theory is that salt water evaporated and then condensed again produces fresh, or almost fresh, water, and that this shows that most of the salty element was not drawn up in the initial evaporation; however, in the case of rain fresh saltiness is added from the dry exhalation from the land. Our author however seems to suggest that the salty constituent in what is evaporated from the sea is converted to fresh water in the clouds (100,7-9); which would seem to vitiate the argument that, since the rain which eventually falls is relatively un-salty, much of the original saltiness must have been left behind in the sea and not included in the original evaporation from the sea.

308. *historia*, 'enquiry'.

309. Aristotle refers specifically – but describing it as a 'story' and not committing itself to its truth – to 'the lake in Palestine', i.e. the Dead Sea.

310. Aristotle here refers to a spring in Chaonia, in North-West Greece.

311. This text is treated as a summary of Aristotelian doctrine by Bruns (1892,1) x. It is discussed and translated into English by Todd (1976,1), who relates it to a passage in Ammonius, *in Int.* 39,13-32. There Alexander is first reported as advancing, against Aristotle's claim at *Int.* loc. cit. that names are conventional, the argument – presumably dialectical – that if sounds are natural the words formed from them are so as well. There follows a reply, distinguishing between sounds and the use we make of them, which Todd argues also derives from Alexander. A similar argument is also reported more briefly in an Arabic text 'On utterances' attributed to Alexander, van Ess 37, published in Badawi (1971) 31; cf. Zimmermann-Brown (1973) 316, Thillet (1984) lxxi. For a distinction in other contexts like that in this *quaestio* between natural endowment and its varying developments cf., with Todd (1976,1) 142, Alexander, *DA* 82,3-5; also *Fat.* 27, 198,3ff., *P.Eth.* 29, 161,14ff., and Aristotle *EN* 2.1, 1103a23. The question whether language was natural or conventional had been a topic of philosophical controversy since the fifth century BC.

312. Or perhaps 'to lay them down on our own authority' (*epi* as in *eph' hêmin*); but cf. *autois* in 101,2.

313. Bruns in his apparatus, though not his actual text, approves Spengel's addition of *êmen*. This may be right, but does not seem essential; the sense is the same in any case.

314. The argument seems to be elliptical; if names were natural, the letters of which they were made up would have to be so too, but they are not. What is not clear is why it should be supposed that the letters are not natural. The author may have in mind the different scripts of different countries, or the phonemes found in one language but not in another; but the relevance of the former at least seems questionable, and the differences in the latter not obvious. See also n. 311 above.

315. i.e. to establish that names are laid down by men, not given by nature.

316. This important text, classed by Bruns (1892,1) x as possibly a self-contained monograph, is discussed by Bruns (1893), Todd (1982), (1984), Sorabji (1989) ch.8, especially 126-8, 136, 139-40, and Inwood (1991) 261-3. I have also benefited greatly from being able to consult and cite Professor Todd's unpublished translation of and comments on this *quaestio* (see the Introduction); where not otherwise indicated, references to 'Todd' in the notes on this *quaestio* are to this translation and the accompanying commentary. Todd suggests, because of parallels in Simplicius' commentary on *Cael.* (285,2-27) where Simplicius was, he argues, using Alexander's commentary on *Phys.* 3.4, that the *quaestio* is actually based on extracts from that commentary; see the Introduction, at n. 23.

The present *quaestio* is concerned to refute two arguments for the infinity of the universe, [A] the dilemma that, whether someone at the supposed edge of the universe can put his hand or throw an object beyond it or not, either way there must be something, if only empty space, beyond; and [B] the argument that whatever is bounded must have something alongside its boundary. Bruns (1893) 9 argues that [A] is a Stoic, [B] an Epicurean argument; but in fact as Todd points out ((1984) 187-7 and nn.) both arguments were used both by the Epicureans, who held that the universe was infinite, and by the Stoics, who used them to argue that there was void outside the universe; cf. below, nn. 317-18. However, as Todd also notes, in Simplicius' report in his commentary on *Cael.*, where Alexander's arguments are directed primarily against the Stoics, only argument [A], not [B], appears, and in his commentary on *Phys.* Simplicius (below n. 318) reports Alexander as saying [B] was the argument primarily used by the Epicureans. In the present *quaestio,* as Todd points out, sections [II] and [III] suggest a primarily anti-Epicurean focus; but Alexander's interest, typically, is in the arguments rather than in the particular schools advocating them. Inwood 263 thus speaks of 'a mixed Stoic/Epicurean account' as the target.

317. cf. Archytas cited by Eudemus ap. Simplicium, *in Phys.* 467,26ff.; Lucretius, 1.968-983; also Alexander ap. Simplicium, *in Cael.* 284,28-285,2, where an argument of this type is attributed to the Stoics, to argue only for void outside the cosmos rather than for unlimited void (Bruns [1893] 3; Todd [1984] 186 n. 9). 101,10-15 form part of *SVF* 2.536.

318. For the argument cf. 104,20ff. below; Aristotle, *Phys.* 3.4, 203b20-2 (reference misprinted at Bruns [1893] 6 n. 3); Epicurus, *ad Hdt.* 41; Lucretius, 2.958-67; Cicero *de Nat. Deorum* 2.103; Alexander ap. Simplicium, *in Phys.* 467,1-3. Cf. Todd (1984) 186 n. 8.

319. Literally 'the opposite of the things that are being asked'.

320. *en hautois* is odd; I follow Todd. Or perhaps 'from (in) their own understanding'.

321. Because a thing can only be a part if there is some ultimate whole of which it is a part.

322. cf. with Bruns (1893) 8, Aristotle, *Phys.* 3.6, 207a1; 'it is not that with nothing outside it, but that which always has something outside it, that is indefinite'; also Sorabji (1988) 139.

323. With the argument of the preceding two paragraphs compare, with Todd (1984) 191 n. 33, Alexander ap. Simplicium, *in Cael.* 285,3-5.

324. cf. Aristotle, *Phys.* 1.6, 189a12-13. (I am grateful to Professor Todd for this reference.) That argument indeed refers to principles infinite in *number*, not extent (I owe this point to Eric Lewis); but so do the arguments in the present section of our text. In an atomist theory the two types of infinity imply each other.

325. For the connection of nature with order cf. Alexander *Fat.* 4, 168,3-5; *in Metaph.* 103,31ff.; Alexander ap. Simplicium, *in Phys.* 311,18-19. Cf. Dooley (1989) 142 n. 306.

326. cf. n. 120 above.

327. Todd here adds '<by nature>', so that 103,11 will be a recapitulation of the present statement. But the text as it stands can be taken as an assertion – admittedly a loosely-formulated one – that things that come to be do not *in general* come to be by chance, even if some do.

328. Bruns (1893) 9 n. 1 suggests 'and of the composite things'; cf. the next note. But for 'things that are' Todd compares 102,25 above.

329. So Schwartz's emendation, accepted by Bruns into his edition. Bruns (1893) 9 however argues that the corruption hides the loss of a larger amount of text, on the grounds that 106,24-30, while referring back to 102,24-103,12, divides into two points what there in our present text appears as one, and that there is nothing in 102,24-103,12 as they stand to correspond to the distinction of four sublunary elements and the heavenly one at 106,26-7. Todd punctuates rather 'What if it is impossible ... unlimited things? How could ...?'

330. That these are the Atomists is shown by comparison with 104,4ff. below, where they are described as also believing in innumerable worlds; cf. Bruns (1893) 8, but also Aristotle, *Phys.* 3.4, 203b26. (I am grateful to Professor Todd for this reference.)

331. So Schwartz's emendation; but Bruns (1893) returns to the MSS text, marked as corrupt, on the grounds that the syntactical structure of this section may have been obscured by a lacuna. See above, n. 329.

332. i.e. the first unlimited plus the second plus the sum of the two will be greater than the first plus the second only; or else, perhaps, a third term can be added if a second can, i.e. if there is a plurality of unlimited things at all (103,22). In the first case the series of increasing terms will have the form a, a+b, a+b+(a+b) ..., in the second a, a+b, a+b+c ... .

333. This would not be so if, unlike Zeno of Elea and the Atomists (Epicurus, *ad*

Hdt. 57) we admitted infinitesimal magnitudes. But, just because the Atomists rejected this possibility, and so postulated indivisible minimum magnitudes, Alexander's argument is appropriate against them.

334. That this comparison between the totality of atoms and that of atoms plus void reflects critics' development of Epicurus' views, rather than his own explicit statements, is argued by Todd (1982), who compares Simplicius, *in Phys.* 618,15-20. Epicurus in fact described void as infinite in extent, the atoms as infinite in *number* (*ad Hdt.* 41).

335. 104,4-8 are cited by Usener, *Epicurea* 301 ad fin.

336. Todd (1976,2) 140 (also id. [1982] 182) compares this argument with Alexander ap. Philoponum, *in GC* 12,6-25.

337. cf. above, n. 318.

338. As it does according to Epicurus, *ad Hdt.* 41; Bruns (1893) 10.104,20-3 are cited by Usener, *Epicurea* 297 ad fin.

339. On these criteria cf Sorabji (1988) 136.

340. Accepting Bruns' conjecture (see Textual Emendations). Without it the sense would be 'an accident of those parts of the totality which have the property of being limited'; but they all do. With Alexander's argument here compare Aristotle, *Phys.* 3.8, 208a11-14 and Simplicius, *in Phys.* 516,14-17 (Todd [1984] 187 n. 12).

341. As happens elsewhere, the reference is vague and the words have to be supplied. Spengel conjectured the plural 'they think it right'.

342. Literally 'a nature'.

343. So Usener, followed by Bruns (1893) 10. Todd, noting the contrast with 'magnitudes' in 105,13, prefers the MSS 'incorporeals', taking 'both movements and times' as explanatory of this.

344. *phantasian … laboi.* Cf. Aristotle, *Phys.* 3.8, 208a16ff.; cf. also id. *Metaph.* 4.5, 1010b10-11, Alexander, *in Metaph.* 313,1-4 ad loc., id. ap. Simplicium, *in Cael.* 286,25-7, and ap. Simplicium, *in Phys.* 517,17-27. Bruns (1893) 6 n. 8, 10; Todd (1984) 189 n. 21-2.

345. Todd deletes 'and those who are awake' on the basis of a comparison with Aristotle *Metaph.* 4.5 and Alexander's comment thereon (see previous note). For empty imaginings of those who are awake one might compare Stoic discussion of the visions of madmen which do not correspond to any external *phantaston* (*SVF* 2.74; I owe this point to Eric Lewis).

346. For the claim, in effect, that the image begs the question cf. Alexander ap. Simplicium, *in Phys.* 285,25-7; below, n. 358.

347. i.e. as we would say, 'dimensions' – length, breadth and height. 106,10-13 form part of *SVF* 2.536.

348. The Stoics defined void as 'extension without *body*'; *SVF* 2.505. Cf. Bruns (1893) p. 10.

349. Literally 'in them'. Todd emends the phrase, but cf. above, n. 35.

350. Or perhaps, reading *ti* for *to* as suggested by Bruns in his apparatus, 'there will not be any void outside the totality'.

351. To describe only the four sublunary elements as possessing matter is distinctly odd in view of the efforts of other *quaestiones* to solve the problems involved in supposing that there is matter in the heavens too; cf. *Quaest.* 1.10, 1.15.

352. cf. above, *Quaest.* 2.18, 2.19, 3.5.

353. cf. Aristotle, *Phys.* 3.5, 204b14-19, 204b35-205a1. (I am grateful to Professor Todd for these references.)

354. See above, n. 329.

355. cf. 104,4ff. above.

356. Bruns (1893) 10 and n. 7 notes the way in which the author comes back yet again to the initial example just when one might have thought him to be rounding off his conclusion.

357. Added by Spengel. See Textual Emendations.

358. cf. Sorabji (1988) 126-7, who describes this as the best answer in antiquity to argument [A]; also Alexander ap. Simplicium, *in Cael.* 285,21-7 with Bruns (1893) 4 and n. 7; Todd (1984) 192 n. 35.

359. This text was translated and discussed briefly at Sharples (1983,1) 118-19, 177-8. It covers similar ground to Alexander, *Fat.* 11, 178,17-28, 12, 14, 183,21-185,7, 15, 186,3-12, and *Mant.* 172,17-174,3.

360. For the claim that the ability to deliberate about and reject appearances is the defining characteristic of human beings cf. Alexander, *Fat.* 178,17-28, 14, 183,30-184,11, *Mant.* 172,19-28. In Alexander's treatment the emphasis, probably through Stoic influence, is not so much on the choice between different courses of action as on the ability to resist assenting to the appearances that impinge upon us. See Sharples (1983,1) 140 and Donini (1987). For the Stoics, indeed, *phantasiai*, here rendered 'appearances', were not confined to sense-impressions; but Alexander is not concerned to give an accurate report of the Stoic position (see Sharples [1983,1] 149-50, and below n. 364).

361. 'always' is required by the argument, for deliberation is certainly *sometimes* followed by assent to the initial appearance; in 107,22 it is only claimed that it *often* is not.

362. To be valid the argument actually requires 'our doing so is the only thing that can do away with what depends on us'.

363. cf. Alexander, *Fat.* 14, 184,21ff.

364. For this contrast between an 'appearance' in the strict sense and what more generally 'appears', cf. *Fat.* 15 186,3-12 and Sharples (1983,1) 149. The passage in *Fat.* is discussed in relation to Alexander's treatment of *phantasia* elsewhere, and the question of his consistency considered, by Modrak (1993).

365. That is, our conception of the moral end, determined by our character, for which we are responsible inasmuch as it is in part the result of our actions; cf. Aristotle, *EN* 3.5, 1114a31-b25 and Alexander, *P.Eth.* 9 129,24-130,2.

366. cf. Alexander, *Fat.* 181,2ff., *Mant.* 182,28f., 183,32ff.; Aristotle, *EN* 3.3, 1112b10f.

367. This *epidromê* or summary (cf. Bruns [1892,1] x) corresponds to *Meteor.* 4.1-7, 378b10-381b25, 382b28-384b23; Alexander's extant commentary on the *Meteorology* devotes 34 pages to 4.1-7 and only 16 to the remaining part of the book, even though that constitutes approximately half of the whole. It is at once apparent from comparison with the Aristotelian text that the author of our *quaestio* has sought to bring out the general outlines of Aristotle's discussion, omitting most of his specific examples; commendable though this aim is, the absence of examples makes the discussion hard to follow, especially since the Greek technical terms – here translated consistently, as far as possible – do not correspond in scope to the English ones. (We would not naturally, for example, apply the same word, *pêgnusthai*, here rendered 'solidify', to what happens to water when frozen and to clay when fired in the kiln.)

368. cf. also Aristotle, *GC* 2.2, 239b24-32, with Furley (1989) 133, and Galen, *de Nat. Fac.* (Helmreich) 1.3, 106,13ff. But see below, nn. 375, 382.

369. Bruns here postulates a lacuna – the words translated above by 'after this he states' actually being 'and after this having stated', and the sentence therefore being incomplete – and supplies 'he gave the account of coming-to-be and passing-away'. It is perhaps as likely that the lengthy sentence-structure has broken down. 'underlying [them]' might also be rendered 'subject [to them]'.

370. In the sense of incomplete cooking, not properly bringing to the boil; I owe the translation to Eric Lewis. Cf. Lee (1952) 306 note b.

371. Or 'change'; see above, nn. 33, 63. But in some passages in the present *quaestio kinêsis* and its cognates have to be rendered by 'movement' (e.g. at 110,16ff.), and elsewhere in the present text 'change' renders *metabolê* (e.g. at 109,2). It seemed best to retain consistent translations within a single *quaestio*.

372. 'innate' (*emphutos*) is here apparently synonymous with 'proper' (*oikeios*) above. Aristotle uses *emphutos* of heat in *Meteor*. 2.2, 355b9, but the word does not occur either in *Meteor*. 4 or in Alexander's commentary thereon.

373. Bruns in his apparatus suggests 'does not influence them; for if it were going to prevail over them [Bruns has "it", the heat in them?] and change them, it would do so by influencing (*kinein*) them'.

374. For the treatment of dry and moist as matter compare Aristotle *Meteor*. 4.1, 378b33ff. (109,3 above is not quite so explicit), and for 'that underlie them' see above, n. 369.

375. That heat is the proper cause of coming-to-be is not stated in so many words in the text of Aristotle here, but is implied by his account of concoction. See also nn. 368, 382.

376. The words supplied between angle brackets, or something like them, are clearly required both by the structure of the argument and by comparison with the text of Aristotle, and have presumably fallen out because of their repetitiveness; they are already absent from MS V.

377. Aristotle (*Meteor*. 4.2, 379b19), as Bruns notes, has 'perfection [produced] from'.

378. *perikarpion* includes everything that surrounds the seed proper, for example the flesh of the apple as opposed to the pips. Cf. Theophrastus, *Hist. Plant.* 1.2.1.

379. e.g. gold, wood and milk: Aristotle, *Meteor*. 4.3, 380b28ff.

380. Bruns prints 'what is concocted in this way' as part of the quotation; but the text of Aristotle has rather 'by dry heat, whenever [the thing] becomes drier on completion'.

381. Or 'process'; but no clear distinction is drawn in what follows between natural processes and what they produce, 'what comes to be by nature' covering both.

382. Aristotle, *Meteor*. 4.5, 382b4-5. See n. 375 above.

383. Water for example would not be regarded as soft, because it yields to objects inserted into it but does so by parting and flowing round. For 'mutual replacement' (*antiperistasis*) see the discussion of Lee (1952) 82-3.

384. Or 'change' (*kinêsis*): above, nn. 63, 371.

385. Added by Spengel.

386. Spengel conjectured 'this'; but cf. above, n. 35. The reference of the pronoun is in any case vague – the fire, or the hot in the things in question?

387. Respectively liquid or moist compounds, like milk, which are thickened by drying, and soft ones like clay, which are solidified or hardened but not made thicker.

388. Aristotle, *Meteor.* 4.6, 383b12, calls these 'millstones', *mulai*.

389. This is the undoubted sense of the text of the *quaestio*, and there is no error in Bruns' report of V here. The text of Aristotle, *Meteorologica* 4.7, 384a20 however has 'if the whey is *not* separated (*mê* for the *quaestio*'s *dê*; N₁ has *men* for *mê*, Fobes ad loc.) it is burned (or "burned away") when boiled by the fire'. The genders show that what is burned is the milk in the *quaestio* but the whey in Aristotle; in the latter case, however, since the two have not been separated it makes no difference – the mixture is what burns. (I take it that Lee [1952] 333 is wrong to translate the text of Aristotle by 'whey ... will *boil* away', suggesting that the whey is boiled off innocuously leaving the solids unaffected.) Alexander's commentary on the *Meteorology* (210,35-6) agrees with the text of Aristotle; and Eric Lewis points out to me that clarified butter, i.e. *that from which the whey has been removed*, can reach a higher temperature before burning than butter which has not been clarified. One suspects that the *quaestio* has modified the argument in a way influenced more by tidiness of presentation than by the physical facts.

390. This may be a later note referring back to the title of this *quaestio*; see above, nn. 12, 367.

391. This *quaestio* seems to be directed against an actual or hypothetical attempt to escape the dilemma for atomist theories, that *either* the indivisible minima of which magnitudes are made up have parts and so are not indivisible, *or* they are not magnitudes at all, by arguing that they are 'as it were' without parts.

392. The supposition must be that 'what is said to be without parts' is, or is implied by the argument of the 'atomists' to be, 'what is as it were without parts' rather than what is without parts, *simpliciter*.

393. Bruns postulates a lacuna before 'if at any rate', but this does not seem necessary. The 'atomists' try to escape the difficulty that a magnitude cannot be composed of things that have no parts (and hence no magnitude either) by saying that their indivisible minima are only 'as it were' without parts; this then explains the claim in the previous sentence that being without parts is just being *as it were* without parts.

394. The other horn of the dilemma; rather than using the formula '*as it were* without parts' to escape the difficulty that the constituents of magnitudes will not be magnitudes at all if they are without parts, it is now suggested that they are not in fact magnitudes, but only 'as it were' magnitudes – that is, as has been shown, not magnitudes at all.

395. This is not strictly logical; it does not follow, from the fact that every magnitude has parts, that what is not [really] a magnitude does not have parts; to avoid the fallacy of affirming the consequent one would rather need the premiss 'every part is a part of a magnitude'. But it was suggested in the previous note that the implied motive of introducing the notion of what is *as it were* a magnitude was precisely to get away from the idea that the constituents of magnitudes themselves had parts.

396. Appealing to the principle that, if A is matter for B (literally 'of ', and so throughout), A must in itself be different from B.

397. The Greek here has the conventional epistolary past tense, looking back from the viewpoint of the recipient of the letter. Professor Barnes points out that the implication of an unnamed addressee may be a matter of convention (found for example in several works of Galen) rather than an indication that the text was actually written as a letter. A number of short texts in the Arabic tradition ascribed to Alexander are described as 'letters' in the titles attached to them.

398. That is to say, if one discusses an intractable argument at all, one is thereby conceding that intractability is a relative, not an absolute matter. With this argument, and especially with its final sentence, one may compare Alexander, *Fat.* 10, 177,1-2 as emended by Langerbeck; cf. Sharples (1983,1) 53-4.

399. Barnes (1982) 39 points out that the example of the drip in Aristotle, *Phys.* 253b14-26 is not in fact a case of the *sorites* (cf. also [Aristotle] *Probl.* 11.28, 902b1). Moreover Simplicius (*in Phys.* 1197,35ff.) records Alexander as *not* interpreting this example as a *sorites*.

400. Because one individual cannot move a ship at all, it does not follow that a number together cannot; cf. Aristotle, *Phys.* 7.5, 250a15ff.

401. The heap (*sôros*) from which the sorites takes its name; if one grain is not a heap, neither are two, nor three, nor four ... .

402. A paradox attributed to Eubulides (Diogenes Laertius 2.108). The interpretation here suggested is clearly 'a man with (say) 3,000 hairs is not bald, so neither is one with 2,999 ... and neither is a man with only one hair'. Cf. Barnes (1982) 37 n. 31.

403. Literally 'a mina'.

404. This is the general sense. The term is however also used for a weight of one-eighth of an obol (LSJ s.v. *khalkos*); *if* this use also applied to money, then, since an obol was one-sixth of a drachma, the point is that a difference of one part in 4,800 is no difference at all – nor two parts, nor three, and so on.

405. *en platei.* The same term and idea are used in a different connection, of human behaviour, by Alexander, *Fat.* 29, 200,1. At Diogenes Laertius 7.76 it means 'in general' as opposed to 'in particular' (cf. Mansfeld [1986], at 370-1; I am grateful to Professor Barnes for drawing my attention to this reference).

406. *epistêmê,* knowledge proper, 'scientific' knowledge. Cf. Aristotle, *Metaph.* 6.2, 1027a20.

407. cf. *Quaest.* 1.23 with Sharples (1983) 185-6.

408. Vitelli marks a lacuna here, and I have provided my own supplement *exempli gratia* to give the general sense.

409. The verbs in all four cases are aorists, but I take them as gnomic aorists. If the reference is to specific examples – and the choice of verbs seems odd if not – 'is moved' could apply to the ship dragged over land; 'is seen' to the small bodies; 'increases' to the *sôros* or heap itself; and 'grows [hair]' to the hairy man coupled above with the bald man. *trephein,* the word here, is often used of growing one's hair (cf. LSJ s.v.), and though there seem no parallels to the omission of an explicit term for 'hair' in such a context, it might have been felt that it could be supplied from the foregoing discussion.

410. Literally 'the whole power', 'the power all together'.

411. Literally 'that existed, were there, before it'.

412. The application to filling is clear enough – the last drop would not fill the jar if the others had not preceded it. And the same presumably applies to the last accession of fitness that gives perfect health (thought of here positively, rather than negatively as the absence of disease).

413. One might suppose that the reference is to Heraclides of Pontus. However, Heraclides' views on the fifth element are unclear (cf. Gottschalk [1980] 106-7); and, significantly, he is not cited on this topic in Simplicius' *de Caelo* commentary, which draws extensively on the commentary by Alexander now lost. The expression in the Greek ('the *logos* against Heraclides') could refer either to a specific work against Heraclides' views or to a section devoted to them from a longer work – conceivably Alexander's lost *de Caelo* commentary; though the suggestion that the discussion of the fifth element formed but one part of an extended discussion of Heraclides' views on, presumably, a variety of topics perhaps suggests the former. The discussion even of the fifth element must have been quite lengthy if there was room for this anti-Stoic digression within it. The alternative is to suppose that the 'Heraclides' in question is in fact the Stoic referred to in the second sentence of the introduction and in the text itself. ('A certain Stoic philosopher', rather than 'this Stoic philosopher', in the second sentence of the introduction might seem odd if this is the same person as 'Heraclides' in the first sentence – I owe this point to Eric Lewis; but it is not perhaps so if the author of the introduction knew of Heraclides *only* as a person named in the text of Alexander he is excerpting.) Alexander says that his adversary is 'leader' (*proïstatai*) of the Stoic school (p. 93,3); the term can indeed just mean 'champion', and is so used later in this text (p. 93,6); but it is the same word *proïstamai* that Alexander uses in speaking of his own appointment as a public teacher of Peripatetic philosophy (*Fat.* 164,14). There is, moreover, a plausible second-century AD candidate, the Stoic teacher Aurelius Heraclides Eupyrides; see Sharples (1990,1) 92-4.

414. Vitelli confessed puzzlement over this sentence. I take it to be an ironic comment by Alexander on the tactics of Stoics who criticise Peripatetics for being at variance with Plato, not realising that they themselves are even more so.

415. Or 'champion' (so four lines below). But see n. 413 above.

416. The basic doctrine comes from *Timaeus* 42E – and was familiar in contemporary Middle Platonism – though the image of the place of observation or 'look-out post' comes from Plato, *Politicus* 272E. Aristotle's unmoved mover did not just retire from concern with the world, like Plato's (if one takes the chronological beginning of the world in the *Timaeus* literally), but was never concerned with it at all. For secondary gods exercising providence in Middle Platonist doctrine cf. above n. 104; but in any case the main point is that for both Plato and Aristotle, unlike the Stoics, the *primary* god is *not* directly concerned with the world.

417. Namely, that it is incorporeal, though not of course immortal. This hardly sounds like substantial agreement; but Alexander goes on to argue that the Stoics disagree with Plato on *both* points.

418. The objection here could either be to the involvement of god in things unworthy of him (for which cf. above, n. 114) or to the claim that the Stoic view implies the existence of two bodies in the same place (for which cf. *Mixt.* 226,34ff.). The first point is more directly relevant to the context, but Alexander is quite ready to make incidental attacks on other aspects of Stoic doctrine (see next note). Vitelli's suggestion in his apparatus would give 'for him, as a body, to pass ...'.

419. The Stoics believed that the souls of virtuous men survived until the periodic consumption of the universe by fire, when they like everything else are re-absorbed into Zeus.

420. I am grateful to Dr Zimmermann for showing me his paper in advance of publication and for permission to refer to its results.

421. So too, in interpretation of Aristotle, Shields (1993) 10-11.

422. cf. the distinction drawn by Whiting (1992) 79-80 between a 'functional' and a 'compositional' definition of *flesh*.

423. cf. Bruns (1892,1) xiii-xiv.

Bibliography

For ease of reference the Bibliography has been arranged alphabetically rather than thematically. Paul Moraux, the doyen of Alexander studies in the present century, intended to devote the third and final volume of his monumental work *Der Aristotelismus* (see Moraux 1973, 1984) entirely to a study of Alexander, but was prevented from completing it by his untimely death. The work is now being completed by various hands. It would have superseded an earlier work, Moraux (1942), which includes some discussion of Alexander's work and writings in general. There is a general account of Alexander in the introduction of Todd (1976), and a general survey in Italian in Donini (1982) 220-48. A full bibliography and survey of current research is given in Sharples (1987).

P. Accattino, 'Alessandro di Afrodisia e la transmissione della forma nella riproduzione animale', *Atti dell' Accademia delle Scienze di Torino* 122, 1988, 79-94.

P. Accattino, 'Alessandro di Afrodisia e gli astri: l'anima e la luce', *Atti dell' Accademia delle Scienze di Torino* 126, 1992, 39-62.

J.L. Ackrill, 'Aristotle's Definitions of *Psuchê*', *Proceedings of the Aristotelian Society* 73, 1972-3, 119-33.

O. Apelt, 'Die kleinen Schriften des Alexander von Aphrodisias', *Rheinisches Museum* 49, 1984, 59-71.

O. Apelt, *Kritische Bemerkungen*, Jena 1906 (*Jahresbericht des Gymnasiums Carolo-Alexandrinum*).

H. von Arnim, *Stoicorum Veterum Fragmenta*, Leipzig 1903-5.

A. Badawi, *La transmission de la philosophie grecque au monde arabe*, Paris 1968.

A. Badawi, *Commentaires sur Aristote perdus en grec et autres épitres*, Beirut 1971.

D.M. Balme, 'Greek Science and Mechanism I: Aristotle on Nature and Chance', *Classical Quarterly* 33, 1939, 129-38.

J. Barnes, 'Medicine, Experience and *Logos*', in J. Barnes et al. (eds), *Science and Speculation*, Cambridge and Paris 1982, 24-68

A.M. Battegazzore, 'Spigolature filologiche e note esegetiche al *De igne* Teofrasteo', *Sandalion* 10-11, 1987-8, 49-66.

E. Bréhier, *Plotinus* (7 vols), Paris 1924-38.

I. Bruns, *Supplementum Aristotelicum* 2.1, Berlin 1887.

I. Bruns (1892,1), *Supplementum Aristotelicum* 2.2, Berlin 1892.

I. Bruns (1892,2), *De Dione Chrysostomo et Aristotele critica et exegetica*, Kiel 1892.

I. Bruns, *Interpretationes variae*, Kiel 1893.

S. Marc Cohen, 'Hylomorphism and Functionalism', in M.C. Nussbaum and A.O. Rorty, eds, *Essays on Aristotle's* De Anima, Oxford 1992, 57-73.

H. Daiber, 'The *Meteorology* of Theophrastus in Syriac and Arabic Translation', in W.W. Fortenbaugh and D. Gutas (eds), *Theophrastus: His Physical, Doxographical, and Scientific Writings*, New Brunswick 1992 (Rutgers University Studies in Classical Humanities, 5), 166-293.

H. Diels, *Doxographi Graeci*, Berlin 1879.

H. Diels and W. Kranz, *Die Fragmente der Vorsokratiker*, Berlin 1952.

A. Dietrich, 'Die arabische Version einer unbekannten Schrift des Alexander von Aphrodisias über die Differentia specifica', *Nachr. der Akademie der Wiss. in Göttingen*, 1964, phil.-hist. Kl., 85-148.

J.M. Dillon, *The Middle Platonists,* London 1977.

P.L. Donini 'Aristotelismo e indeterminismo in Alessandro di Afrodisia', in *Aristoteles: Werk und Wirkung, Paul Moraux gewidmet,* ed. J. Wiesner, vol. 2, Berlin 1987, 72-89.

W. Dooley, *Alexander of Aphrodisias: On Aristotle Metaphysics 1*, London 1989.

M. Dragona-Monachou, *The Stoic Arguments for the Existence and Providence of the Gods*, Athens 1976.

D.E. Eichholz, 'Aristotle's Theory of Metals and Minerals', *Classical Quarterly* 43, 1949, 141-6.

J. Ellis, 'Alexander's Defense of Aristotle's Categories', *Phronesis* 39 (1994) 69-89.

S. Fazzo and H. Wiesner, 'Alexander of Aphrodisias in the Kindî-circle and in al-Kindî's Cosmology', *Arabic Sciences and Philosophy* 3 (1993) 119-53.

S. Fazzo and M. Zonta, *Alessandro di Afrodisia, Sulla Providenza*, Milan (forthcoming).

G. Fine, *On Ideas: Aristotle's Criticism of Plato's Theory of Forms*, Oxford 1993.

E.S. Forster, *Aristotle: On Sophistical Refutations, On Coming-to-be and Passing Away*, and D.J. Furley, *Pseudo-Aristotle On the Cosmos*, London and Cambridge, Mass., 1955.

W.W. Fortenbaugh, P.M. Huby, R.W. Sharples, D. Gutas (eds), *Theophrastus of Eresus. Sources for his Life, Writings, Thought and Influence*, Leiden 1992.

D. Frede, 'Could Paris (son of Priam) have Chosen Otherwise?', *Oxford Studies in Ancient Philosophy* 2, 1984, 279-92.

J. Freudenthal, 'Die durch Averroes erhaltenen Fragmente Alexanders zur Metaphysik des Aristoteles untersucht und übersetzt', *Abh. Berlin* 1884, phil.-hist. Kl., no. 1.

D.J. Furley, *Cosmic Problems,* Cambridge 1989.

H. Gätje, 'Zur arabischen Überlieferung des Alexander von Aphrodisias', *Zeitschrift der deutschen morgenlandischen Gesellschaft* 116, 1966, 255-78.

R. George, 'An argument for divine omniscience in Aristotle', *Apeiron* 22, 1989, 61-74.

M.L. Gill, 'Aristotle on Matters of Life and Death', in John J. Cleary and Daniel C. Shartin (eds), *Proceedings of the Boston Area Colloquium in Ancient Philosophy* 4, 1988, 187-205.

M.L. Gill, *Aristotle on Matter: The Paradox of Unity*, Princeton 1989.

H.B. Gottschalk, 'Strato of Lampsacus: Some Texts', *Proceedings of the Leeds Philosophical and Literary Society, Literary and Historical Section,* 11.6, 1965, 95-182.

H.B. Gottschalk, *Heraclides of Pontus*, Oxford 1980.

D.W. Hamlyn, *Aristotle: De Anima books II and III²*, Oxford 1993.

A. Hasnawi, 'Alexandre d'Aphrodise *vs* Jean Philopon: notes sur quelques traités d'Alexandre "perdus" en grec, conservés en arabe', *Arabic Sciences and Philosophy* 4 (1994) 53-109.

P. Henry, 'Une comparaison chez Aristote, Alexandre et Plotin', in *Les sources de Plotin* (Entretiens Hardt, 5), Geneva 1960, 427-49.

J.L. Ideler, *Physici et medici graeci minores*, Berlin 1841, repr. Amsterdam 1963.

K. Ierodiakonou, 'Medicine as a Stochastic Art' in Ph.J. van der Eijk, H.J. Horstmanshoff, P.H. Schrijvers (eds), *Ancient Medicine in its Socio-Cultural Context*, Amsterdam (forthcoming).

148 *Bibliography*

B. Inwood, 'Chrysippus on Extension and the Void', *Revue Internationale de Philosophie* 178, 1991, 245-66.

H.H. Joachim, *Aristotle on Coming to Be and Passing Away*, Oxford 1922.

L. Judson, 'Chance' and 'Always or for the most part', in L. Judson (ed.), *Aristotle's Physics: A Collection of Essays*, Oxford 1991, 73-99.

H.S. Lang, *Aristotle's Physics and its Medieval Varieties*, Albany 1992.

J. Lear, *Aristotle: the Desire to Understand*, Cambridge 1988.

H.D.P. Lee, *Aristotle: Meteorologica*, Cambridge, Mass. and London 1952.

A.C. Lloyd, *Form and Universal in Aristotle*, Liverpool 1980.

A.A. Long and D.N. Sedley, *The Hellenistic Philosophers*, Cambridge 1987.

J. Longrigg, 'Elementary Physics in the Lyceum and Stoa', *Isis* 66, 1975, 211-29.

E.P. Mahoney, 'Nicoletto Vernia and Agostino Nifo on Alexander of Aphrodisias: an unnoticed dispute', *Rivista critica di storia della filosofia* 23, 1968, 269-96.

J. Mansfeld, 'Diogenes Laertius and Stoic Philosophy', *Elenchos* 7, 1986, 297-382.

A. Martini and D. Bassi, *Catalogus codicum graecorum bibliothecae Ambrosianae*, vol. 2, Milan 1906.

T. Maudlin, 'De Anima 3.1: is any sense missing?', *Phronesis* 31, 1986, 51-67.

P. Merlan, 'Zwei Untersuchungen zu Alexander von Aphrodisias', *Philologus* 113, 1969, 85-91.

D.K.W. Modrak, 'Alexander on *Phantasia:* a Hopeless Muddle or a Better Account?', *Southern Journal of Philosophy* 31 (1993), supplement, 173-97.

E. Montanari, 'Per un editione del *Peri kraseos* di Alessandro di Afrodisia', *Atti e memoria dell' accademia toscana di scienze e lettere La Colombaria*, 36, 1971, 17-58.

P. Moraux, *Alexandre d'Aphrodise: Exégète de la noétique d'Aristote*, Liège and Paris 1942.

R. Norman, 'Aristotle's Philosopher-God', *Phronesis* 14, 1969, 67-74.

S. Pines, *A New Fragment of Xenocrates and its Implications*, Philadelphia 1961 (*Trans. American Philosophical Society*, 51.2).

K. Praechter. Review of Bruns (1892,2), *Berliner Philologische Wochenschrift* 14, 1894, 714f.

A. Radl, *Der Magnetstein in der Antike*, Stuttgart 1988 (*Boethius*, vol. 19).

H. Robinson, 'Form and the immateriality of the intellect from Aristotle to Aquinas', in Blumenthal, H. and Robinson, H. (eds) *Aristotle and the Later Tradition*, Oxford 1991 (*Oxford Studies in Ancient Philosophy*, supplementary volume), 207-26.

Sir David Ross (ed.), *Aristotle: De Anima*, Oxford 1961.

H.-J. Ruland, *Die arabischen Fassungen zweier Schriften des Alexander von Aphrodisias*, diss. Saarbrücken 1976.

H.-J. Ruland, 'Die arabische Ubersetzung der Schrift des Alexander von Aphrodisias uber die Sinneswahrnehmung', *Nachr. Gottingen*, phil.-hist. Kl. [1978] no. 5, pp. 161-225.

H.-J. Ruland, Zwei arabischen Fassungen der Abhandlung des Alexander von Aphrodisias über die universalia, *Nachr. der Akademie der Wiss. in Göttingen*, phil.-hist. Kl., 1979, no. 10.

R.W. Sharples, 'Responsibility, Chance and Not-being (Alexander of Aphrodisias *mantissa* 169-172)', *Bulletin of the Institute of Classical Studies* 22, 1975, 37-64.

R.W. Sharples, 'Alexander of Aphrodisias De fato: Some Parallels', *Classical Quarterly* n.s. 28, 1978, 243-66.

R.W. Sharples, 'If What is Earlier, Then of Necessity What is Later? Some ancient discussions of Aristotle, *De generatione et corruptione* 2.11', *Bulletin of the Institute of Classical Studies* 26, 1979, 27-44.

R.W. Sharples, 'Alexander of Aphrodisias' Second Treatment of Fate? *De anima libri mantissa*, pp. 179-186 Bruns', *Bulletin of the Institute of Classical Studies* 27, 1980, 76-94.

R.W. Sharples, 'Alexander of Aphrodisias on Divine Providence: Two Problems', *Class. Quart.* 32, 1982, 198-211.

R.W. Sharples (1983,1) *Alexander of Aphrodisias* On Fate, London 1983.

R.W. Sharples (1983,2) 'Alexander of Aphrodisias, *Quaestiones* on Possibility, II', *Bulletin of the Institute of Classical Studies* 30, 1983, 99-110.

R.W. Sharples (1983,3) 'The Unmoved Mover and the Motion of the Heavens in Alexander of Aphrodisias', *Apeiron* 17, 1983, 62-6.

R.W. Sharples (1983,4) 'Nemesius of Emesa and Some Theories of Divine Providence', *Vigiliae Christianae* 37, 1983, 141-56.

R.W. Sharples, 'Theophrastus on the Heavens', in *Aristoteles, Werk und Wirkung: Paul Moraux gewidmet,* ed. J. Wiesner, Berlin 1985, 577-93.

R.W. Sharples (1987,1), 'Alexander of Aphrodisias: Scholasticism and Innovation', *Aufstieg und Niedergang der römischen Welt*, vol. II.36.1, Berlin 1987, 1176-1243.

R.W. Sharples (1987,2), 'Could Alexander (Follower of Aristotle) Have Done Better? A response to Professor Frede and others', *Oxford Studies in Ancient Philosophy* 5, 1987, 197-216.

R.W. Sharples (1990,1), 'The School of Alexander', in R. Sorabji (ed.), *Aristotle Transformed*, London 1990, 83-111.

R.W. Sharples (1990,2), *Alexander of Aphrodisias: Ethical Problems*, London 1990.

R.W. Sharples, *Alexander of Aphrodisias: Quaestiones 1.1-2.15,* London 1992.

C. Shields, 'The Homonymy of the Body in Aristotle', *Archiv für Geschichte der Philosophie* 75, 1993, 1-30.

R. Sorabji, *Aristotle On Memory,* London 1972.

R. Sorabji, *Necessity, Cause and Blame*, London 1980.

R. Sorabji, *Time, Creation and the Continuum*, London 1983.

R. Sorabji, *Matter, Space and Motion*, London 1988.

G. Théry, *Autour du decret de 1210: II, Alexandre d'Aphrodise* (*Bibliothèque Thomiste* 7), Le Saulchoir Kain, 1926.

P. Thillet, 'Élements pour l'histoire du texte du *De fato* d'Alexandre d'Aphrodise', *Revue d'histoire des textes* 12, 1982, 13-56.

P. Thillet, *Alexandre d'Aphrodise: Traité du Destin*, Paris 1984.

C. Thurot, 'Alexandre d'Aphrodisias, Commentaire sur le traité d'Aristote *De sensu et sensibili*, édité avec la vieille translation latine', *Notices et extraits des MSS de la Bibliothèque Nationale* 25, 1875, no. 2.

R.B. Todd (1976,1), 'Alexander of Aphrodisias on *De interpretatione* 16a26-9', *Hermes* 104, 1976, 140-6.

R.B. Todd (1976,2), *Alexander of Aphrodisias on Stoic Physics,* Leiden 1976.

R.B. Todd, 'Infinite Body and Infinite Void: Epicurean Physics and Peripatetic Polemic', *Liverpool Classical Monthly* 7, 1982, 82-4.

R.B. Todd, 'Alexander of Aphrodisias and the Case for the Infinite Universe (*Quaestiones* 3.12)', *Eranos* 82, 1984, 185-93.

J. Van Ess, 'Über einige neue Fragmente des Alexander von Aphrodisias und des Proklos in arabischer Übersetzung', *Der Islam* 42, 1966, 148-68.

G. Vitelli, 'Frammenti di Alessandro di Afrodisia nel cod. Riccard. 63', *Studi Italiani di Filologia Classica* 2, 1895, 379-81.

G. Vitelli, 'Due Frammenti di Alessandro di Afrodisia', in *Festschrift Theodor Gomperz*, Vienna 1902, 90-3.

M.J. White, *Agency and Integrality,* Dordrecht 1985.

J. Whiting, 'Living Bodies', in M.C. Nussbaum and A.O. Rorty, eds, *Essays on Aristotle's* De Anima, Oxford 1992, 75-91.

C. Wildberg, *John Philoponus' Criticism of Aristotle's Theory of Ether,* Berlin 1988.

B. Williams, 'Hylomorphism', *Oxford Studies in Ancient Philosophy* 4 (1986) 189-99.

F.W. Zimmermann, 'Proclus Arabus rides again', *Arabic Sciences and Philosophy* 4 (1994) 9-51.

F.W. Zimmermann and H.V.B. Brown, 'Neue arabische Übersetzungstexte aus dem Bereich der spätantiken griechischen Philosophen', *Der Islam* 50, 1973, 313-24.

Appendix
The Commentators*

The 15,000 pages of the Ancient Greek Commentaries on Aristotle are the largest corpus of Ancient Greek philosophy that has not been translated into English or other European languages. The standard edition (*Commentaria in Aristotelem Graeca*, or *CAG*) was produced by Hermann Diels as general editor under the auspices of the Prussian Academy in Berlin. Arrangements have now been made to translate at least a large proportion of this corpus, along with some other Greek and Latin commentaries not included in the Berlin edition, and some closely related non-commentary works by the commentators.

The works are not just commentaries on Aristotle, although they are invaluable in that capacity too. One of the ways of doing philosophy between A.D. 200 and 600, when the most important items were produced, was by writing commentaries. The works therefore represent the thought of the Peripatetic and Neoplatonist schools, as well as expounding Aristotle. Furthermore, they embed fragments from all periods of Ancient Greek philosophical thought: this is how many of the Presocratic fragments were assembled, for example. Thus they provide a panorama of every period of Ancient Greek philosophy.

The philosophy of the period from A.D.200 to 600 has not yet been intensively explored by philosophers in English-speaking countries, yet it is full of interest for physics, metaphysics, logic, psychology, ethics and religion. The contrast with the study of the Presocratics is striking. Initially the incomplete Presocratic fragments might well have seemed less promising, but their interest is now widely known, thanks to the philological and philosophical effort that has been concentrated upon them. The incomparably vaster corpus which preserved so many of those fragments offers at least as much interest, but is still relatively little known.

The commentaries represent a missing link in the history of philosophy: the Latin-speaking Middle Ages obtained their knowledge of Aristotle at least partly through the medium of the commentaries. Without an appreciation of this, mediaeval interpretations of Aristotle will not be understood. Again, the ancient commentaries are the unsuspected source of ideas which have been thought, wrongly, to originate in the later mediaeval period. It has been supposed, for example, that Bonaventure in the thirteenth century invented the ingenious arguments based on the concept of infinity which attempt to prove the Christian view that the universe had a beginning. In fact, Bonaventure is merely repeating arguments devised

* Reprinted from the Editor's General Introduction to the series in Christian Wildberg, *Philoponus Against Aristotle on the Eternity of the World*, London and Ithaca, N.Y., 1987.

by the commentator Philoponus 700 years earlier and preserved in the meantime by the Arabs. Bonaventure even uses Philoponus' original examples. Again, the introduction of impetus theory into dynamics, which has been called a scientific revolution, has been held to be an independent invention of the Latin West, even if it was earlier discovered by the Arabs or their predecessors. But recent work has traced a plausible route by which it could have passed from Philoponus, via the Arabs, to the West.

The new availability of the commentaries in the sixteenth century, thanks to printing and to fresh Latin translations, helped to fuel the Renaissance break from Aristotelian science. For the commentators record not only Aristotle's theories, but also rival ones, while Philoponus as a Christian devises rival theories of his own and accordingly is mentioned in Galileo's early works more frequently than Plato.[1]

It is not only for their philosophy that the works are of interest. Historians will find information about the history of schools, their methods of teaching and writing and the practices of an oral tradition.[2] Linguists will find the indexes and translations an aid for studying the development of word meanings, almost wholly uncharted in Liddell and Scott's *Lexicon*, and for checking shifts in grammatical usage.

Given the wide range of interests to which the volumes will appeal, the aim is to produce readable translations, and to avoid so far as possible presupposing any knowledge of Greek. Notes will explain points of meaning, give cross-references to other works, and suggest alternative interpretations of the text where the translator does not have a clear preference. The introduction to each volume will include an explanation why the work was chosen for translation: none will be chosen simply because it is there. Two of the Greek texts are currently being re-edited – those of Simplicius *in Physica* and *in de Caelo* – and new readings will be exploited by

1. See Fritz Zimmermann, 'Philoponus' impetus theory in the Arabic tradition'; Charles Schmitt, 'Philoponus' commentary on Aristotle's *Physics* in the sixteenth century', and Richard Sorabji, 'John Philoponus', in Richard Sorabji (ed.), *Philoponus and the Rejection of Aristotelian Science* (London and Ithaca, N.Y. 1987).

2. See e.g. Karl Praechter, 'Die griechischen Aristoteleskommentare', *Byzantinische Zeitschrift* 18 (1909), 516-38 (translated into English in R. Sorabji (ed.), *Aristotle Transformed: the ancient commentators and their influence* (London and Ithaca, N.Y. 1990); M. Plezia, *de Commentariis Isagogicis* (Cracow 1947); M. Richard, '*Apo Phônês*', *Byzantion* 20 (1950), 191-222; É. Evrard, *L'Ecole d'Olympiodore et la composition du commentaire à la physique de Jean Philopon*, Diss. (Liège 1957); L.G. Westerink, *Anonymous Prolegomena to Platonic Philosophy* (Amsterdam 1962) (new revised edition, translated into French, Collection Budé; part of the revised introduction, in English, is included in *Aristotle Transformed*); A.-J. Festugière, 'Modes de composition des commentaires de Proclus', *Museum Helveticum* 20 (1963), 77-100, repr. in his *Études* (1971), 551-74; P. Hadot, 'Les divisions des parties de la philosophie dans l'antiquité', *Museum Helveticum* 36 (1979), 201-23; I. Hadot, 'La division néoplatonicienne des écrits d'Aristote', in J. Wiesner (ed.), *Aristoteles Werk und Wirkung* (Paul Moraux gewidmet), vol. 2 (Berlin 1986); I. Hadot, 'Les introductions aux commentaires exégétiques chez les auteurs néoplatoniciens et les auteurs chrétiens', in M. Tardieu (ed.), *Les règles de l'interprétation* (Paris 1987), 99-119. These topics are treated, and a bibliography supplied, in *Aristotle Transformed*.

translators as they become available. Each volume will also contain a list of proposed emendations to the standard text. Indexes will be of more uniform extent as between volumes than is the case with the Berlin edition, and there will be three of them: an English-Greek glossary, a Greek-English index, and a subject index.

The commentaries fall into three main groups. The first group is by authors in the Aristotelian tradition up to the fourth century A.D. This includes the earliest extant commentary, that by Aspasius in the first half of the second century A.D. on the *Nicomachean Ethics*. The anonymous commentary on Books 2, 3, 4 and 5 of the *Nicomachean Ethics*, in *CAG* vol. 20, is derived from Adrastus, a generation later.[3] The commentaries by Alexander of Aphrodisias (appointed to his chair between A.D. 198 and 209) represent the fullest flowering of the Aristotelian tradition. To his successors Alexander was The Commentator *par excellence*. To give but one example (not from a commentary) of his skill at defending and elaborating Aristotle's views, one might refer to his defence of Aristotle's claim that space is finite against the objection that an edge of space is conceptually problematic.[4] Themistius (*fl*. late 340s to 384 or 385) saw himself as the inventor of paraphrase, wrongly thinking that the job of commentary was completed.[5] In fact, the Neoplatonists were to introduce new dimensions into commentary. Themistius' own relation to the Neoplatonist as opposed to the Aristotelian tradition is a matter of controversy,[6] but it would be agreed that his commentaries show far less bias than the full-blown Neoplatonist ones. They are also far more informative than the designation 'paraphrase' might suggest, and it has been estimated that Philoponus' *Physics* commentary draws silently on Themistius six hundred times.[7] The pseudo-Alexandrian commentary on *Metaphysics* 6-14, of unknown

3. Anthony Kenny, *The Aristotelian Ethics* (Oxford 1978), 37, n.3: Paul Moraux, *Der Aristotelismus bei den Griechen*, vol. 2 (Berlin 1984), 323-30.

4. Alexander, *Quaestiones* 3.12, discussed in my *Matter, Space and Motion* (London and Ithaca, N.Y. 1988). For Alexander see R.W. Sharples, 'Alexander of Aphrodisias: scholasticism and innovation', in W. Haase (ed.), *Aufstieg und Niedergang der römischen Welt*, part 2 *Principat*, vol. 36.2, *Philosophie und Wissenschaften* (1987).

5. Themistius *in An. Post.* 1,2-12. See H.J. Blumenthal, 'Photius on Themistius (Cod. 74): did Themistius write commentaries on Aristotle?', *Hermes* 107 (1979), 168-82.

6. For different views, see H.J. Blumenthal, 'Themistius, the last Peripatetic commentator on Aristotle?', in Glen W. Bowersock, Walter Burkert, Michael C.J. Putnam, *Arktouros, Hellenic Studies Presented to Bernard M.W. Knox* (Berlin and N.Y., 1979), 391-400; E.P. Mahoney, 'Themistius and the agent intellect in James of Viterbo and other thirteenth-century philosophers: (Saint Thomas Aquinas, Siger of Brabant and Henry Bate)', *Augustiniana* 23 (1973), 422-67, at 428-31; id., 'Neoplatonism, the Greek commentators and Renaissance Aristotelianism', in D.J. O'Meara (ed.), *Neoplatonism and Christian Thought* (Albany N.Y. 1982), 169-77 and 264-82, esp. n. 1, 264-6; Robert Todd, introduction to translation of Themistius *in DA* 3.4-8, in *Two Greek Aristotelian Commentators on the Intellect*, trans. Frederick M. Schroeder and Robert B. Todd (Toronto 1990).

7. H. Vitelli, *CAG* 17, p. 992, s.v. Themistius.

authorship, has been placed by some in the same group of commentaries as being earlier than the fifth century.[8]

By far the largest group of extant commentaries is that of the Neoplatonists up to the sixth century A.D. Nearly all the major Neoplatonists, apart from Plotinus (the founder of Neoplatonism), wrote commentaries on Aristotle, although those of Iamblichus (*c.* 250–*c.* 325) survive only in fragments, and those of three Athenians, Plutarchus (died 432), his pupil Proclus (410–485) and the Athenian Damascius (*c.* 462–after 538), are lost.[9] As a result of these losses, most of the extant Neoplatonist commentaries come from the late fifth and the sixth centuries and a good proportion from Alexandria. There are commentaries by Plotinus' disciple and editor Porphyry (232–309), by Iamblichus' pupil Dexippus (*c.* 330), by Proclus' teacher Syrianus (died *c.* 437), by Proclus' pupil Ammonius (435/445–517/526), by Ammonius' three pupils Philoponus (*c.* 490 to 570s), Simplicius (wrote after 532, probably after 538) and Asclepius (sixth century), by Ammonius' next but one successor Olympiodorus (495/505–after 565), by Elias (*fl.* 541?), by David (second half of the sixth century, or beginning of the seventh) and by Stephanus (took the chair in Constantinople *c.* 610). Further, a commentary on the *Nicomachean Ethics* has been ascribed to Heliodorus of Prusa, an unknown pre-fourteenth-century figure, and there is a commentary by Simplicius' colleague Priscian of Lydia on Aristotle's successor Theophrastus. Of these commentators some of the last were Christians (Philoponus, Elias, David and Stephanus), but they were Christians writing in the Neoplatonist tradition, as was also Boethius who produced a number of commentaries in Latin before his death in 525 or 526.

The third group comes from a much later period in Byzantium. The Berlin edition includes only three out of more than a dozen commentators described in Hunger's *Byzantinisches Handbuch*.[10] The two most important are Eustratius (1050/1060–*c.*1120), and Michael of Ephesus. It has been suggested that these two belong to a circle organised by the princess

---

8. The similarities to Syrianus (died *c.* 437) have suggested to some that it predates Syrianus (most recently Leonardo Tarán, review of Paul Moraux, *Der Aristotelismus*, vol.1 in *Gnomon* 46 (1981), 721-50 at 750), to others that it draws on him (most recently P. Thillet, in the Budé edition of Alexander *de Fato*, p. lvii). Praechter ascribed it to Michael of Ephesus (eleventh or twelfth century), in his review of *CAG* 22.2, in *Göttingische Gelehrte Anzeiger* 168 (1906), 861-907.

9. The Iamblichus fragments are collected in Greek by Bent Dalsgaard Larsen, *Jamblique de Chalcis, Exégète et Philosophe* (Aarhus 1972), vol. 2. Most are taken from Simplicius, and will accordingly be translated in due course. The evidence on Damascius' commentaries is given in L.G. Westerink, *The Greek Commentaries on Plato's Phaedo*, vol. 2, Damascius (Amsterdam 1977), 11-12; on Proclus' in L.G. Westerink, *Anonymous Prolegomena to Platonic Philosophy* (Amsterdam 1962), xii, n. 22; on Plutarchus' in H.M. Blumenthal, 'Neoplatonic elements in the de Anima commentaries', *Phronesis* 21 (1976), 75.

10. Herbert Hunger, *Die hochsprachliche profane Literatur der Byzantiner*, vol. 1 (= *Byzantinisches Handbuch*, part 5, vol. 1) (Munich 1978), 25-41. See also B.N. Tatakis, *La Philosophie Byzantine* (Paris 1949).

Anna Comnena in the twelfth century, and accordingly the completion of Michael's commentaries has been redated from 1040 to 1138.[11] His commentaries include areas where gaps had been left. Not all of these gap-fillers are extant, but we have commentaries on the neglected biological works, on the *Sophistici Elenchi*, and a small fragment of one on the *Politics*. The lost *Rhetoric* commentary had a few antecedents, but the *Rhetoric* too had been comparatively neglected. Another product of this period may have been the composite commentary on the *Nicomachean Ethics* (*CAG* 20) by various hands, including Eustratius and Michael, along with some earlier commentators, and an improvisation for Book 7. Whereas Michael follows Alexander and the conventional Aristotelian tradition, Eustratius' commentary introduces Platonist, Christian and anti-Islamic elements.[12]

The composite commentary was to be translated into Latin in the next century by Robert Grosseteste in England. But Latin translations of various logical commentaries were made from the Greek still earlier by James of Venice (*fl. c.* 1130), a contemporary of Michael of Ephesus, who may have known him in Constantinople. And later in that century other commentaries and works by commentators were being translated from Arabic versions by Gerard of Cremona (died 1187).[13] So the twelfth century resumed the transmission which had been interrupted at Boethius' death in the sixth century.

The Neoplatonist commentaries of the main group were initiated by Porphyry. His master Plotinus had discussed Aristotle, but in a very independent way, devoting three whole treatises (*Enneads* 6.1-3) to attacking Aristotle's classification of the things in the universe into categories. These categories took no account of Plato's world of Ideas, were inferior to Plato's classifications in the *Sophist* and could anyhow be collapsed, some

---

11. R. Browning, 'An unpublished funeral oration on Anna Comnena', *Proceedings of the Cambridge Philological Society* n.s. 8 (1962), 1-12, esp. 6-7.

12. R. Browning, op. cit. H.D.P. Mercken, *The Greek Commentaries of the Nicomachean Ethics of Aristotle in the Latin Translation of Grosseteste, Corpus Latinum Commentariorum in Aristotelem Graecorum* VI 1 (Leiden 1973), ch. 1, 'The compilation of Greek commentaries on Aristotle's Nicomachean Ethics'. Sten Ebbesen, 'Anonymi Aurelianensis I Commentarium in *Sophisticos Elenchos*', *Cahiers de l'Institut Moyen Age Grecque et Latin* 34 (1979), 'Boethius, Jacobus Veneticus, Michael Ephesius and "Alexander" ', pp. v-xiii; id., *Commentators and Commentaries on Aristotle's Sophistici Elenchi*, 3 parts, *Corpus Latinum Commentariorum in Aristotelem Graecorum*, vol. 7 (Leiden 1981); A. Preus, *Aristotle and Michael of Ephesus on the Movement and Progression of Animals* (Hildesheim 1981), introduction.

13. For Grosseteste, see Mercken as in n. 12. For James of Venice, see Ebbesen as in n. 12, and L. Minio-Paluello, 'Jacobus Veneticus Grecus', *Traditio* 8 (1952), 265-304; id., 'Giacomo Veneto e l'Aristotelismo Latino', in Pertusi (ed.), *Venezia e l'Oriente fra tardo Medioevo e Rinascimento* (Florence 1966), 53-74, both reprinted in his *Opuscula* (1972). For Gerard of Cremona, see M. Steinschneider, *Die europäischen Übersetzungen aus dem arabischen bis Mitte des 17. Jahrhunderts* (repr. Graz 1956); E. Gilson, *History of Christian Philosophy in the Middle Ages* (London 1955), 235-6 and more generally 181-246. For the translators in general, see Bernard G. Dod, 'Aristoteles Latinus', in N. Kretzmann, A. Kenny, J. Pinborg (eds), *The Cambridge History of Latin Medieval Philosophy* (Cambridge 1982).

of them into others. Porphyry replied that Aristotle's categories could apply perfectly well to the world of intelligibles and he took them as in general defensible.[14] He wrote two commentaries on the *Categories*, one lost, and an introduction to it, the *Isagôgê*, as well as commentaries, now lost, on a number of other Aristotelian works. This proved decisive in making Aristotle a necessary subject for Neoplatonist lectures and commentary. Proclus, who was an exceptionally quick student, is said to have taken two years over his Aristotle studies, which were called the Lesser Mysteries, and which preceded the Greater Mysteries of Plato.[15] By the time of Ammonius, the commentaries reflect a teaching curriculum which begins with Porphyry's *Isagôgê* and Aristotle's *Categories*, and is explicitly said to have as its final goal a (mystical) ascent to the supreme Neoplatonist deity, the One.[16] The curriculum would have progressed from Aristotle to Plato, and would have culminated in Plato's *Timaeus* and *Parmenides*. The latter was read as being about the One, and both works were established in this place in the curriculum at least by the time of Iamblichus, if not earlier.[17]

Before Porphyry, it had been undecided how far a Platonist should accept Aristotle's scheme of categories. But now the proposition began to gain force that there was a harmony between Plato and Aristotle on most things.[18] Not for the only time in the history of philosophy, a perfectly crazy proposition proved philosophically fruitful. The views of Plato and of Aristotle had both to be transmuted into a new Neoplatonist philosophy in order to exhibit the supposed harmony. Iamblichus denied that Aristotle contradicted Plato on the theory of Ideas.[19] This was too much for Syrianus and his pupil Proclus. While accepting harmony in many areas,[20] they could see that there was disagreement on this issue and also on the issue of whether God was causally responsible for the existence of the ordered

14. See P. Hadot, 'L'harmonie des philosophies de Plotin et d'Aristote selon Porphyre dans le commentaire de Dexippe sur les Catégories', in *Plotino e il neoplatonismo in Oriente e in Occidente* (Rome 1974), 31-47; A.C. Lloyd, 'Neoplatonic logic and Aristotelian logic', *Phronesis* 1 (1955-6), 58-79 and 146-60.

15. Marinus, *Life of Proclus* ch. 13, 157,41 (Boissonade).

16. The introductions to the *Isagôgê* by Ammonius, Elias and David, and to the *Categories* by Ammonius, Simplicius, Philoponus, Olympiodorus and Elias are discussed by L.G. Westerink, *Anonymous Prolegomena* and I. Hadot, 'Les Introductions', see n. 2 above.

17. Proclus in *Alcibiadem 1* p. 11 (Creuzer); Westerink, *Anonymous Prolegomena*, ch. 26, 12f. For the Neoplatonist curriculum see Westerink, Festugière, P. Hadot and I. Hadot in n. 2.

18. See e.g. P. Hadot (1974), as in n. 14 above; H.J. Blumenthal, 'Neoplatonic elements in the de Anima commentaries', *Phronesis* 21 (1976), 64-87; H.A. Davidson, 'The principle that a finite body can contain only finite power', in S. Stein and R. Loewe (eds), *Studies in Jewish Religious and Intellectual History presented to A. Altmann* (Alabama 1979), 75-92; Carlos Steel, 'Proclus et Aristotle', Proceedings of the Congrès Proclus held in Paris 1985, J. Pépin and H.D. Saffrey (eds), *Proclus, lecteur et interprète des anciens* (Paris 1987), 213-25; Koenraad Verrycken, *God en Wereld in de Wijsbegeerte van Ioannes Philoponus*, Ph.D. Diss. (Louvain 1985).

19. Iamblichus ap. Elian in *Cat.* 123,1-3.

20. Syrianus in *Metaph.* 80,4-7; Proclus in *Tim.* 1.6,21-7,16.

physical cosmos, which Aristotle denied. But even on these issues, Proclus' pupil Ammonius was to claim harmony, and, though the debate was not clear cut,[21] his claim was on the whole to prevail. Aristotle, he maintained, accepted Plato's Ideas,[22] at least in the form of principles (*logoi*) in the divine intellect, and these principles were in turn causally responsible for the beginningless existence of the physical universe. Ammonius wrote a whole book to show that Aristotle's God was thus an efficent cause, and though the book is lost, some of its principal arguments are preserved by Simplicius.[23] This tradition helped to make it possible for Aquinas to claim Aristotle's God as a Creator, albeit not in the sense of giving the universe a beginning, but in the sense of being causally responsible for its beginningless existence.[24] Thus what started as a desire to harmonise Aristotle with Plato finished by making Aristotle safe for Christianity. In Simplicius, who goes further than anyone,[25] it is a formally stated duty of the commentator to display the harmony of Plato and Aristotle in most things.[26] Philoponus, who with his independent mind had thought better of his earlier belief in harmony, is castigated by Simplicius for neglecting this duty.[27]

The idea of harmony was extended beyond Plato and Aristotle to Plato and the Presocratics. Plato's pupils Speusippus and Xenocrates saw Plato as being in the Pythagorean tradition.[28] From the third to first centuries B.C., pseudo-Pythagorean writings present Platonic and Aristotelian doctrines as if they were the ideas of Pythagoras and his pupils,[29] and these forgeries were later taken by the Neoplatonists as genuine. Plotinus saw the Presocratics as precursors of his own views,[30] but Iamblichus went far beyond him by writing ten volumes on Pythagorean philosophy.[31] Thereafter Proclus sought to unify the whole of

---

21. Asclepius sometimes accepts Syranius' interpretation (*in Metaph.* 433,9-436,6); which is, however, qualified, since Syrianus thinks Aristotle is realy committed willy-nilly to much of Plato's view (*in Metaph.* 117,25-118,11; ap. Asclepium *in Metaph.* 433,16; 450,22); Philoponus repents of his early claim that Plato is not the target of Aristotle's attack, and accepts that Plato is rightly attacked for treating ideas as independent entities outside the divine Intellect (*in DA* 37,18-31; *in Phys.* 225,4-226,11; *contra Procl.* 26,24-32,13; *in An. Post.* 242,14-243,25).

22. Asclepius *in Metaph.* from the voice of (i.e. from the lectures of) Ammonius 69,17-21; 71,28; cf. Zacharias *Ammonius, Patrologia Graeca* vol. 85 col. 952 (Colonna).

23. Simplicius *in Phys.* 1361,11-1363,12. See H.A. Davidson; Carlos Steel; Koenraad Verrycken in n. 18 above.

24. See Richard Sorabji, *Matter, Space and Motion* (London and Ithaca, N.Y. 1988), ch. 15.

25. See e.g. H.J. Blumenthal in n. 18 above.

26. Simplicius *in Cat.* 7,23-32.

27. Simplicius *in Cael.* 84,11-14; 159,2-9. On Philoponus' *volte face* see n. 21 above.

28. See e.g. Walter Burkert, *Weisheit und Wissenschaft* (Nürnberg 1962), translated as *Lore and Science in Ancient Pythagoreanism* (Cambridge Mass. 1972), 83-96.

29. See Holger Thesleff, *An Introduction to the Pythagorean Writings of the Hellenistic Period* (Åbo 1961); Thomas Alexander Szlezák, *Pseudo-Archytas über die Kategorien*, Peripatoi vol. 4 (Berlin and New York 1972).

30. Plotinus e.g. 4.8.1; 5.1.8 (10-27); 5.1.9.

31. See Dominic O'Meara, *Pythagoras Revived: Mathematics and Philosophy in Late Antiquity* (Oxford 1989).

Greek philosophy by presenting it as a continuous clarification of divine revelation[32] and Simplicius argued for the same general unity in order to rebut Christian charges of contradictions in pagan philosophy.[33]

Later Neoplatonist commentaries tend to reflect their origin in a teaching curriculum:[34] from the time of Philoponus, the discussion is often divided up into lectures, which are subdivided into studies of doctrine and of text. A general account of Aristotle's philosophy is prefixed to the *Categories* commentaries and divided, according to a formula of Proclus,[35] into ten questions. It is here that commentators explain the eventual purpose of studying Aristotle (ascent to the One) and state (if they do) the requirement of displaying the harmony of Plato and Aristotle. After the ten-point introduction to Aristotle, the *Categories* is given a six-point introduction, whose antecedents go back earlier than Neoplatonism, and which requires the commentator to find a unitary theme or scope (*skopos*) for the treatise. The arrangements for late commentaries on Plato are similar. Since the Plato commentaries form part of a single curriculum they should be studied alongside those on Aristotle. Here the situation is easier, not only because the extant corpus is very much smaller, but also because it has been comparatively well served by French and English translators.[36]

Given the theological motive of the curriculum and the pressure to harmonise Plato with Aristotle, it can be seen how these commentaries are a major source for Neoplatonist ideas. This in turn means that it is not safe to extract from them the fragments of the Presocratics, or of other authors, without making allowance for the Neoplatonist background against which the fragments were originally selected for discussion. For different reasons, analogous warnings apply to fragments preserved by the pre-Neoplatonist commentator Alexander.[37] It will be another advantage of the present translations that they will make it easier to check the distorting effect of a commentator's background.

Although the Neoplatonist commentators conflate the views of Aristotle with those of Neoplatonism, Philoponus alludes to a certain convention

32. See Christian Guérard, 'Parménide d'Elée selon les Néoplatoniciens', forthcoming.

33. Simplicius *in Phys.* 28,32-29,5; 640,12-18. Such thinkers as Epicurus and the Sceptics, however, were not subject to harmonisation.

34. See the literature in n. 2 above.

35. ap. Elian *in Cat.* 107,24-6.

36. English: Calcidius *in Tim.* (parts by van Winden; den Boeft); Iamblichus fragments (Dillon); Proclus *in Tim.* (Thomas Taylor); Proclus *in Parm.* (Dillon); Proclus *in Parm.*, end of 7th book, from the Latin (Klibansky, Labowsky, Anscombe); Proclus *in Alcib. 1* (O'Neill); Olympiodorus and Damascius *in Phaedonem* (Westerink); Damascius *in Philebum* (Westerink); *Anonymous Prolegomena to Platonic Philosophy* (Westerink). See also extracts in Thomas Taylor, *The Works of Plato*, 5 vols. (1804). French: Proclus *in Tim.* and *in Rempublicam* (Festugière); *in Parm.* (Chaignet); Anon. *in Parm* (P. Hadot); Damascius *in Parm.* (Chaignet).

37. For Alexander's treatment of the Stoics, see Robert B. Todd, *Alexander of Aphrodisias on Stoic Physics* (Leiden 1976), 24-9.

when he quotes Plutarchus expressing disapproval of Alexander for expounding his own philosophical doctrines in a commentary on Aristotle.[38] But this does not stop Philoponus from later inserting into his own commentaries on the *Physics* and *Meteorology* his arguments in favour of the Christian view of Creation. Of course, the commentators also wrote independent works of their own, in which their views are expressed independently of the exegesis of Aristotle. Some of these independent works will be included in the present series of translations.

The distorting Neoplatonist context does not prevent the commentaries from being incomparable guides to Aristotle. The introductions to Aristotle's philosophy insist that commentators must have a minutely detailed knowledge of the entire Aristotelian corpus, and this they certainly have. Commentators are also enjoined neither to accept nor reject what Aristotle says too readily, but to consider it in depth and without partiality. The commentaries draw one's attention to hundreds of phrases, sentences and ideas in Aristotle, which one could easily have passed over, however often one read him. The scholar who makes the right allowance for the distorting context will learn far more about Aristotle than he would be likely to on his own.

The relations of Neoplatonist commentators to the Christians were subtle. Porphyry wrote a treatise explicitly against the Christians in 15 books, but an order to burn it was issued in 448, and later Neoplatonists were more circumspect. Among the last commentators in the main group, we have noted several Christians. Of these the most important were Boethius and Philoponus. It was Boethius' programme to transmit Greek learning to Latin-speakers. By the time of his premature death by execution, he had provided Latin translations of Aristotle's logical works, together with commentaries in Latin but in the Neoplatonist style on Porphyry's *Isagôgê* and on Aristotle's *Categories* and *de Interpretatione*, and interpretations of the *Prior* and *Posterior Analytics*, *Topics* and *Sophistici Elenchi*. The interruption of his work meant that knowledge of Aristotle among Latin-speakers was confined for many centuries to the logical works. Philoponus is important both for his proofs of the Creation and for his progressive replacement of Aristotelian science with rival theories, which were taken up at first by the Arabs and came fully into their own in the West only in the sixteenth century.

Recent work has rejected the idea that in Alexandria the Neoplatonists compromised with Christian monotheism by collapsing the distinction between their two highest deities, the One and the Intellect. Simplicius (who left Alexandria for Athens) and the Alexandrians Ammonius and Asclepius appear to have acknowledged their beliefs quite openly, as later

---

38. Philoponus *in DA* 21,20-3.

did the Alexandrian Olympiodorus, despite the presence of Christian students in their classes.[39]

The teaching of Simplicius in Athens and that of the whole pagan Neoplatonist school there was stopped by the Christian Emperor Justinian in 529. This was the very year in which the Christian Philoponus in Alexandria issued his proofs of Creation against the earlier Athenian Neoplatonist Proclus. Archaeological evidence has been offered that, after their temporary stay in Ctesiphon (in present-day Iraq), the Athenian Neoplatonists did not return to their house in Athens, and further evidence has been offered that Simplicius went to Harrān (Carrhae), in present-day Turkey near the Iraq border.[40] Wherever he went, his commentaries are a treasurehouse of information about the preceding thousand years of Greek philosophy, information which he painstakingly recorded after the closure in Athens, and which would otherwise have been lost. He had every reason to feel bitter about Christianity, and in fact he sees it and Philoponus, its representative, as irreverent. They deny the divinity of the heavens and prefer the physical relics of dead martyrs.[41] His own commentaries by contrast culminate in devout prayers.

Two collections of articles by various hands have been published, to make the work of the commentators better known. The first is devoted to Philoponus;[42] the second is about the commentators in general, and goes into greater detail on some of the issues briefly mentioned here.[43]

---

39. For Simplicius, see I. Hadot, *Le Problème du Néoplatonisme Alexandrin: Hiéroclès et Simplicius* (Paris 1978); for Ammonius and Asclepius, Koenraad Verrycken, *God en wereld in de Wijsbegeerte van Ioannes Philoponus*, Ph.D. Diss. (Louvain 1985); for Olympiodorus, L.G. Westerink, *Anonymous Prolegomena to Platonic Philosophy* (Amsterdam 1962).

40. Alison Frantz, 'Pagan philosophers in Christian Athens', *Proceedings of the American Philosophical Society* 119 (1975), 29-38; M. Tardieu, 'Témoins orientaux du *Premier Alcibiade* à Harrān et à Nag 'Hammādi', *Journal Asiatique* 274 (1986); id., 'Les calendriers en usage à Harrān d'après les sources arabes et le commentaire de Simplicius à la *Physique* d'Aristote', in I. Hadot (ed.), *Simplicius, sa vie, son oeuvre, sa survie* (Berlin 1987), 40-57; id., *Coutumes nautiques mésopotamiennes chez Simplicius*, in preparation. The opposing view that Simplicius returned to Athens is most fully argued by Alan Cameron, 'The last day of the Academy at Athens', *Proceedings of the Cambridge Philological Society* 195, n.s. 15 (1969), 7-29.

41. Simplicius *in Cael.* 26,4-7; 70,16-18; 90,1-18; 370,29-371,4. See on his whole attitude Philippe Hoffmann, 'Simplicius' polemics', in Richard Sorabji (ed.), *Philoponus and the Rejection of Aristotelian Science* (London and Ithaca, N.Y. 1987).

42. Richard Sorabji (ed.), *Philoponus and the Rejection of Aristotelian Science* (London and Ithaca, N.Y. 1987).

43. Richard Sorabji (ed.), *Aristotle Transformed: the ancient commentators and their influence* (London and Ithaca, N.Y. 1990). The lists of texts and previous translations of the commentaries included in Wildberg, *Philoponus Against Aristotle on the Eternity of the World* (pp. 12ff.) are not included here. The list of translations should be augmented by: F.L.S. Bridgman, Heliodorus (?) in *Ethica Nicomachea*, London 1807.

I am grateful for comments to Henry Blumenthal, Victor Caston, I. Hadot, Paul Mercken, Alain Segonds, Robert Sharples, Robert Todd, L.G. Westerink and Christian Wildberg.

English-Greek Glossary

abandon: *aphistasthai*
able: *dunasthai, hoios te*
above: *anôthen*
absent, be: *apeinai*
absurd, absurdity: *adoxos, atopos, atopia, paralogos*
abundance: *plêthos*
accede: *prosienai*
accept: *dekhesthai*
accident, accidental: *sumbainein, sumbebekos, kata sumbebekos*
accompaniment: *sumptôma*
account: *logos*
accustomed, being: *sunêtheia*
achieve: *tunkhanein*
acquire: *ekhein*
act: *poiein, prattein, energein*
action: *poiêsis*
active: *energês, poiêtikos*; be active: *energein*; activity: *energeia, energein*
actual, actually: *energeia(i), entelekheia(i)*; be actual: *energein*; actuality: *energeia, entelekheia*
add: *epipherein, prostithenai*; added: *epaktos*; be added: *prosginesthai, proskeisthai*; addition: *prosthêkê, prosthesis*
adequate: *hikanos*
adjacent: *sunekhês*; be adjacent: *parakeisthai*
admit: *dekhesthai, homologein, paradekhesthai*; capable of admitting: *dektikos*
admixture: *mixis*
advanced, be: *prolambanein*
advantage, gain: *euporein*
adviser: *sumboulos*
affected, be: *paskhein*; affection, being affected: *pathos, pathêsis*; capable of being affected: *pathêtos*; that cannot be affected: *apathês*
affinity with, having: *enarthmios*
against: *para, pros*; up against: *para*

agree: *homologein*
air: *aêr*
akin: *sungenês*
Alexander: *Alexandros*
alien: *allotrios*
alike: *homoios*; make alike: *homoioun*
alive, be: *zên*
all: *hapas, hosos, pas*; all together: *athroos*; not at all: *oud' holôs*
allow: *ean*
along with, exist: *sunuparkhein*
already: *êdê*; be or exist already: *phthanein*; say or mention already: *prolegein*; already said: *proeiremenos*
alter, alteration, being altered: *alloioun, alloiôsis*
altogether: *holôs, pantapasin*
always: *aei*
amber: *elektron*
amount, great: *polus*
animal: *zôion*
anomalous situation: *anômalia*
another: *allos, heteros*
answer, answering, give answer: *apokrisis, apokrinesthai*
apart from: *khôris*
Apollonia, of: *Apollôniates*
apparent: *phaneros*; become apparent: *phainesthai*
appeal to: *pistousthai*
appear, appear in: *phainesthai, emphainesthai*
appearance: *emphasis, phantasia, phantasma*
appetite, be object of: *oregesthai*
appetite, object of: *orektos*
appetition: *orexis*
apply: *ekhein epi, prospherein*; (term): *kategorein, legein*; apply to: *parakolouthein*
apprehend: *antilambanesthai, lambanein*; apprehending, can apprehend: *antilêptikos*

apprehension: *antilêpsis*
approach: *prosodos, prosienai*
approved, be: *dokein*
argue: *dialegesthai*; argue against:
  antilegein
argument: *logos*
Aristotle: *Aristotelês*
art: *tekhnê*; product of art, in
  accordance with art: *tekhnikos*
artificial: *kheirokmêtos*
artisan: *tekhnitês*
as far as: *hoson*
as it were: *hoion, hoionei*
as many as: *hosos, tosoutos ... hosos*
as many times: *tosautakis*
as many ways, in: *tosautakhôs*
as much: *hosos, tosoutos*
ash: *tephra*
ashamed, be: *aideisthai*
ask: *apaitein, epizêtein, erôtan, zêtein*
asleep, be: *koimasthai*
assent: *sunkatathesis,*
  sunkatatithesthai
assert: *phanai*
assign: *anatithenai*
assistance: *boêtheia*
assume: *lambanein*; be assumed:
  keisthai
at any rate: *amelei, goun*
at odds with, be: *makhesthai*
at once: *euthus, eutheôs*
atom: *atomon*
attack: *epitrekhein*
attempt (to show, argue): *epikheirêsis*
attend to: *ephistasthai*; attention:
  epistasis; come to attention of:
  peripiptein
attract: *epagesthai, ephelkesthai,*
  helkein; attracting: *helxis, holkê*
attribute: *anatithenai*
autumn: *metopôron, metopôrinos*
awake, be: *egeiresthai*
aware of, be: *gnôrizein*
away with; do away with: *anairein*

bald man: *phalakros*
base: *basis*
be, being: *einai, ekhein* + adverb,
  ginesthai, huparkhein
beat out: *elaunein*
become: *ginesthai*
before: *prôtos*; exist before:

proüparkhein; say or mention
  before: *prolegein*
beget: *gennan*
beginning: *arkhê*
being: *ousia*; beings: *onta*
believe: *pisteuein*
belong: *huparkhein*; belong per
  accidens: *sumbainein*
bench: *bathron*
benefit: *ôphelia, ôphelein*
best: *aristos*
better: *ameinôn, beltiôn*
between: *metaxu*
beyond: *epekeina*
bitter: *pikros*; bitterness: *pikrotês*
black: *melas*
blackness: *melania*
bladder: *kustis*
blame: *memphesthai, psegein; psogos*
blending: *krasis*; well blended:
  eukratos
blood: *haima*
body: *sôma*; of body: *sômatikos*
boil: *hepsein*; boiling: *hepsêsis*
book: *biblion*; (division of work): *logos*
both: *amphô, amphoteros, hekateros*
brackish: *platus*
breadth: *platos*
breaking up: *dialusis*
breath: *pneuma*
brief: *brakhus*; briefly: *en brakhei*
broader sense, in: *koinoteron*
bronze: *khalkos*
brought about, be: *ginesthai*
build: *oikodomein*
builder: *oikodomos*
burn: *kaiein, ekkaiein, puroun*; burn
  off: *apokaiein*; burn thoroughly:
  sunkaiein; what can be burned:
  kaustos
business, make it one's: *ergon*
  poieisthai
buy: *ôneisthai, priasthai*

call: *kalein, legein*; call in:
  paralambanein; be called: *ekhein*
  (*epônumian*)
can: *ekhein* + infin., *hoios te*
capable, be: *dunasthai*; capable of
  admitting or receiving: *dektikos*;
  capacity: *dunamis, dunamei*
carried, be: *pheresthai*; be carried

down: *katapheresthai*; be carried down with: *sunkatapheresthai*; be carried up with: *sunanapheresthai*; carry up: *anapherein*; carrying, being carried: *phora*

cattle: *bous*

cause: *aitia, aitios, aition*

cease: *dialeipein, pauesthai*; cease to be: *phtheiresthai*; ceasing to be: *phthora*

centre: *kentron*

chaff: *akhuros*

champion: *proïstasthai*

chance: *automatos*

change: *kinein, metaballein, metatithenai*; *kinêsis, metabolê*; change of name: *metonomasia*; causing change: *kinêtikos*

characteristic: *idios*

chief points: *kephalaia*

child: *pais*

choice: *proairesis*

circle: *kuklos*; moving in circle: *kuklophorêtikos*

circumference: *periphereia*

circumstance: *peristasis*

cite: *paratithesthai*

city: *polis*

claim: *axioun*

clay: *pêlos*

clear: *dêlos, prodêlos, enargês, gnôrimos, phaneros*

cloud: *nephos*

cold: *psukhos*; coldness: *psukhrotês*

collect: *lambanein*

collection, what collects: *athroisma, sustêma*

colour: *khrôma, khrônnunai*

combination: *sunthesis*

combine: *sunkrinein, suntithenai*; be combined with: *prosginesthai*

come: *pheresthai*; come from: *ginesthai apo*; come to be, come about: *ginesthai*; coming to be: *genesis*; come to be in: *enginesthai*; come to have: *ginesthai* + dative; coming to know: *gnôsis*; coming together: *sunodos*; subject to coming to be, that has come to be: *genêtos*; not subject to coming to be: *agenêtos*

commensurateness: *summetria*; commensurate: *summetros*

commentary: *exêgêsis, hupomnêma*

common: *koinos*

companions: *hetairoi*

complete: *plêroun, apoplêroun, sumplêroun, telos epitithenai, teleios, teleioun*; completely: *pantelôs*; completion, completeness: *teleiôsis*

compose: *sunistanai, suntithenai*; be composed of: *einai ek, sunkeisthai*; composite: *sunthetos*; composition: *sunthesis, sustasis*; compound, compounded: *sunamphoteros*

compress: *sunthlibein*; compressed: *brakhus*; compression: *pilêsis*

comprise: *sunekhein*

conception: *prolêpsis*

concern: *epimeleia*

conclude: *lambanein*

concoct: *peptein, pessein, pettein*; concoction: *pepsis*; inconcoction: *apepsia*; unconcocted: *apeptos*

condensation, condense: *sustasis, sunistasthai, sustellein*

conditional: *sunnêmenon*; conditionally: *ex hupotheseôs*

confident, be: *tharrein*

confirmation: *kuros*

conflagration: *ekpurôsis*

conflict, be in: *enantiousthai*

consequence: *akolouthia*; be consequent: *hepesthai*

consider: *theôrein*; consideration: *episkepsis, skepsis*

constitute: *sunistanai*

consume, exhaust: *analiskein*

consumed, be: *apanaliskesthai*

contact: *haphê*; be in contact, come into contact: *haptesthai*

contemplate: *theôrein*; contemplating: *theôrêtikos*

contempt, behave with: *epêreazein*

contingent: *endekhomenos*

continual: *athroos*; continue: *proienai*; continuous: *sunekhês*; continuously: *aei*

contrary, subordinate: *hupenantios*

contrast: *antithesis*

contribute: *sunergein, suntelein*; contribution: *sunteleia*

control: *kratein*; in control: *kurios*

conversely: *empalin*

conversion: *metabolê*
convey: *pherein*
conviction, convince: *pistis*
cool: *psukhein*
cooling: *psuxis*
copper coin: *khalkos*
corporeal: *sôma, sômatikos*
counter-example, be:
  antimartureisthai
counterfeit: *kibdêlos*
cow: *bous*
cowherd: *boukolos*
craftsman: *dêmiourgos*
create: *poiein*; creative: *poiêtikos*
criticise: *legein ... kata*
cupping-glass: *sikua*
cycle: *kuklos, periodos*; come round in
  cycle: *anakuklousthai*

darkness: *skotos*
day: *hêmera*
decay: *sêpsis, sêpesthai*
decide, decision: *prokrinein*
define: *horizein, diorizein, periorizein*;
  definite something: *tode ti*
deliberate: *bouleuesthai*; deliberation:
  boulê; deliberative, capable of
  deliberation: *bouleutikos*
delineation: *perigraphê*
demand: *apaitein, axioun*
Democritus: *Dêmokritos*
demonstration: *deixis, apodeixis*
dense: *pakhus*; make dense: *puknoun*;
  density: *pakhutês, puknotês*
deny: *ou phanai*
depart: *apienai, exienai, existasthai*;
  departure: *ekstasis*
depend on: *artasthai, keisthai en*;
  depending on: *epi*
depth: *bathos*
derive, deriving: *para, ekhein apo,
  ekhein para, einai para, pherein*; be
  derived from: *ginesthai apo*
deserving: *axios*
desire: *ephesis, ephiesthai*; object of
  desire: *epithumêtos*
destroy: *phtheirein*; destruction:
  phthora
determination: *horos*
determine, (make) determinate:
  dialambanein, horizein, diorizein
develop: *proagein*

dialectical attempt: *logou epikheirêsis*
die: *thnêskein*
differ: *allôs ekhein, diaperein*;
  difference, differentiation:
  diaphora; different: *alloios, allos,
  diaphoros, heteros*; at different
  times: *allote*
difficulty: *aporia*; raise difficulty:
  aporein
dig: *orussein*
Diogenes: *Diogenês*
disagreement: *diaphônia*
discover: *heuriskein*; discovery:
  heuresis
discuss: *legein*; discuss in detail:
  diarthroun; discussion: *logos*
disperse: *diakrinein*
disposition: *hexis*
disproportion: *asummetria*
dispute: *amphisbetêsis*
dissolution: *analusis*; dissolve: *luein,
  analuein, dialuein*; that can be
  dissolved: *lutos*
distinction: *diairesis*; distinguish,
  draw or make distinction: *diairein,
  diorizein*
divide: *diairein*; divisible: *diairetos*;
  division: *diairesis, tomê*
divine (heavenly): *theios*
do: *poiein, prattein*
doctrine: *dogma*
doing away with: *anairesis, anairetikos*
double: *diplasios*
downwards: *katô*
drachma, drachma coin: *drakhma*;
  hundred drachmas, mina: *mna*
draw (line): *agein*; draw to self, draw
  in: *epispasthai*; draw, draw in: *span*;
  draw up: *anagein, tassein*
drink: *pinein*
drop of water: *stagôn*
dry: *xêros, xêrainein*; dry moisture out
  of: *exikmazein*; dryness: *xêrotês*
dung: *kopros*

each: *hekastos, pas, thateros*; each (of
  two): *hekateros*; each other: *allêlous*
earth: *gê*
earthenware: *keramos*
earthy: *geôdês*
easily moved: *eukinêtos*
easy: *rhaidios*

effect: *ergon*
effervescence: *zesis*
efficient: *poiêtikos*
effluence: *aporrhoia*; form effluence:
   aporrhein
effort, make every: *poiein to par' autas*
either way: *amphoterôs*
element, elemental: *stoikheion*
else; something else: *allos, heteros*
emit: *aphienai*
Empedocles: *Empedoklês*
empty: *kenos*
encounter: *peripiptein*
end: *telos*; failure to achieve end:
   ateleia
enmattered: *enulos*
enquire: *zêtein*; enquiry: *pragmateia*
enter in: *eisienai*
entire: *pas*
equal, equivalent: *isos*; equal in
   number: *isarithmos*
equinox: *isêmeria*
error: *diamartia*
escape notice: *lanthanein*
especially: *allôs te kai*
essence: *ti ên einai*
establish: *kataskeuazein, paristanai,*
   pistousthai, poieisthai kataskeuên,
   prokataballein, sunistanai;
   establishing, establishment:
   kataskeuê, pistis, sustasis
eternal, everlasting: *aïdios*; eternity:
   aïdiotês
evaporate: *diatmein, exatmizein;*
   evaporate along with: *sunexatmizein*
every: *hekastos, pas*; in every case:
   pantôs; in every way or respect:
   pantêi; everywhere: *pantakhou;*
   make every effort: *poiein to par'*
   autas
evidence: *marturia, marturion*
exact: *akribês*
examine: *exetazein*
example, for: *hoion, hoionei, ei tukhoi*
exceed: *huperekhein*; be excessive:
   huperballein
exclude: *anairein*
excrement: *hupostasis*
exhalation, exhale: *anathumiasis,*
   anathumiasthai
exhaust: *analiskein*
exist: *einai, huparkhein,*

huphistasthai; exist along with:
   sunuparkhein; existence:
   hupostasis; real existence: *huparxis*
expect: *prosdokan*
explain: *apodidonai, diexienai;*
   explanation: *exêgêsis*
express: *legein*
extend around: *periteinesthai*
extension: *diastasis, diastêma*
external: *ektos*

failure to achieve: *apotukhia*
fall outside: *ekpiptein*
fall short: *apodein*
fallacy, commit: *paralogizesthai*
false: *pseudês, pseudos*; false opinion:
   pseudodoxia; falsity of argument:
   pseudologia
familiar, familiarity: *suntrophos,*
   suntrophia
fan: *rhipizein*
far, further away: *porrô*
fear: *phobos*
ferment: *zein*
few: *oligos*
fifth: *pemptos*
fill: *plêroun*; filling up: *plêrôsis*
final: *teleutaios*
finally: *telos*
find: *heuriskein*
fine: *kalos*; (= rare) *leptos*; fineness:
   leptotês
fire: *pur*; heavenly fire: *hupekkauma*
first: *prôtos*; in the first place: *tên*
   arkhên
fit: *epharmozein*; fit in: *enarmozein*
five: *pente*
flame: *phlox*
flavour: *khumos*
flesh: *sarx*
float upon: *epokheisthai*
flow: *rhein*; flow away: *aporrhein*; flow
   in: *epirrhein*; flow this way and
   that: *metarrhein, metarrhusis*
follow: *akolouthein, hepesthai;*
   following: *akolouthos*; what follows:
   akolouthia
foot (length): *pous*
force: *bia*; have force: *dunasthai*
foreknowledge: *prognôsis*
forethought: *pronoia*; exercise or be

object of forethought: *pronoein,*
pronoeisthai
form: *eidos*; give or create form:
eidopoiein
four: *tessares*; in four ways: *tetrakhôs*;
fourth: *tetartos*
free man: *eleutheros*
fruit: *karpos*
full: *plêrês*
function: *ergon*
further: *epi pleon*

general: *koinos*; generally, in general:
katholou, koinêi
general (military), be: *stratêgein*
genus: *genos*
geometrician: *geômetros*
get: *lambanein*
give, provide: *didonai, apodidonai*;
give (answer): *poieisthai*; give
(explanation): *legein*; give up:
aphiesthai
go: *ienai*; go back to: *epanienai*; go
forward: *prosienai*; go on: *metienai,*
proienai; go on to: *ienai epi*
goal: *skopos*
goat: *aix*
goatherd: *aipolos*
god: *theos*
going to, be: *mellein*
gold: *khrusos*
good: *agathos*
govern: *kubernan*
gradual(ly): *para mikron*
grant (in argument): *sunkhôrein*
graze: *nemein*
great deal, great amount: *polus*;
greater: *meizôn, pleôn*; greatest:
pleistos
grow, grow naturally: *phuein,*
phuesthai, trephein
gut: *koilia*

hairy man: *komêtês*
half: *hêmisus*
hand: *kheir*
happen: *ginesthai, sumbainein,*
tunkhanein; happen to:
epiginesthai; have happen to one:
paskhein
harbour: *limên*
hard: *sklêros*

harmony, be in: *sunaidein*
haul ship up on land: *neolkein*
have: *ekhein, ginesthai* + dative; have
to: *dein, opheilein*; have as position:
legein
heading: *epigraphê*
health: *hugeia*
heap: *sôros*
hear: *akouein*; that can be heard:
akoustos; hearing: *akoê*
heat: *thermotês, thermainein, thermos*;
heat first: *prothermainein*
heavenly: *theios*; heavenly fire:
hupekkauma
heavy: *barus*; heaviness: *baros*
Heracleia: *Hêrakleia*
Heraclides: *Hêrakleidês*
here: *autou, entautha*; things here:
tade
high: *hupsêlos*
hinder: *empodizein*
hold back: *epekhein*
hollow: *koilos*
honey: *meli*
honour: *timê*; honourable: *timios*
horn: *keras*
horse: *hippos*
horse-trainer: *hipponomos*
hot: *thermos*; red-hot: *pepurômenos*
house: *oikia*
human being: *anthrôpos*
hurtle: *pheresthai*

identity of names: *homônumia*
ignorant: *anepistêmôn*
image: *eikôn, phantasia*; having no
image: *aphantastos*
imagine: *phantasian lambanein*
imitate: *mimeisthai*; imitation:
mimêsis
immortality: *athanasia*
impeding, impede: *empodôn*
imperfect: *atelês*; imperfection: *ateleia*
imperishable: *aphthartos*;
imperishability: *aphtharsia*
impinge: *epiballein, prospiptein*
impious: *asebês*
impossible: *adunatos*
impression: *phantasia, phantasma*
impulse: *hormê*
in front: *emprosthen*
inactivity: *argia*

inappropriate: *allotrios*
include: *lambanein, periekhein, perilambanein, sullambanein*
incomplete: *ateles*; incompleteness: *ateleia*
inconcoction: *apepsia*
incorporeal: *asômatos*
increase: *auxein, sunauxanein, auxêsis*
indefinite: *apeiros*; indefinitely: *epi apeiron*
indeterminate, indeterminacy: *aoristos*
indicate, indicative, indication: *deiknunai, sêmainein, deiktikos, dêlôtikos, mênutikos*
individual: *kath' hekasta*; individually: *kat' arithmon, idiâi, kat' idian*
indivisible: *adiairetos, atomon*
induction: *epagôgê*
inevitable: *anankaios*
infer: *lambanein*
infinite, infinity: *apeiros*
influence: *kinein*; have influence: *dunasthai*
influx: *epikhusis*
infrequent: *spanios*
initial: *prôtos*
innate: *emphutos*
inseparable: *akhôristos*
insoluble: *alutos*
instrument: *organon*; instrument of sensation: *aisthêtêrion*
intellect, intellection: *nous, noêsis*; exercise intellect: *noein*; intellectual: *noetikos*; object of intellect: *noêtos*
intensification: *epitasis*
intermediate: *metaxu*
internal: *entos*
intervening: *metaxu*
intractable: *aporos*
introduce: *eisagein*
invite: *parakalein*
involve: *einai meta*
ipso facto: *êdê*
iron: *sidêros*; iron-like: *sidêritis*
irrational: *alogos, paralogos*
itself; by/in itself: *kath' hauto*; not itself: *ouketi*

joining together: *harmonia*
judge, judging, judgement: *krinein,*

krisis, kritikos; form a judgement: *epikrinein*
just for this reason: *êdê*
just like: *paraplêsios*
juxtaposition: *parathesis, sunthesis*

keep: *phulassein*
killed, be: *apollusthai*
kind: *eidos, genos, phusis*
kindle: *exaptein*
know: *eidenai*; knowledge, knowing about: *epistêmê, gnôsis*; knowledgeable: *epistêmôn*; make known: *gnôrizein*

lack, lacking: *aporia, endeia, endeês*; be lacking: *leipein, ekleipein*
laid down, be: *keisthai*
land: *gê*
last: *eskhatos*
later: *husteron*
latitude: *platos*
lay down: *tithesthai*; such as to lay down: *thetikos*; laying down, laid down: *thesis*
lead: *agein, apagein*; lead to: *ginesthai eis*
lead (metal): *molibdos*
leader, be: *proïstasthai*
learn: *manthanein*; learning: *mathêsis*
leave: *leipein, kataleipein*; leave out: *paraleipein*; leave behind: *hupoleipein*
lecture: *akroasis*
leisure: *skholê*
length: *mêkos*
less, lesser: *elattôn, hêttôn, oligos*
letter: *stoikheion*
liable, be: *enekhesthai*
lid, rest on like: *epipômatizein*
life: *zôê*
light: *phôs*
light (not heavy): *kouphos*
like: *hoios, homoios*; make like: *homoioun*
likely: *eikos*
limb: *melos, meros*
limit, be limited: *peras, perainein*
line: *grammê*
little: *oligos*
living creature: *zôion*
locate: *tithenai, tithesthai*

log: *xulon*
logically: *logos*
long: *makros*
longer: *eti*
look: *blepein*; look for: *epizêtein*
lose: *apoballein*
luck: *tukhê*
lye: *konia*

magnet: *lithos*
magnitude: *megethos*
make: *poiein, parekhein*; maker: *poiêtês*
malleable: *elatos*
manner: *tropos*
many: *polus*; in many ways: *pollakhôs*
master: *despotês*
material, matter: *hulê, hulikos*; possessing matter: *enulos*; matter (in hand): *pragma*
mean: *legein, sêmainein*; have meaning: *dunasthai*
measure: *metron*
melt: *têkein*; that can be melted: *têktos*; melting: *diakhusis, têxis*
menses, menstrual blood: *emmênon*
mention: *legein, paratithesthai*; mention before or already: *prolegein*
Meteorology: *Meteôrologika*
milk: *gala*
mina, hundred drachmas: *mna*
minor: *oligos*
mirror: *katoptron*
misdeed: *hamartanein*
missing, be: *leipein*
mix: *mignunai*; mix in: *katamignunai, enkatamignunai*; mixed: *miktos*; mixing, mixture: *mixis*
moist, moisture: *hugron, hugrotês, ikmas*; become moist, be made moist: *hugrainesthai*
more: *pleôn*; no more: *ouden mallon*
moreover: *eti*
mortal, mortality: *thnêtos*
most: *pleistos*; for the most part: *epi pleiston*
motion, movement: *kinêsis*; move: *kinein*; easily moved: *eukinêtos*
much: *polus*
must: *dein, khrênai*
mutual replacement: *antiperistasis*
mythographer: *theologos*

name: *onoma, epônumia, onomazein*; change of name: *metonomasia*; identity of names: *homônumia*; plurality of names: *poluônumia*
nation: *ethnos*
nature, natural: *phusis, phusikos*; natural philosopher: *phusikos*; in one's nature: *sumphutos*; be, do or grow by nature, naturally: *phuein, phuesthai*
near: *engus*
necessary, necessity: *ananke, anankaios*
need: *dein, deisthai*
neither: *oudeteros*
next: *akolouthos, hexês, ephexês*
no longer: *ouketi*
no way, in: *medamôs*
not at all: *oud' holôs*
not itself: *ouketi*
note: *lambanein*; note in addition: *epilambanein, proslambanein*
nothing: *mêden*
nourishment: *trophê*
now: *êdê*
number: *arithmos, plêthos*; certain number: *posos*; equal in number: *isarithmos*
nutritive: *threptikos*

objection: *enstasis*
objective, be: *prokeisthai*
obscure: *asaphês*
observe: *katagignôskein*; place of observation: *periôpê*
obtain: *tunkhanein*
occupy: *katekhein*
occur: *ginesthai*
often: *pollakis*
oil: *elaion*
old age: *gêras*
olive-oil: *elaion*
omit: *kataleipein*
one: *heis*; one (of two): *heteros, thateros*; one another: *allêlous*; one … another: *allos … allos*
opinion: *doxa*
oppose: *antibainein*; be opposed, be opposite: *antikeisthai, enantiousthai*; opposed, opposite, opponent, opposition: *enantios, enantiôsis*

or rather, or else: *ê*
order, ordering, ordered sequence:
 tassein, taxis; in an ordered way:
 tetagmenôs; orderly: *eutaktos*
organic: *organikos*
organise: *dioikein*
origin: *arkhê, genesis*
other: *allos*; the other: *heteros*; other
 than one's own: *allotrios*
ought: *dein*
outside: *ektos, exô*; from outside:
 exôthen; pass outwards: *exienai*
overcome: *kratein*
overpower: *katiskhuein*
oversee: *epitropeuein*
own, own proper: *idios, oikeios*; in own
 right: *kath' hauto, kat' oikeion logon*

pair: *duas*; be paired: *sunduazesthai*
pale yellow: *ôkhros*
part: *meros, morion*; divisible into
 parts: *meristos*; without parts, that
 have no parts: *amerês*
participate: *metekhein*
particular: *kath' hekasta, kata meros,
 en merei*
pass away: *phtheiresthai*; pass away
 along with: *sumphtheiresthai*;
 passing away: *phthora*; subject to
 passing away: *phthartos*; not
 subject to passing away: *aphthartos*
pass outwards: *exienai*
pass over: *hupertithesthai*
pass through: *phoitan*
passage: *diodos*; (of text) *lexis*
passive: *pathêtikos*; be passive:
 paskhein
pasture: *boskein*
path: *hodos*
peculiar: *idios*
penetrate: *eisduesthai, enduesthai*
per accidens: *kata sumbebêkos*
per se: *kath' hauto*
perceive by senses: *aisthanesthai*;
 perceptible by sense: *aisthêtos*
percolate: *dietheisthai*
perfect: *teleios, teleioun*; perfection:
 teleiôsis; less perfect: *atelês*
perform (actions): *energein*
perhaps: *isôs, mêpote*
perish: *phtheiresthai*; perishable:
 phthartos

permanence: *monê*; be permanent:
 histasthai
persuade: *peithein*; persuasion:
 pithanotês
philosopher: *philosophos*; natural
 philosopher: *phusikos*
Physics, on: *phusikos*
place: *khôra, topos, tithenai, tithesthai*
plant: *phuton*
Plato: *Platôn*
plausible: *eulogos*; plausibility:
 pithanotês
plurality: *pleôn, plêthos*
point (geometrical): *sêmeion, stigmê*;
 point (of thing said): *nous*; have a
 point: *legein ti*
poor: *penês*
pore: *poros*
position: *proairesis*; have as position:
 legein
possess: *ekhein*
possessing matter: *enulos*
possible: *hoios te*; be possible:
 dunasthai, einai, endekhesthai
postpone: *hupertithesthai*
postulate: *tithesthai*
potentiality, potentially: *dunamis,
 dunamei*; be potentially, have
 potential: *dunasthai*
power: *dunamis, dunamei, exousia*
practice: *askêsis*
praise: *epainos, epainein*
precede: *proüparkhein*; preceding the
 final: *metaxu tou teleutaiou*
predicate: *katêgorein*
preponderance: *pleôn, pleonektein*
presence, be present: *parousia,
 pareinai, huparkhein*; be present in:
 enuparkhein
preserve: *phulassein, sôzein, sôstikos,
 têrein*; preservation: *sôtêria*
prevail, prevailing: *kratein, pleonexia*
prevent: *kôluein*
previously mentioned: *proeirêmenos*
primary, primarily: *prôtos,
 proêgoumenos*; prime matter: *prôtê
 hulê*
principal: *kurios*
principle: *arkhê*
privation: *sterêsis*; of privation:
 sterêtikos
problem: *problêma*

proceed: *proieinai*
proclaim: *kêruttein*
produce: *ergazesthai, gennan, poiein*;
be produced by: *ginesthai ek*;
producing: *poiêtikos*; product: *ergon*
profess: *hupiskhneisthai*
progress, progression: *epididonai,
epidosis, proödos*
proper: *idios, oikeios*; proper, in
proper sense: *kurios*; property:
idiotês; be property: *huparkhein,
sumbainein*
proportion: *logos*; be proportionate:
ekhein logon; proportioning:
summetria
propose: *protithesthai*; proposition:
protasis
provide: *perekhein*
providence: *pronoia*; exercise or be
object of providence: *pronoein,
pronoeisthai*
proximate: *prosekhês*
punishment: *kolasis*
pupil (of eye): *korê*
pure: *katharos*; purify: *kathairein*
push away: *apôthein*
put forward: *legein*
put together: *suntithenai*; be put
together: *sunkeisthai*; putting
together: *sunthesis*

qualification, quality: *poiotês, poios*;
without qualification: *haplôs, pantôs*
quantity: *posotês, posos*
quench: *sbennunai*
question: *erôtêsis*; put or pose
question: *erôtan*

rain: *hudôr, huein*
raise (point): *kinein*
rank with: *suntassein*
rare: *araios, manos*
rational: *logikos, logos*
rawness: *ômotês*
reach: *lambanein*
ready: *hetoimos*
reality: *alêtheia, einai, hupostasis*;
real being: *ousia*; real existence:
huparxis, hupostasis; real thing:
pragma
reason (cause): *aitia, aitios, aition*; for

reason: *kharin*; make reason:
aitiasthai
reason (rationality), reasonable: *logos,
eulogos*
recede: *apienai, apokhôrein*; receding:
aphodos
receive: *analambanein, dekhesthai,
lambanein*; capable of receiving:
dektikos; reception: *lêpsis*; receptive:
dektikos
recently: *prôiên*
reciprocity: *antidosis, allêlous*
reckon in: *sunkatarithmein*
recognise: *gignôskein*
recollection: *anamnêsis*
recorded observations: *historia*
red-hot: *pepurômenos*
reduce: *meioun*
refer: *anagein*; reference: *anaphora*;
be referred: *anaphoran ekhein*
reflection: *phrontis*
refute: *elenkhein*
region: *meros*; in our region: *par'
hêmin*
reject: *apôthein, parapempein*
relate: *anapherein, anaphoran
poieisthai*; related, relative, in
relation: *pros*; relation: *skhesis*
remain: *menein, diamenein,
emmenein*; remain behind:
hupomenein; be remaining:
hupoleipein
remark: *mnêmoneuein*
remind: *hupomimnêskein*
removal: *anairesis*
remove: *anairein, khôrizein,
paraluein*; be removed:
methistasthai; be removed from:
aphistasthai
reply: *logos*
request: *axioun*
require: *axioun, dein, deisthai*
residue: *perittôma, perittôsis*
resist: *antibainein, antikoptein,
enistasthai, hupenantiousthai*;
resistant: *antibatikos*
resolution, resolve: *lusis, luein,
apoluesthai*
respire: *anapnein*
rest, being at rest: *stasis*; stay at rest,
be at rest: *êremein, histasthai*
rest, the rest: *allos*

result: *ginesthai, sumbainein, loipos*
resume: *analambanein*
retain: *katekhein*
retarded, be: *hupoleipein*
return: *anakamptein*
reverse way, in: *empalin*
revolution: *periphora*
right: *axios, dikaios, orthos*; be right: *kalôs ekhein*; think right: *axioun*
ripe: *pepôn*; ripen: *pepainein*; ripening: *pepansis*
river: *potamos*
roast: *optein*; roasting: *optêsis*
rottenness: *saprotês*
route: *hodos*
run: *trekhein*
runner: *dromeus*
rust: *iousthai*

sake of, for: *heneka, kharin*; for sake of something: *heneka tou*
salt: *hals*; saltiness: *halmurotês*; salty, salt: *halmuros*
same: *autos*; in same way: *hôsautôs*
satisfy: *areskein*
say: *legein, phanai*; say before, say already: *prolegein*; that should be said: *rhêteos*
scatter: *diaphorein*
science: *epistêmê*
scorching: *stateusis*
sea: *thalassa*
searching: *zêtêsis*
second, secondary: *deuteros, heteros*
sect: *proairesis*
see: *horan*; be seen: *phainesthai*; that can be seen: *horatos*
seed: *sperma*; body surrounding seed: *perikarpion*
seek: *zêtein*
seem: *dokein, phainesthai*
self: *autos*; be self-aware: *sunaisthanesthai*; self-awareness: *sunaisthêsis*
sense, sensation, sense-experience, sense-perception: *aisthêsis, aisthanesthai*; of or possessing sensation, able to sense, sensory: *aisthêtikos*; sensed, object of sense, that can be sensed, sensible: *aisthêtos*; incapable of being sensed:

anaisthêtos; sense-organ: *aisthêtêrion*
separate: *khôrizein*; separate out: *ekkrinein, sunekkrinein*; that can be separated: *khôristos*; separation: *khôrismos*; separation out: *ekkrisis*
servant: *oiketês*
service: *hupêresia*
set before: *prokataballein*
set out: *ektithesthai*
settle out: *huphizanein*
several: *pleôn*; in several ways, in: *pleonakhôs*
shape: *morphê, skhêma*
share: *koinônein*; sharing: *koinônia*; sharing in: *koinos*
sheep: *probata*
shepherd: *poimên*
ship: *ploion*
shoot: *toxeuein*
should: *dein*
show: *deiknunai, endeiknunai*
shrink back: *oknein*
sight: *opsis*; object of sight: *horatos*; of sight: *horatikos*
sign: *sêmeion*
similar: *homoios*, similar: *paraplêsios*; similarity: *homoiotês*
simmering: *molusis, molunsis*
simple: *haplous*
simultaneously: *hama*
single: *heis*
sink: *katapheresthai*
slave: *doulos*
small: *mikros, oligos*
smear: *khriein*
smell: *osmê*; sense of smell: *osphrêsis*; that can be smelled: *osphrêtos*
snow: *khiôn*
so great: *tosoutos*
Socrates (as example): *Sôkratês*
soda: *nitron*
soft: *malakos*; soften: *malattein*; that can be softened: *malaktos*; that cannot be softened: *amalaktos*
solid: *stereos*; solidity: *stereotês*; solidify: *pêgnunai*; solidification: *pêxis*; causing solidification: *pêktikos*; solidified: *pêktos*
solstice: *tropai*
soluble: *lutos*
sophism: *sophisma*

sorites: *sôreitês*
sort: *phusis*; sort of thing, of the sort:
  hopoios; of certain sort: *poios*; of this
  sort: *toioutos, toiosde*
soul: *psukhê*; possessing soul:
  empsukhos; without soul: *apsukhos*
sound: *hugiês*
south wind: *notos*; from south wind:
  notios
space: *khôra*
speak: *legein, phanai*; speak about:
  poieisthai logon; speak against:
  enantia legein
species: *eidos*
spherical: *sphairikos*
spontaneous: *automatos*
spread out: *diaduesthai*
spring (season): *ear*; (water) *pêgê*;
  from springs: *pêgaios*
squeeze out: *ekthlibein*
stand: *histasthai*; stand aloof from:
  aphistasthai
start: *arkhesthai*; starting-point: *arkhê*
state (condition): *diathesis*; state
  (assert): *legein, apodidonai*
still: *eti*
Stoa, Stoic: *Stoa, Stôïkos*
stochastic: *stokhastikos*
stone: *lithos*
stop: *histasthai*
straight away: *antikrus, euthus,*
  eutheôs
straight line, in: *euthus*
straits: *stena*
stretch out: *ekteinein*
strongly: *sphodra*
subject: *hupokeimenon*; be subject:
  hupokeisthai
subordinate contrary: *hupenantios*
subsequently: *husteron*
substance: *ousia*
substrate: *hupokeimenon*
subtract: *aphairein*; subtraction:
  aphairesis
succession: *diadokhê*
such as: *hopoios*
sufficient: *hikanos*; be sufficient:
  arkein
suitability: *epitêdeiotês*
summary: *epidromê*
summer: *theros, therinos*
sun: *hêlios*

supervene: *epiginesthai*
supply: *khorêgia*
support: *antibainein, boêthein*
suppose, make supposition:
  lambanein, hupolambanein,
  tithesthai, hupotithesthai; I
  suppose: *isôs, skhedon*; be supposed:
  hupokeisthai; supposition:
  hupothesis
surface: *epipedon, epiphaneia*; be on
  surface: *epipolazein*
surpass: *huperballein*
surrender: *endidonai*
surround: *periekhein, perikeisthai*;
  surroundings: *periekhon*
sweat: *hidrôs*
sweet, sweetness: *glukus, glukutês*
swiftly; more swiftly: *thatton*
swineherd: *subôtês*
syllable: *sullabê*
syllogism: *sullogismos*

take, take on: *lambanein*; take away:
  aphairein; take in addition:
  proslambanein; take together:
  sullambanein; taking on: *analêpsis*
tangible: *haptos*
task: *ergon*
taste: *geusis*; that can be tasted:
  geustos
teach: *didaskein*; teaching: *didaskalia*
term: *onoma*
terminus: *peras*
that is (= i.e.): *hoion, hoionei*
theoretical: *theôrêtika*
thereafter: *loipon*
therefore: *êdê*
thick: *pakhus*; thicken: *pakhunein*;
  thickening: *pakhunsis*
thing: *pragma*; things that are: *onta*
think: *dokein, hêgeisthai,*
  hupolambanein, noein, nomizein,
  oiesthai, phronein; think right:
  axioun
third: *tritos*
thought, thinking: *ennoia, epinoia*
thousand: *khilia*
three: *treis*; threesome: *trias*
thunderbolt: *keraunos*
timber: *hulê, xulon*
time: *khronos*; appropriate time: *kairos*
title: *epigraphein*

together: *hama, homou*; cannot exist
together: *asunuparktos*; take
together: *sullambanein*
totality: *pas*
touch: *haphê, haptesthai*; of touch:
haptikos; that can be touched:
haptos
transfer: *metapherein*
transition: *metabolê*; make transition:
metaballein
transmission: *diadosis*
transmit: *diadidonai, diapempein*
travel: *ienai, pheresthai*; travel
through: *diienai*
treasure: *thêsauros*
treble: *triplasios*
true, truth: *alêthês, alêtheia*; true
philosopher: *anêr philosophos*
try: *peirasthai*
turn, in: *para meros*
twice: *dis*
two: *duo*; in two ways: *dikhôs*; twofold:
dittos
type: *tropos*

ultimate: *eskhatos*
unable, be: *adunatein*
unalloyed: *eilikrinês*
unconcocted: *apeptos*
unconvincing: *apithanos*
undelineable: *aperigraphos*
under, falling under: *hupo*
undergo: *paskhein*
underlie: *hupokeisthai*
understand: *akouein, epistasthai*;
understanding: *dianoia, epistêmê,
epistêmôn, gnôsis*; understood:
epistêtos
undifferentiated: *adiaphoros*
unfinished: *atelês*
unforeseen: *aproöratos*
unify: *henoun*
uninterrupted: *anepileiptos*
unit: *monas*
universal: *katholou*; universally: *kata
pantos*
unlike: *anomoios*
unlimited, unlimitedness: *apeiros,
apeiria*; unlimited times, unlimited
number: *apeirakis*
unmixed: *amiktos*

unmoved: *akinêtos*; be unmoving:
akinêtizein
unreasonable: *alogos*
unvarying: *homalos*
unyielding: *mê eiktos*; unyielding
quality: *antitupia*
up to (depending on): *epi*
upper hand, gain: *epikratein,
pleonektein*
upwards: *anô*
urine: *ouron*
use, make use of: *khrêsthai*; useful:
khrêsimos
utter: *legein*

vapourised, be: *atmizein*
vein: *phleps*
very: *autos*
vinegar: *oxos*
violence, due to: *biaios*
virtue: *aretê*
void: *kenon*; containing much void:
polukenos

wash: *plunein*
water: *hudôr*; living in water: *enudros*;
watery: *hudatôdês*
way: *tropos*; in certain way: *poios*
weak: *asthenês*; weaken: *marainein*;
weakness: *astheneia*
wealthy: *plousios*
wear down: *katatribein*
well: *kalôs*; well blended: *eukratos*;
well-being: *eu einai*
well (for water): *phrear*
whatsoever: *tukhon*
whey: *orros*
whichever: *hopoteros*
white, whiteness: *leukos, leukotês*;
make whiter: *leukainein*
whole: *holos, pas*; of the whole *athroos*
willing, be: *ethelein*
win: *nikan*
wine: *oinos*
winter: *kheimôn, kheimerinos*
wish: *boulesthai, boulêsis, thelein*
withering: *auansis*
without: *khôris*
womb: *hustera*
wonder: *thaumazein*
word: *rhêma*
world: *kosmos*

worth, worthy: *axios*
write: *graphein*; write before:
  prographein
wrong, do: *hamartanein*

yearly: *eniausios*
yellow, pale: *ôkhros*
yield: *hupeikein*

Greek-English Index

* emendation; < > supplied in text; [ ] deleted. Adverbs are not generally indexed separately from the adjectives from which they are formed. References are to *quaestio* numbers (in **bold** type) and to the page and line numbers of Bruns' text, which appear in the margin of this translation.

adiairetos, indivisible, **3.9** 94,16; 95,30-2; 96,18-19; 97,14
adiaphoros, undifferentiated, **3.9** 96,26
adoxos, absurd, absurdity, **fr.1 Vitelli** 91,18.24
adunatein, be unable, **3.9** 97,29
adunatos, impossible, **3.9** 95,25; 97,1.7.20.27-8.32.35; **3.12** 103,12; 106,3
aei, always, continuously, **2.18** 62,30*.34; **2.19** 63,19; **2.22** 71,7; **2.25** 76,19; **3** 80,10; **3.5** 87,23.27-8.<29>; 88,1.7; **3.10** 100,5; **3.12** 103,9; **fr.1 Vitelli** 91,26; repeatedly, **fr.1 Vitelli** 91,20
aêr, air, **2.23** 72,12.24; 73,20; 74,7.9.13.16; **2.24** 75,13.22; **3.6** 89,33; 90,23.26.32; 91,3.7.13-15; **3.14** 108,19; 110,13.16.18; 113,9; 114,13.20-1.24.27.33; 115,20-1
agathos, good, **2.21** 69,1; 70,4
agein, lead, **3.2** 81,15; **3.13** 107,11-12; draw (line), **3.9** 96,15.17
agenêtos, not subject to coming-to-be, **2.18** 62,23; **2.19** 63,19
aideisthai, be ashamed, **fr.2 Vitelli** 92,13-14
aïdios, eternal, everlasting, 45,15; **2.18** 62,29.34 63,3; **2.19** 63,8.10; **2.22** 72,1; **3.5**, 87,27; 88,7-8.16.15; 89,21
aïdiotês, eternity, **2.19** 63,24,
aipolos, goatherd, **2.21** 67,33
aisthanesthai, sense, have sensation or sense-experience, perceive by senses 80,13.17; **3.3** 82,35-6; 83,4; 84,17-18; 85,4.6.9.14.20.25-6.35; 86,25; **3.6** 89,31; 90,6.13.21.25; 91,1.5-6.9-10.14; **3.7** 91,25-31.33-4; 92,2-5.8-9.11-12.14-15.17-19.26-7; 93,12.15.18.20-2; **3.8** 94,3; **3.9** 94,11.14.25-6.29-32; 95,1.8-13.15-17.19-20.22.24.28; 96,5; 97,10-11.16; **3.12** 101,20-1; 102,6
aisthêsis, sense, sensation, sense-perception or sense-experience, **2.23** 74,28; **3** 80,7.14.16; **3.3** 82,22-5.27-8.32-3.35-6; 83,1.3-5.[6].7.13.16.18; 84,18.34; 85,3.22.29.31; 85,3.8.15-16.22.26.29.31; 86,2.4.7-8.10.16.24.27-8.[29].31.33; **3.6** 89,26-7.29; 90,2.5.7-8.10.12.14.17.20-1.25; 91,7.16-17.19-20; **3.7** 91,32; 92,1.7-8.10.12-13.16.25.30-1.33-5; 93,5-6.10-12.14.17-19.21; **3.8** 93,23.25-6.29-30 94,5.8; **3.9** 94,19.25; 95,1.6.12.17-18; 96,4.7.12.18.28-9.35-6; 98,6; **3.12** 101,14.16-17.23.27-9.33.36; 102,4-5; 104,19-20; 105,8-9.12.18.23; **3.13** 107,9-10; 108,4; **fr.1 Vitelli** 91,25
aisthêtêrion, sense-organ, instrument of sensation **3.3** 82,35; 86,7; **3.6** 89,29-30; 90,4.6.10-11.13-17.19-20.24.26-30.34. 36.38-9; 91,5.9.11-12.16.18-19.21-2;

3.4 87,15; **3.12** 105,33; 106,39; **3.14** 112,20

antibatikos, resistant, **2.17** 62,4

antidosis, reciprocity, **2.21** 68,29

antikeisthai, be opposed, be opposite, **2.20** 64,8-9; **3.4** 87,13-14; **3.6** 90,16; **3.12** 101,16; **3.14** 111,12.15.17-19.33; 112,1

antikoptein, resist, **3.4** 87,15-16

antikrus, straight away, **3.6** 90,18

antilambanesthai, apprehend, **3.6** 91,4-5.8; **3.7** 92,21

antilegein, argue against, **fr.2** Vitelli 93,1

antilêpsis, apprehension, apprehend, **3.6** 91,4; **3.7** 91,30.32; 93,13; **3.8** 93,27

antilêptikos, apprehending, can apprehend **3.3**, 85,8; **3.12** 101,33

antimartureisthai, be counter-example, **3.12** 101,18

antiperistasis, mutual replacement, **3.10** 98,34; **3.14** 112,21

antithesis, contrast, **3.4** 87,18

antitupia, unyielding quality, **2.17** 62,3

aoristos, indeterminate, -acy, **3.5** 89,18; **3.14** 111,29; 112,15; **fr.1** Vitelli 92,6

apagein, lead, **fr.1** Vitelli 91,19.23

apaitein, ask, demand, **2.21** 70,7-8.11; **fr.1** Vitelli 92,2

apanaliskesthai, be consumed, **2.23** 73,14

apathês, that cannot be affected, **3.6** 91,23

apeinai, be absent, **3.12** 102,9-10.17-18

apeirakis, unlimited times, unlimited number, **3.12** 103,14; 104,7

apeiria, what is unlimited, unlimitedness, **3.12** 103,8.12; 104,15

apeiros, infinite, infinity, indefinite, unlimited **2.22** 71,5.10.15.19.24-5; 3 80,21; **3.5** 88,1.3.5.8.20.22.31; **3.7** 92,15.18; **3.12** 101,9-10; 102,26.28.30; 103,1.6-7.12-14.16-18.20-4.26-8. 31-2.35; 104,1.3-11; 106,2.25.28; **3.15** 116,8; **fr.1** Vitelli 92,3

apeiron, epi, indefinitely, **2.20** 65,3; **3.12** 103,25-6.33

apepsia, inconcoction, **3.14** 108,32; 109,11.17.<18>; 111,1.5.12.15-16.20.22.26.32; 112,1

apeptos, unconcocted, **3.10** 99,26.29.32.35.37; 100,2

aperigraphos, undelineable, **fr.1** Vitelli 92,7

aphairein, take away, subtract, **2.21** 69,8; **fr.1** Vitelli 91,23

aphairesis, subtraction, **fr.1** Vitelli 91,17-18.22-3

aphantastos, having no image, **3.12** 101,16

aphienai, emit, **2.23** 73,12-13.18.20.27.29; *aphiesthai*, give up, **2.21** 68,19

aphistasthai, stand aloof from, be removed from, abandon, **2.21** 67,16; 70,32-3; **3.12** 101,33-4; **fr.2** Vitelli 92,6-7

aphodos, receding, 80,8; **3.4** 87,1.8

aphtharsia, imperishability, **2.19** 63,28

aphthartos, imperishable, not subject to passing away **2.19** 63,19; **2.20** 64,23-4.30-1; **2.28** 78,20-1; **fr.2** Vitelli 93,14

apienai, depart, recede, **2.26** 76,29; **3.4** 87,3.6.21; **3.7** 92,30; **3.14** 113,24

apithanos, unconvincing, **fr.1** Vitelli 91,27-8

apoballein, lose, **2.24** 75,20

apodein, fall short, **2.21** 67,[28]

apodeixis, demonstration, **3.12** 105,36

apodidonai, give, state, explain, **2.27** 77,6.9; **3.3** 82,32; 85,7.21.30.34; 86,28.33; **3.10** 99,11; **3.14** 109,1.34; 114,20; 115,3.12-13

apokaiein, burn off, **2.23** 73,14

apokhôrein, recede, **3.4** 87,14

apokrinesthai, answer, give answer, **2.21** 65,22; 66,4.10; **3.12** 106,37

apokrisis, answer, answering, **2.21** 66,8.16; 68,17; 70,14-15

Apolloniatês, of Apollonia, **2.23** 73,11

apollusthai, be killed, **2.21** 66,30

apoluesthai, resolve, **3.15** 115,32

apoplêroun, complete, completion, **2.16** 61,23

107,27; 108,8; **3.14** 109,22; 110,20;
111,29; **3.15** 115,27.30; 116,9; **fr.1**
Vitelli 91,17; 92,12-13.17; **fr.2**
Vitelli 92,1; *autou*, here, **2.17** 62,7
auxein, increase, **3.12** 103,33-4; **fr.1**
Vitelli 91,18; 92,10
auxêsis, increase, **3.2** 81,26; **3.12**,
103,26
axios, deserving, right, worth, worthy
2.21 65,21; 68,17; 69,3; 70,1.15.19;
fr.1 Vitelli 91,16; **fr.2 Vitelli** 92,13
axioun, claim, think right, demand,
request, require **2.21** 67,8; 70,29;
3.9 96,12; **3.12** 104,16.22.30;
105,19.22; **fr.1 Vitelli** 91,6; **fr.2**
Vitelli 93,15

baros, heaviness, **3.10** 99,16
barus, heavy, **3.10** 100,14-15
basis, base, **2.18** 63,7
bathos, depth, **3.12** 106,5.23
bathron, bench, **2.20** 64,3
beltiôn, better, **3.3** 84,31-3; **3.4** 87,18;
3.12 105,35
bia, force, **2.23** 74,6.25
biaios, due to violence, **3.14** 109,19
biblion, book, **fr.2 Vitelli** 92,10
blepein, look, **3.9** 97,2-3
boêtheia, assistance, **2.19** 63,23
boêthein, support, **3.12** 101,29
boskein, pasture, **2.21** 67,34
boukolos, cowherd, **2.21** 67,32
boulê, deliberation, **3.13** 107,18.21
boulêsis, wish, **2.21** 67,15
boulesthai, wish, **2.21** 67,20.21; **3.3**
83,17; 85,16.18
bouleuesthai, deliberate, **3.13**
107,15.20.22.26.29-32.35-6;
108,5-6.12.14
bouleutikos, deliberative, capable of
deliberation **3.13** 107,8.18
bous, cow, cattle, **2.21** 67,33
brakhus, brief, compressed, **3.9**
96,11; **3.12** 105,5; 106,35; *en
brakhei*, briefly, **fr.1 Vitelli** 90,4

deiknunai, show, indicate, **2.18** 63,4;
2.21 65,19; 66,12;
· 70,12.16.20.22.25.27; 71,1;
2.22 71,9.34; **2.24** 75,33; 76,7-8;
2.26 76,26;
2.27 77,<5>.8.11-13.15.19.22.30;

2.28 79,14; **3** 80,14.17; **3.3**
83,10.17.23.27.31; 84,7.13-14.34;
85,2.21-2.35; 86,17.23 **3.5** 87,32;
88,23; **3.6** 89,26;
90,17.19-20.27.29-30.34; 91,12.17;
3.7 92,1.25.33; 93,8; **3.9** 94,10-11;
95,7.14.27.34; 96,8; **3.10** 98,29;
99,6.10.18.33 100,11; **3.12** 101,10;
105,5.13; 106,1.9.24.28.30-1; **3.14**
108,20.26; 111,27; 112,6; 114,15.29;
fr.2 Vitelli 92,9; 93,14-15
deiktikos, indicative, indication, **3.14**
114,35-115,1
dein, have to, must, should, ought
2.18 62,31; **2.21** 65,22; 66,4; **2.22**
71,17; 72,4; **2.24** 76,9; **3.2** 82,4.8; **3.3**
84,11; 85,18; 86,11.27.31; **3.4** 87,6;
3.6 91,2; **3.9** 95,22; **3.10** 99,30.32.37;
3.11 101,3.5; **3.12** 101,22.27; **3.14**
112,31; *dein, deisthai*, need, require,
2.16 61,18.27; **2.17** 62,9; **2.19**
63,12.14.16.21.23; **2.21** 67,7; 68,34;
3.2 81,28; **3.3** 86,9; **3.5** 89,19; **3.6**
91,9.21; **3.12** 106,19-20; **3.13** 107,12
deixis, demonstration, **2.27** 77,24
dekhesthai, admit, accept, receive,
2.20 64,10-12; **2.23** 73,8.20-2.25;
2.24 75,4; **2.28** 79,11; **3.3** 83,21-2;
3.7 92,28; **3.9** 95,23.26.37; 96,2;
97,20.22.28; 98,1.4; **3.11** 100,31;
3.12 103,1.7
dektikos, receptive, capable of
receiving or admitting **2.20** 65,13;
2.28 78,14; 79,8; **3.3** 85,1; **3.9**
95,29.36; **3.11** 100,30.33; **3.12**
106,12-13.16
dêlos, clear, **2.18** 62,16; **2.20** 65,8;
2.21 66,9; 67,11; 68,12.15-16; **3.3**
84,16; **3.10** 99,21; **3.11** 100,28; **3.12**
104,14.17; **3.13** 107,35; 108,12.16;
3.14 113,13; **3.15** 115,29
dêlôtikos, indicative, **2.22** 72,4; **3.3**
86,19; **3.5** 87,27
dêmiourgos, craftsman, **2.21** 66,32-3
Dêmokritos, Democritus, **2.23** 72,28
despotês, master, **2.21**
68,23.25.28-30.32-3
deuteros, second, secondary,
45,20.23; **2.21** 69,26; **2.22** 71,3;
2.24 74,31; **2.25** 76,11;
2.27 77,13.16.26-7.<29>; **3** 80,3.6;
3.2 81,4.8-9; **3.3** 82,21; 84,36; 85,25;

endidonai, surrender, **3.12** 106,35
enduesthai, penetrate, **2.23** 73,1
enekhesthai, be liable, **3.12** 104,18
energeia, activity, actuality, actual, actually, **2.18** 62,28-29.31-32; **2.20** 64,17.18; 65,8; **2.21** 66,24; 68,21-2.24.30-2.34; 69,4.12-13.20; **2.28** 79,11; **3.2** 81,<8>.18.23-4.27; 82,2.5.9.<10>.13.18-20; **3.3** 83,5-7.9.19.28; 84,1-2.4.10.17.20-1.27.36; 85,4.29; 86,1.9-10.13-14.17-18.22.24.31.33; **3.7** 92,4-5.8-11.20.33-4; 93,1.6.10.19; **3.9** 95,20; 96,2.35; **3.13** 108,4; **3.15** 116,2.4; **fr.1 Vitelli** 92,5.9
energein, be active, be actual; act, activity; perform actions, **2.21** 66,23; 68,22.24.30; 69,4.12.21; **2.24** 76,1; **3.2** 81,20.25; 82,15.19; **3.3** 83,22.24-5.30; 84,4; 85,18.24-5; 86,12; **3.7** 92,6; **3.9** 94,17
energês, active, **2.24** 76,2
enginesthai, come to be in, **3.9** 98,1
engus, near, **3.4** 87,3
enuparkhein, be present in, **3.14** 113,2
eniausios, yearly, **3.4** 87,20
enistasthai, resist, **3.12** 101,22
enkatamignunai, mix in, **3.10** 100,3.5
ennoia, thought, **2.21** 66,32
enstasis, objection, **3.12** 101,24
entautha, here, in the sublunary region, **2.21** 70,1-2; **3.6** 90,1
entelekheia, actuality, actual, actually, **2.27** 77,7.9-10.13; **3.2** 80,5; 81,7.12.15; **3.3** 83,16-17.31; 84,6-7; 85,32; 86,30.34; **3.14** 112,13
entos, internal, **3.14** 112,36; 113,1.6
enudros, living in water, **3.6** 91,7.15
enulos, possessing matter, enmattered, **2.24** 75,5; **2.28** 78,13.27; 79,10.13; **3.12** 106,26-7
epagesthai, attract, **3.14** 110,7
epagôgê, induction, **2.27** 77,28
epainein, praise, **3.13** 108,4-5.7
epainos, praise, **3.13** 108,6
epaktos, added, **3.14** 112,33
epanienai, go back to, **3.14** 112,30
epekeina, beyond, **3.12** 101,11.19; 104,17; 105,20.30

epekhein, hold back, **2.23** 72,24
epêreazein, behave with contempt, **fr.1 Vitelli** 92,7
epharmozein, fit, **3.3** 85,21; **3.9** 97,9
ephelkesthai, attract, **2.23** 74,12
ephesis, desire, **2.19** 63,20;2.23 74,25
ephexês, next, **3.3** 83,7.15.32; **3.6** 91,12; **3.9** 95,13; **3.14** 113,33; 114,17
ephiesthai, desire, **2.23** 74,29
ephistasthai, attend to, **fr.1 Vitelli** 90,3-4
epi, depending on, up to (other meanings not indexed), **2.16** 61,19.27; **2.17** 62,11*; **2.21** 70,4; **3** 80,22; **3.3** 85,14-15.17.20; **3.13** 107,5-7.21.25.27.31; 108,5.7.12-14.16
epiballein, impinge, **3.9** 96,34
epididonai, progress, **3.3** 86,21.26
epidosis, progression, progress, 80,5; **3.2** 81,6.12.22; **3.3** 84,1.5.10.18.24
epidromê, summary, 80,23; **3.14** 108,17; 115,[23]
epiginesthai, happen to, supervene, **2.28** 79,17; **3.14** 112,29
epigraphê, heading, **fr.2 Vitelli** 92,10.13
epigraphein, title, **3.14** 108,21-2
epikheirêsis, attempt to show, attempt to argue, 80,20; **3.11** 100,25; **3.12** 105,17.22
epikhusis, influx, **3.10** 99,4
epikratein, upper hand, gain, **2.20** 64,21; 65,15
epikrinein, form a judgement, **fr.1 Vitelli** 90,4
epilambanein, note in addition, **3.3** 83,15-16; **3.6** 90,30
epimeleia, concern, **2.21** 65,20
epinoia, thought, thinking, **2.28** 79,18; **3.12** 106,7
epipedon, surface, **3.12** 106,22
epiphaneia, surface, **3.14** 112,20-1
epipherein, add, **3.9** 95,33-4; 96,9
epipolazein, be on surface, **2.23** 74,8; **3.10** 99,15
epipômatizein, rest on like lid, **2.23** 72,13.23
epirrhein, flow in, **3.10** 99,4
episkepsis, consideration, **fr.2 Vitelli** 92,2
epispasthai, draw to self, draw in, **2.23** 73,23; 74,8-9; **3.14** 110,7

epistasis, attention, **2.21** 71,2

epistasthai, understand, **3.3** 83,27

epistêmê, knowledge, science, understanding 80,4; **3.2** 81,5-6.11; 82,5; **3.3**, 83,22; 84,4.7; 85,2.9; **3.11** 100,30-3; **3.12** 102,27; **fr.1 Vitelli** 91,26

epistêmôn, knowledgeable, understanding, **3.3** 83,20-4.26; **3.11** 100,33; **fr.1 Vitelli** 91,4

epistêtos, understood, **3.12** 102,28

epitasis, intensification, **2.17** 62,3

epitêdeiotês, suitability, **3.2** 81,10

epithumêtos, object of desire, **2.23** 74,21

epitrekhein, attack, **fr.2 Vitelli** 92,6

epitropeuein, oversee, **fr.2 Vitelli** 93,12

epizêtein, look for, ask, **2.21** 70,17; **2.23** 72,17

epokheisthai, float upon, **3.14** 114,21; 115,21

epônumia, name, **3.2** 81,16

êremein, stay at rest, be at rest, **2.18** 62,21; **3.14** 110,17

ergazesthai, produce, **3.14** 110,29

ergon, effect, function, product, task, **2.16** 61,25; **2.20** 64,8-9.15; **2.28** 79,17; **3.13** 107,34; 108,6; **3.14** 108,31; 111,3.5; *ergon poieisthai*, make it one's business, **2.21** 70,25

erôtan, ask, put or pose question, **2.21** 65,22; 66,5; 68,17; 70,12-13; **3.12** 101,17; **fr.1 Vitelli** 91,6.28*; 92,1

erôtêsis, question, **2.21** 66,11-13.21; 67,8; 68,17*; 70,13

eskhatos, last, ultimate, **2.22** 71,12.19.30; **3.9** 96,31; 97,5.10.14

ethelein, thelein, willing, be, **2.23** 72,27; **3.12** 101,10

ethnos, nation, **3.11** 101,6

eti, longer, moreover, still, **3.5** 88,21; **3.12** 103,34; 104,13*; 105,7; **3.15** 115,27*

eu einai, well-being, **2.19** 63,14.16.22

eukinêtos, easily moved, **2.23** 72,32

eukratos, well blended, **3.14** 110,26

eulogos, reasonable, plausible, **2.17** 62,8; **2.18** 62,36; **2.23** 74,1; **3.2** 82,6; **3.7** 93,11; **3.12** 102,6; 106,20; **3.13** 107,23; **3.14** 109,<16>; 111,1; 113,22; **fr.1 Vitelli** 91,21; **fr.2 Vitelli** 93,1

euporein, advantage, gain, **2.21** 70,31

eutaktos, orderly, **2.19** 63,24-6

euthus, in straight line, **2.22** 72,1; **3.5** 87,30.32-88,1.5.10-11.20.22-3; **3.9** 96,15.22.30; *euthus, eutheôs*, at once, straight away, **3.2** 82,18-19; **3.3** 85,2; **3.12** 104,1; **fr.2 Vitelli** 93,17

exaptein, kindle, **2.17** 62,7; **3.14** 110,19

exatmizein, evaporate, **3.14** 113,30; 114,3.26.32; 114,26; 115,13

exêgêsis, explanation, commentary, 45,20.23.24; **2.22** 71,3; **2.24** 74,31; **2.25** 76,12; **3** 80,3.6.12.14.17; **3.2** 81,4.17; **3.3** 82,21; **3.6** 89,25; **3.7** 91,24; **3.9** 94,10

exetazein, examine, **3.12** 106,36

exienai, depart, pass outwards, **2.23** 74,11; **3.14** 110,5; 113,35

exikmazein, dry moisture out of, **2.23** 74,27

existasthai, depart, **2.18** 62,27

exô, outside, **2.23** 73,3; **3.7** 93,22; **3.12** 104,17; 106,34

exôthen, outside, from outside, **2.20** 64,13; 65,14; **2.23** 73,12; **3.3** 85,5; **3.7** 93,13; **3.12** 102,21-2

exousia, power, **3.13** 107,36

gala, milk, **3.14** 114,[33].35; 115,1

gê, earth, land, **2.24** 75,13; **3.6** 90,28; 91,17; **3.10** 98,22.26.28; 99,1.9.11-12.29; 100,1.3; **3.14** 108,19; 110,4; 112,17; 113,15.26.35 114,8.14-16.19.32-5; 115,2.20

genesis, coming-to-be, origin, 45,20; **2.18** 62,19; **2.20** 64,6.13.31; 65.6-8; **2.21** 68,20; 70,14; **2.22** 71,3.10; **2.24** 75,17; **2.28** 79,15; **3** 80,8-9; **3.2** 81,29-31; 82,1-3.7-8; **3.3** 84,23.28; **3.4** 87,2-5.7.10-11.13-15.17.19; **3.5** 87,25; 88,9.18.20; 89,20.22; **3.10** 100,12; **3.14** 108,18.20.23; 109,2.11; 110,27.30.32-3.35; 114,8; 115,17; **fr.2 Vitelli** 93,12

genêtos, subject to coming-to-be, that has come to be, **2.18** 62,19; **2.19** 63,23; **2.20** 64,1.24

hamartanein, do wrong, misdeed,
  3.13 108,15
hapas, all, **2.20** 64,20.27; **3.12** 101,21;
  3.14 109,18; **fr.1 Vitelli** 92,9
haphê, touch, contact, **2.23** 74,6; **3.6**
  89,27-8.31; 90,8-9.21; **3.8** 93,31
haplous, simple, **2.20**
  64,24.26.28-9.32; 65,12; **2.24**
  75,5.17; **2.28** 78,24; **3.6** 89,32;
  90,2.25.27.31; 91,13.20; **3.12**
  106,2.25.28; **3.14** 108,24; 109,2;
  haplôs, without qualification, **2.18**
  62,32; **2.21** 67,[25]; **2.22**
  71,6.12-14.20; 72,5-6; **3** 80,10; **3.5**
  87,22.24; 88,5.26.32.34; **3.8** 94,5;
  3.12 103,22; **fr.1 Vitelli** 92,4
haptesthai, touch, be in contact,
  come into contact **2.23** 74,7.11; **3.6**
  89,30.32; 90,21.23.31; **3.12** 104,1
haptikos, of touch, **3.6** 90,24
haptos, tangible, that can be touched,
  3.6 89,28; 90,8-9.33; **3.9** 95,5
harmonia, joining together, **2.20**
  64,38
hêgeisthai, think, **2.21** 67,8; 70,30;
  fr.2 Vitelli 93,10
heis, one, single (only significant
  usages indexed), **2.21** 68,10; **3.7**
  92,33; **3.9** 94,20-1.24;
  95,8.13.21.28-9.32-3.35;
  96,10.13.16.18-20.26.29.36;
  97,12.15-16.18; 98,8.10.12.14; **3.12**
  103,24.27; 104,9; 106,6; **fr.1 Vitelli**
  91,20.22-3; 92,17
hekastos, each, every, **2.17** 62,14;
  2.21 68,9; **2.22** 71,16.31; **2.23** 73,17;
  2.24 75,4-5.28; **2.27** 77,17; **2.28**
  78,13.17; **3.2** 81,23-4.31; **3.3** 82,26;
  85,7; 86,2; **3.4** 87,10-11; **3.5** 89,20;
  3.7 92,13; **3.8** 94,3; **3.9** 94,28; **3.9**
  96,17.25; 97,15.18; 98,9.15; **3.10**
  99,13-14; **3.11** 100,29; **3.12**
  101,26.31; 103,29; 104,6.8-9.12; **3.14**
  108,26.29; 109,3.32.35;
  110,5.8.11.19; 111,8.11.19.33; **fr.1
  Vitelli** 91,7.9.14.30
hekateros, each (of two), both, **2.21**
  68,33; **3.3** 85,3; **3.9** 97,4; **3.12**
  102,16; **3.14** 108,29.32; 110,1; 112,15
hêlios, sun, **2.23** 74,18.20; **3** 80,8; **3.4**
  87,1.3.11.20; **3.10** 98,22.24; 99,14;
  100,2

helkein, attract, **2.23** 72,9;
  73,9.11-12.15.17-20.22.24.26.28-31;
  74,1.3-5.9.14.16-17.20.23.25
helxis, attracting, **2.23** 73,23
hêmera, day, **3.10** 99,14
hêmisus, half, **3.12** 103,32
heneka, for sake of, **2.21**
  67,18.19.20.[27]; 68,24; **3.2** 81,24;
  heneka tou, for sake of something,
  3.12 102,21; 103,3
henoun, unify, **2.20** 64,33; **3.14** 114,8
hepesthai, follow, be consequent,
  2.16 61,12.14.18; **2.21** 66,33; 69,32;
  70,3.22; **2.22** 71,21.30; **2.23**
  72,14.17-18; 73,4.31; **3.5** 89,14.17;
  3.6 90,16-17; **3.7** 93,20-1; **3.12**
  102,28; 103,14; 104,15; 105,7.36;
  3.13 107,10.20.26; **3.15** 116,12; **fr.2
  Vitelli** 93,5
hepsein, boil, **3.14** 111,31; 115,1-2
hepsêsis, boiling, **3.14**
  111,5.15.28.31-3
Hêrakleia, Heracleia, 45,22; **2.23** 72,9
Hêrakleides, Heraclides, **fr.2 Vitelli**
  92,1
hetairoi, companions, **2.21** 65,18
heteros, one (of two), the other,
  another, second, different,
  (something) else, **2.21** 67,[27]; **2.22**
  71,7; **2.23** 72,28; **2.24** 75,1; **2.28**
  78,5.23.30; **3.2** 81,13.17; **3.3**
  84,11.22; **3.6** 89,33; 90,35; 91,9; **3.7**
  91,27; **3.14** 108,29; *heteros ...
  heteros*, one ... the other, **3.9** 96,3-4
hetoimos, ready, **2.21** 65,21
hêtton, less, **3.14** 110,20
heuresis, discovery, **3.1** 81,2
heuriskein, find, discover, **2.21**
  66,29-30; 70,10; **3.9** 95,2; 96,30-1;
  3.13 108,2; **fr.1 Vitelli** 90,4
hexês, next, **3.7** 92,32; **3.14** 112,21
hexis, disposition, **3.2**
  81,9.10.20.23-4.27.29;
  82,2.11-14.17-18; **3.3**
  84,2.20.25.27.31.35.37-8; 85,1-2.24;
  86,22
hidrôs, sweat, **3.10** 98,24.26; 99,22.27
hikanos, adequate, sufficient, **2.21**
  67,8; 70,18; **2.27** 77,8; **3.11** 101,7;
  3.12 102,3.7.24; 105,27
hipponomos, horse-trainer, **2.21**
  67,33

hippos, horse, **3.5** 88,13; **3.12** 103,3.6

histasthai, be at rest, stand, stop, be permanent, **2.18** 62,36; 63,7; **2.25** 76,19; **3.5** 88,3-4 89,9; **3.12** 105,33

historia, recorded observations, **3.10** 100,20

hodos, route, **2.24** 75,33; path, **3.14** 109,13

hoion, hoionei, as it were, for example, that is (= i.e.), 80,24; **3.6** 89,33; 90,23; **3.15** 115,25-6.30-1.33-5; 116,1.3-4.6.8.10; **fr.1** Vitelli 91,28 92,9

hoios, like, **3.3** 85,31, 86,34; *hoios te*, possible, able, can, **2.20** 64,30; **2.21** 65,34; 66,1; 70,5*.15.17.29; **2.22** 72,1; **2.28** 78,16; **3.3** 85,8; **3.5** 88,5.8.11.13.23.33; **3.6** 90,19.28; 91,5.12.16.18.20; **3.7** 92,8; **3.9** 94,15-16.17; 95,7.9.11.21.34; 96,32.37; 97,6.22; 98,2-3; **3.11** 100,28; **3.12** 102,32; 103,2.16.36; 104,24; 105,11; 106,1-2.4.21.25-6; **fr.1** Vitelli 90,3

holkê, attraction, **2.23** 74,5

holos, whole, altogether, **2.25** 76,19; **2.28** 78,33; **3.12** 101,26; 102,7-16.21; 107,2; **fr.1** Vitelli 91,7.14-15; *oud' holôs*, not at all, **2.19** 63,15; **2.24** 75,6; **3.8** 94,4

homalos, unvarying, **2.18** 62,29

homoios, similar, like, alike, 45,8; **2.16** 61,1.5.8.10-11.21; **2.18** 62,34; **2.21** 67,33; 68,3; **2.22** 71,17; **2.23** 72,29-30; 73,1.8.10; 74,4.22; **2.27** 77,24; **2.28** 78,6.37; **3** 80,6.8; **3.3** 82,21.30; 83,6.11-12.15.20.23; 84,1.5; 85,4.7.24.32-3; 86,6.16.22.35; **3.4** 87,1; **3.5** 89,13.16.18; **3.7** 93,16; **3.9** 94,28; 95,4.24; 96,29; 97,7.14.16; **3.10** 100,2; **3.12** 101,30; 103,9; 105,10.28; 106,22; **3.14** 110,9.12.16.27; 111,9; **3.15** 115,26-7

homoiotês, similarity, **2.23** 73,4

homoioun, like, alike, make, **2.18** 62,28; **3.3** 85,33

homologein, agree, admit, **2.21** 68,12; **3.12** 105,10; **fr.1** Vitelli 91,21

homônumia, identity of names, **3.11** 101,8

homou, together, **2.21** 70,33; **3.9** 97,33

hopoios, sort of thing, of the sort,

such as, **3.12** 106,23; **3.13** 107,16; **3.14** 114,10

hopoteros, whichever, **3.14** 112,10

horan, see, **2.20** 64,2; 65,12; **2.21** 69,2; **2.23** 74,24; **3.3** 85,7; **3.7** 91,26-7.33-4; 92,2-3.5-7.15.20-1.23.27-8.30; 93,15.17; **3.9** 97,4; **3.12** 103,10-11; 104,29; **fr.1** Vitelli 91,30-2; 92,10

horatikos, of sight, **3.7** 92,8.20

horatos, that can be seen, object of sight, **3.6** 90,33; 91,14; **3.7** 91,34; 92,7-8.23; **3.9** 95,3

horizein, define, determine, (make) determinate **2.16** 61.20; **2.21** 67,4; **3.5** 89,4.9.12.14.18; **3.12** 102,17; **3.14** 109,25.27-8; 110,35.20; 111,11.28.31; 112,14.18.22-3; **fr.1** Vitelli 91,25; 92,1-3

hormê, impulse, **3.12** 107,2

horos, determination, **fr.1** Vitelli 92,2

hôsautôs, in same way, same, **fr.1** Vitelli 91,22.27

hosos, as many as, as much as, all, **3.6** 89,30; 90,21; **3.10** 98,31; 99,26; 100,<9>.17; **3.12** 102,7; 104,12; **3.13** 108,10; **3.14** 112,9.32-3; 113,20.35; 114,1.6.14-15.21.29.31; 115,8-10.12; *hoson*, as far as, **3.13** 107,17

hudatôdês, watery, **3.14** 114,26-7

hudôr, water, rain, **2.23** 72,26; 74,8.18; 75,13; **3.6** 89,33; 90,23.26.31; 91,6-7.13-14.16; **3.10** 98,18.25.27.30.34; 99,7.9-10.12.17-19.23.31-2.35; 100,3-4.6.8.10-11.14.22-3; **3.14** 108,19; 110,23; 111,29-30; 112,16.32-3; 113,9.11-12.14-15.18.20.25-6; 114,10.12.14.18.21.24.28.30.33-4; 115,8-10.20.21

huein, rain, rain-water, **3.10** 100,<9>.10

hugeia, health, **fr.1** Vitelli 92,17

hugiês, sound, **2.21** 66,10; **3.5** 88,21

hugrainesthai, become moist, be made moist, **3.14** 112,27, 113,7-9

hugros, moist, moisture, **2.23** 73,17-19.24.27; 74,11.16; **3.14** 108,33; 109,8.25.28; 110,6-7.31.34; 111,29; 112,8.12.14.16;

113,3.10.16.18.24-5.30-1;
114,3.7.9.32; 115,14-15
hugrotês, moisture, **2.23** 73,25; **3.10**
98,21; **3.14** 108,25.28; 109,4.20-2;
111,20.27-8; 112,6
hulê, matter, material, 45,27; **2.17**
62,3.6.11; **2.20** 64,7-8.17.20; 65,13;
2.24 74,33;
75,3.6.9-11.13.17.20.23-4.34-5;
76,7.9; **2.27** 77,5.27.30; **2.28** 77,31-2;
78,2.7.9.12.16.20.22.30-2.37;
79,1.10.15-16; **3.5** 89,15; **3.7**
92,29.35; 93,2.11; **3.9** 95,21; **3.12**
106,12.21; **3.14** 109,3.7.9-10; 110,32;
111,19; 112,24; **3.15** 116,9; **fr.1**
Vitelli 90,2, 91,1; timber, **3.10**
99,30; *prôtê hulê*, prime matter,
2.24 75,6-8.(18)
hulikos, material, **3.3** 84,25.27.37
huparkhein, be, exist, belong, be
property, be present, **2.18**, 62,15;
3.9 94,21; **3.11** 100,29; **3.12**
101,25-6; 104,28-9; 106,10; **3.14**
111,29; **fr.1** Vitelli 91,6-8.14
huparxis, real existence, **3.12** 106,11
hupeikein, yield, **3.14** 112,20-1
hupekkauma, heavenly fire, 45,11;
2.17 61,29.32
hupenantios, subordinate contrary,
3.4 87,9
hupenantiousthai, resist, **3.13**
107,34
huperballein, surpass, be excessive,
3.12 104,14; **3.14** 114,4
huperekhein, exceed, **3.12** 103,19.24
hupêresia, service, **3.2** 81,28
hupertithesthai, postpone, pass
over, **2.21** 70,6; **3.3** 85,19
huphistasthai, exist, **2.17** 62,13;
2.28 79,15-16; **3.12** 106,3.21
huphizanein, settle out, **3.10** 99,21
hupiskhneisthai, profess, **2.21** 70,34
hupo, under, falling under, **2.21**
68,7.10; **2.28** 77,33; 79,3; **3.3** 84,23;
3.14 111,13-14.<15>.16
hupokeisthai, underlie, be subject,
be supposed, **2.20**
64,10.14.16-18.20.28; 65,12-13; **2.22**
72,6; **2.24** 75,7-9.13.17.25; 76,8; **2.27**
77,6.23-4.27; **2.28** 78,8.10.17-18.26;
79,8; **3.6** 90,16; **3.7** 92,29; **3.8** 94,7;
3.14 110,30; 111,3; *hupokeimenon*,

substrate, subject, **2.26** 76,26.30;
3.9 95,31; **3.14** 109,3.9-10
hupolambanein, suppose, think,
2.21 70,29; **3.9** 97,33; **3.10** 99,8.37;
3.12 103,15
hupoleipein, leave, leave behind, be
remaining, be retarded, **3.5** 89,9-10;
3.10 98,23; 99,16; **3.12** 103,18; **3.14**
109,23; 114,26
hupomenein, remain, remain behind,
2.28 78,35; **3.7** 92,30; **3.10** 100,7.9
hupomimnêskein, remind, **2.21**
66,18; **3.14** 108,23; 112,8.24
hupomnêma, commentary, 45,21;
2.22 71,5
hupostasis, existence, real existence,
reality, **2.24** 75,18; **2.28** 78,19-20;
79,16; **3.3** 85,9-11; **3.12** 106,6;
excrement, **3.10** 99,36; 100,1.18-19
hupothesis, supposition, **3.12** 104,15;
105,31; *ex hupotheseos*,
conditionally, **2.22** 71,7.16; **3** 80,10;
3.5 87,22; 89,1
hupotithesthai, suppose, make
supposition, **2.23** 72,30; **3.12** 101,10;
104,1; 105,29.31-2.35
hupsêlos, high, **3.10** 99,2.4
hustera, womb, **2.23** 74,14
husteron, later, subsequently, **2.21**
68,13; **2.22** 71,6.9-11.23.29.32;
72,7-8; **3.5** 88,15.21-2.25-9.31-5;
89,1-2.4.23-4; **3.6** 90,30; **3.12** 103,2

idios, own, proper, peculiar,
characteristic, **2.16** 61,25; **2.23**
72,18; **3.3** 85,10; **3.7** 92,12; 93,19;
3.8 93,25; **3.9** 96,25; **3.12** 102,4.31;
fr.1 Vitelli 91,2; *idiâi*, individually,
3.3 82,26; **3.12** 104,8; *kat' idian*,
individually, **3.3** 86,2-3
idiotês, property, **3.10** 99,25
ienai, go, travel, **2.22** 71,5; **3.10** 99,8;
ienai epi, go on to, **3.3** 85,30; **3.14**
110,27-8; 112,23
ikmas, moisture, **2.23** 73,12.16.30;
74,1
iousthai, rust, **2.23** 73,15
isarithmos, equal in number, **3.6**
90,34
isemeria, equinox, **3.5** 89,6-7
isos, equal, equivalent, **2.16** 61,15;
2.22 71,24; **3.3** 84,12-13; 85,34; **3.12**

83,2; **3.9** 94,13.23.29; 96,23-4; 97,6;
3.12 103,10; 106,4.7; **3.14** 113,22;
114,2; 115,1
khrênai, must, **2.21** 65,22; 70,8; **2.27**
77,17; **3.2** 82,4.7; **3.3** 84,14.30; **3.12**
102,1; 105,3; 106,35; **3.13** 108,2;
3.14 111,10
khrêsimos, useful, **3.3** 82,32; 83,12-13
khrêsthai, use, make use of, **2.24**
75,33; **3.3** 85,27; 86,27; **3.7**
92,24.[32]; **3.9** 94,22; **3.12** 101,35;
102,2; 105,12.23.36-106,1; **3.13**
108,13
khriein, smear, **2.23** 73,15-16
khrôma, colour, **3.7** 92,3.5.21.24; **3.12**
106,14
khrônnunai, colour, **3.7** 92,22-4.27-8
khronos, time, **2.23** 74,27; **3.5** 89,12;
3.9 95,14; 96,3; 97,31; **3.12** 105,15;
3.14 114,25
khrusos, gold, **fr.1 Vitelli** 91,30
khumos, flavour, **3.10** 98,27; 99,20;
3.12 106,15
kibdêlos, counterfeit, **2.21** 65,34
kinein, move, change, influence, raise
(point), **2.18** 62,30.34-37; 63,1.3;
2.19 63,20; **2.21** 65,29-30; 69,9; **2.23**
72,13.19-21.23.27; 73,2.3;
74,2.6.11.23-4; **2.25** 76,19; **3.2**
81,25-6; 82,8; **3.3** 82,27; 83,8.18;
84,15-16; 86,5.11-14; **3.5** 89,5; **3.7**
93,2-3; **3.9** 95,25; **3.14** 110,14.16.18;
fr.1 Vitelli 92,10
kinêsis, movement, motion, change,
45,14; **2.18**
62,15-16.20.21-2.25.29.31; 63,2.4;
2.19 63,20.25; **2.25** 76,14.16,21-2;
3.2 81,18.19.26.28-9;
82,3-4.6-8.16.20; **3.3** 82,27; 83,19;
84,22; 86,2.13; **3.5** 89,11.14.16-17;
3.7 93,2.4; **3.9** 95,25; 96,35;
97,14.16-17; **3.10** 98,22.24.34;
99,2.5.14; **3.12** 105,14; **3.13** 108,4;
3.14 109,32; 110,19; 112,25
kinêtikos, causing change, **3.3** 83,9
koilia, gut, **3.10** 100,19
koilos, hollow, **3.10** 99,3
koimasthai, be asleep, **3.12** 105,28
koinônein, share, **2.18** 62,32; **2.21**
68,11
koinônia, sharing, **2.28** 78,34
koinos, common, general, sharing in,

2.20 64,20; **2.21** 68,9; **2.28** 77,32-3;
78,1.3.7-9.12-13.15.19.28; 79,3.5; **3.3**
85,12-13.21-22.25; 86,27; **3.13**
108,1; **3.14** 110,27; 111,12.31;
114,33-4; *koinêi*, in general, **3.3**
82,23; *koinoteron*, in broader sense,
3.3 84,18
kolasis, punishment, **3.13** 108,15
kôluein, prevent, **3.9** 97,25-6 98,4;
3.12 101,12-13; 105,20; 106,37-8
komêtês, hairy man, **fr.1 Vitelli** 91,12
konia, lye, **3.10** 100,18; **3.14** 114,31
kopros, dung, **3.14** 110,4
korê, pupil (of eye), **3.6** 91,14; **3.9** 97,3
kosmos, world, 45,15; **2.19**
63,8.10.15.17.25; **2.20** 64,1;
65,7.10-11; **3.12** 101,11-12;
104,6.8.12; 106,31-3
kouphos, light, **2.23** 74,9.13; **3.10**
99,14; 100,4
krasis, blending, **2.20** 64,25; **3.12**
106,30
kratein, control, overcome, prevail
3.10, 99,29; **3.12** 102,20-1.24; **3.12**
105,30; **3.14** 109,7.9-10.21.27;
110,13-14.17.22.33.35
krinein, judge, judging, **3.9**
94,13.21.23.26.29-32;
95,2-3.6-7.9.12-13.15.17-19.24.27-8;
96,4.19.23.<24>.27;
97,11.26.28.30.36; 98,1.5.10-11;
3.13 107,14
krisis, judging, judgement, **3.9** 95,1.7;
97,18.26.29.32.34; 98,3.6.10; **3.13**
107,14
kritikos, judging, judge, **3.9** 96,25
kubernan, govern, **2.19** 63,26
kuklophorêtikos, moving in circle,
3.12 106,27
kuklos, cycle, circle, 80,11;
3.5 87,23.25; 88,18; 89,3.4.14;
3.9 96,15-16.29
kurios, in control, **3.11** 100,35; **3.13**
107,31.35.37; 108,1.11; principal,
3.6 90,3; proper, in proper sense,
2.18 62,35; **2.21** 65,26-7.30; **2.24**
75,7-8; **3.2** 82,14-15; **3.3** 83,18.25;
85,28.34-5; 86,28; **3.4**
87,10.13-14.17; **3.12** 106,8; **3.13**
108,3; **3.14** 109,15.17; 110,33
kuros, confirmation, **fr.1 Vitelli**
92,11.15

kustis, bladder, **3.10** 99,20

lambanein, apprehend, assume, collect, conclude, get, include, infer, note, reach, receive, suppose, take, take on, **2.22** 71,22.33; 72,2.8; **2.23** 72,30; **2.24** 76,1.3.6; **2.27** 77,2-4.24.28; **2.28** 78,1.12.18; 79,9.13; **3.3** 82,26.28; 83,4-6.9.33; 84,12; 86,4.8.10.13; **3.5** 88,4; **3.6** 90,11.18.20.24.37; 91,10; **3.7** 92,27; 93,13.17; **3.9** 94,25; 95,5.12.18.21.27; 96,5.14.18.21.28.30; 97,7.19; **3.10** 98,28; 99,22-3.30.33; **3.12** 102,13; 104,19.26-7; 105,7; 106,8.11; 107,2; **3.14** 112,14-15.25.28.30.32.34; 113,8; 114,12.29; **3.15** 115,30; **fr.1 Vitelli** 91,25.29

lanthanein, escape notice, **fr.2 Vitelli** 92,12

legein, say, speak, state; apply (term), call, discuss, express, give (explanation, reason), have as position, mean, mention, put forward, utter, **2.16** 61,4; **2.17** 61,33; 62,9; **2.20** 64,1; **2.21** 65,21.23-5.27-9.31-4; 66,5.7.9.14-15.19-22.25-6; 67,4.10.14.16.30; 68,5.7-9.12-15.18-19.21-3.27.29.34; 69,2.11.15.19.21.29.32-3; 70,3.8.10.13.16.21.24.28.31; 71,1-2; **2.22** 71,26.28.34; **2.23** 72,12.19-20.25-6; 73,9; 74,5; **2.24** 74,32; 75,2.4.29.31; **2.25** 76,20.22; **2.27** 77,2.18.20-1.25-6.29; **3** 80,3.7; **3.2** 81,5.8.10.13.17.30; 82,5.7; **3.3** 82,22-4.26; 83,4.8.18.20.22-7.35; 84,5.11.13-14.19.29-30.33.36; 85,4.20-3.26.31.34; 86,3.4.11.13.21.27.29.31; **3.4** 87,17; **3.5** 88,12; 89,9.12; **3.6** 89,33; 90,4.6.9.13.23; **3.7** 92,14.31.33; **3.8** 93,28-9; 95,33; 96,7.8.12.27; 97,5.9.35; **3.10** 98,17.20-1; 99,8.31; **3.11** 101,3-4; **3.12** 101,14; 102,5.8.12-13.16; 103,15-17.26.28; 104,1-2.5; 105,8-9.14; 106,5-6.12.37-8; 107,23; 108,1.3; **3.14** 108,18.31-2.34; 109,15.<18>.34; 110,20.23.27-8;

111,1-2.7.10-12.14-17.23.25.31.34-112,1; 112,5.13.19.23.28.31; 113,5.7.12.33; 114,5.9.22.34; 115,6.16.18.20.[23]; **3.15** 115,31.33.35; 116,12; **fr.1 Vitelli** 91,1.24; 92,1.9; **fr.2 Vitelli** 92,2.7.11*.14; 93,2.5.7.13.16; *legein ti*, have a point, **3.12** 104,22; *legein ... kata*, criticise, **fr.2 Vitelli** 92,3

leipein, be lacking, be missing, **3.6** 90,20.30; **3.14** 115,[23]; leave, **3.12** 104,<2>

lêpsis, reception, **3.7** 93,10.16; **3.9** 96,6-7

leptos, fine, **2.23** 72,31; **3.10** 99,13

leptotês, fineness, **2.23** 73,3

leukainein, make whiter, **3.14** 114,26

leukos, white, whiteness, **2.21** 69,8; **3.9** 94,17-18.27; 97,3.21.29-30.33-5

leukotês, whiteness, **3.9** 95,23.26

lexis, passage, 45,20.23-4.<25-6>; **2.22** 71,3.5; **2.24** 74,31; **2.25** 76,11; **2.26** 76,24.27; **2.27** 77,1; **3** 80,3.6.12.14.17; **3.2** 81,4; **3.3** 82,21; **3.6** 89,25; **3.7** 91,24; **3.9** 94,10; 96,11

limên, harbour, **3.10** 100,21

lithos, magnet, 45,22; **2.23** 72,9.11-12.15.18.20-1.23.30-1; 73,3-4.6-7.18.24.26.29; 74,6.12.14-15.20.25-7; stone, **3.14** 114,8.17; 115,5; **fr.1 Vitelli** 91,11

logikos, rational, **3.13** 107,6-8

logos, argument, account, discussion, reply; reason, reasonable, rational; logically, **2.21** 65,18; 66,7.35; 67,7; 70,6-7.19.24.27.30.34; **2.25** 76,13; **2.27** 77,6.9.18.20; **2.28** 78,33; 79,2; **3.3** 82,25; 85,22.27.30.34; 86,27-8.33; **3.6** 90,4; **3.7** 92,34; 93,16; **3.9** 95,29.35; **3.12** 101,10.18.22.32.34; 105,4.12.16.18.36; 106,9; **3.13** 107,13-14; 108,2; **3.14** 109,34; 110,28; 111,14; 112,6.30; **fr.1 Vitelli** 90,1; 91,1-3.5.10.17.19.23.26.29; 92,17; **fr.2 Vitelli** 92,1.7.8; book (division of work), **3.2** 81,4; proportion, **3.14** 109,5.9; *logou epikheirêsis*, dialectical attempt, **3.12** 105,17.22

loipos, result, **3.12** 103,31; *loipon*, thereafter, **3.5** 88,7

peripiptein, encounter, come to attention of, **3.12** 101,18.20

peristasis, circumstance, **2.20** 65,14

periteinesthai, extend around, **3.10** 99,12

perittôma, residue, **3.10** 99,32.35; 100,16.20

perittôsis, residue, **3.10** 100,2.6.11

pessein, pettein, concoct, **3.14** 109,21; 110,34; 111,20.36

pêxis, solidification, **3.14** 112,23.26.30; 113,13.22.28; 115,10

phainesthai, appear, become apparent, be seen, seem, **2.21** 66,9; 70,20; **3.10** 99,21; **3.12** 103,9; 104,23; 105,24.27; **3.13** 107,16; 108,1-2; **3.15** 115,28; **fr.1 Vitelli** 91,5

phalakros, bald man, **fr.1 Vitelli** 91,12

phanai, say, speak, assert, **2.20** 64,1; **2.21** 65,25; 66,20; 67,6; 68,5.16-17; 69,27; 70,6.9.11.18; **2.23** 73,12; **3.8** 93,30; **3.10** 98,24; **3.12** 101,35; 106,13.23; **3.14** 111,3; 112,31; 114,9; **fr.1 Vitelli** 91,2.16; **fr.2 Vitelli** 92,4; 93,10; *ou phanai*, deny, **2.21** 65,24

phaneros, apparent, clear, **2.21** 66,12; **2.24** 76,5; **3.3** 85,27; **3.10** 98,35; 99,1; **fr.2 Vitelli** 92,11

phantasia, appearance, image, impression, **3.7** 92,31; **3.12** 101,14.29; 105,23.31.35; **3.13** 107,9.13.15.17.20.22-4.26-7.30.32-5.37; 108,2-4.6-7.9; *phantasian lambanein*, imagine, **3.12** 105,25

phantasma, appearance, impression, **3.1** 81,2; **3.12** 105,28; **3.13** 107,14

pherein, convey, **2.17** 62,11; **3.9** 97,14.25; derive, **3.12** 101,23-4; *pheresthai*, be carried, travel, come, hurtle, **2.18** 62,26; **2.21** 66,31; **2.23** 72,11-12.15.17.22.25.29; 73,1.3.5-6; 74,13.25; **3.10** 98,33; 99,10; 100,24

philosophos, philosopher, **fr.2 Vitelli** 92,3.14; 93,6

phleps, vein, **2.23** 74,15

phlox, flame, **2.17** 62,1

phobos, fear, **2.21** 70,31

phoitan, pass through, **fr.2 Vitelli**, 93,16

phora, carrying, being carried **2.23** 73,1.5

phôs, light, **3.7** 92,27

phrear, well, **3.10** 98,32 99,3

phronein, think, **3.2** 81,13-14.16; **3.3** 84,15.21

phrontis, reflection, **2.21** 71,2

phthanein, be already, exist already, **2.28** 79,2.5

phthartos, perishable; subject to passing away, **2.19** 63,23; **2.28** 78,22.34; **fr.2 Vitelli** 93,17

phtheirein, destroy, **3.3** 83,35 86,26; *phtheiresthai*, pass away, perish, cease to be, **2.20** 64,2.5.12-14; **2.28** 78,34-6; **3.4** 87,7.11-12.21; **3.5** 88,9; **3.14** 109,20.30; **fr.2 Vitelli** 93,17-18

phthora, passing away, destruction, ceasing to be, 45,20; **2.20** 64,4.12.14; 65,5; **2.21** 70,14; **2.22** 71,4; **2.28** 78,23.33; 79,15; **3** 80,9; **3.3** 83,33; 86,20; **3.4** 87,2.4-7.11-13.15.17.19; **3.5** 87,25; **3.14** 108,18.23; 109,13.19.26.34; 110,27.30.36

phuein, phuesthai, be or do by nature, naturally, **2.23** 73,12; **3.3** 83,28; **fr.1 Vitelli** 91,25 92,1; grow, grow naturally, **3.10** 99,37; **3.14** 108,35

phulassein, keep, preserve, **2.19** 63,28; **2.20** 64,3.11.22; 65,4

phusikos, natural, **2.18** 62,17-19.35; **2.20** 64,10.14; **2.24** 76,1-4.6; **2.25** 76,14.17.20-1; **2.27** 77,7; **3.12** 106,7; **3.14** 109,2; 110,25.31; 111,18; natural philosopher, **3.10** 98,21; *On Physics* (title) **3.7** 93,8

phusis, nature, natural, kind, sort, 45,14; **2.17** 62,5; **2.18** 62,15-16.18.23-24.26-7.33-4.37; 63,2.4.6; **2.19** 63,10-11.19.21; **2.20** 64,14-16; 65,14; **2.21** 69,20; **2.23** 74,19.29; **2.28** 77,33; 79,5; **3.2** 82,13-14; **3.3** 83,20; 84,12.29.31-2; **3.4** 87,14; **3.10** 98,18.32; 99,11; 100,23; **3.11** 100,26.29-31.36; 101,1-5; **3.12** 101,<32>; 102,31; 103,4.6.11; 105,1.4.7.13; 106,32; 107,4; **3.13** 107,13; **3.14** 109,1.4.12-13.18-20.27.32-3; 112,26; 114,10-11.13; **3.15** 115,34; **fr.1 Vitelli** 91,2; 92,12

phuton, plant, **3.14** 109,15
pikros, bitter, **3.9** 94,27-8; **3.10** 99,36
pikrotês, bitterness, **3.9** 95,24
pilêsis, compression, **2.17** 62,7
pinein, drink, **3.10** 99,23
pisteuein, believe, **fr.2 Vitelli** 93,5
pistis, conviction, convince,
　establishment of argument, **3.12**
　101,26; 105,5
pistousthai, establish, **2.27** 77,28;
　appeal to, **3.10** 100,16.19
pithanotês, plausibility, persuasion,
　3.12 101,13-15.18; 105,5; 106,35;
　fr.1 Vitelli 91,15
Platôn, Plato, **2.21** 70,34; **fr. 2**
　Vitelli 92,3-4.6.8.13.15;
　93,1-2.4.9-10; (as example), **3.5**
　88,13.19
platos, breadth, **3.12** 106,4; latitude,
　fr.1 Vitelli 91,25; 92,1
platus, brackish, **3.10** 100,12.13
pleistos, most, greatest, **2.23** 73,13;
　2.27 77,19; **3.5** 89,22; **3.10** 100,7.15;
　fr.1 Vitelli 91,3; *epi pleiston*, for
　the most part, **3.12** 102,32; 103,9-10
pleôn, more, greater, several,
　plurality, preponderance, **2.21**
　70,10-11; **2.23** 73,4.13.18-19.30;
　74,2; **2.28** 77,32; **3** 80,14; **3.5** 89,19;
　3.6 89,26; 90,19.32.35; 91,5; **3.7**
　92,1.10.13; **3.9** 95,22.28;
　97,17-18.20; **3.10** 100,13; **3.12**
　103,21-2.27; 104,4; 106,1.25-6.31;
　3.14 109,29; 110,12.21-2.35; 112,10;
　113,35; 114,14-16.19.28.30.35;
　115,2; **fr.2 Vitelli** 93,8; *epi pleon*,
　further, **3.3** 85,19-20
pleonakhôs, in several ways, **3.14**
　111,1.32
pleonektein, gain upper hand,
　preponderance, **2.20** 65,3;
　3.14 112,11
pleonexia, prevailing, prevail, **3.14**
　109,30-1
plêrês, full, **3.10** 100,1; **3.14** 114,20
plêrôsis, filling up, **fr.1 Vitelli** 92,17
plêroun, complete, **2.21** 70,19; fill,
　2.23 74,3
plêthos, abundance, **3.14** 110,1;
　112,4; plurality, number, **3.9** 98,14;
　fr.1 Vitelli 91,10.13
ploion, ship, **fr.1 Vitelli** 91,11

plousios, wealthy, **fr.1 Vitelli**
　91,12.32-3; 92,1.4-5
plunein, wash, **3.10** 99,24
pneuma, breath, **3.14** 111,30; 113,10
poiein, act, create, do, make, produce,
　45,9; **2.16** 61,2.5.15-16.24-6; **2.18**
　62,33; **2.20** 64,8; **2.21** 66,22.24;
　67,18.19.21; 68,4.18; 69,5.24; **2.23**
　74,17.21; **2.28** 78,3-4; 79,14; **3.3**
　83,14.17.33; 86,9.19; **3.7** 92,17;
　93,3.5.7; **3.9** 95,7; 97,26; 98,10; **3.10**
　99,31; 100,24; **3.12** 101,34-5;
　103,31.36; 104,9; 106,8; **3.13**
　107,11-12.21; 108,15; **3.14** 108,30;
　109,5; 111,3; 113,11; 114,21.25; **3.15**
　116,11; **fr.2 Vitelli** 93,15; give
　(answer), **2.21** 66,8; *poieisthai*
　kataskeuên, establish, **3.12** 105,5;
　poieisthai logon, speak about, **3.14**
　111,13
poiêsis, action, **3.7** 93,6
poiêtês, maker, **2.21** 66,32
poiêtikos, active, creative, efficient,
　producing, **2.16** 61,20; **3.2** 82,17; **3.3**
　86,14; **3.5** 89,22; **3.14** 108,27.31;
　109,2.12.16.26.36; 110,32;
　112,18.27-8
poimên, shepherd, **2.21** 67,32
poios, of a certain sort, in a certain
　way, **2.24** 75,12; **3.11** 101,7; quality,
　3.3 84,16
poiotês, qualification, quality, **2.20**
　64,18.21.27; **2.28** 78,26; **3.10** 98,26;
　100,6
polis, city, **fr.1 Vitelli** 91,9
pollakhôs, in many ways, **3.13** 107,34
pollakis, often, **3.7** 92,30; **3.13** 107,22
polukenos, containing much void,
　2.23 72,32
poluônumia, plurality of names,
　3.11 101,8
polus, much, many, great deal, great
　amount, **2.16** 61,19; **2.21** 67,7.15;
　69,3; 70,1.15; **2.23** 73,9; 74,29; **3.2**
　81,25; 82,6; **3.9**
　96,13-14.16.22-4.29-30; 97,15.18;
　98,8.12.14; **3.10** 98,21; 100,16; **3.12**
　101,30.36; 103,14; 104,13; 106,39;
　3.13 107,32.34; **3.14** 110,20;
　114,13.21; **fr.1 Vitelli** 91,19-21; **fr.2**
　Vitelli 93,3

3.6 89,33; 90,1.25.27; 91,13.21.23;
3.9 96,31.33; 97,7.9.11.13.16.19.22;
3.10 99,23.26.34; **3.12** 105,14*;
106,1.3-4.7-8.12-13.15.18.25-7.32-5;
3.14 108,36; 110,31; 112,8.18.22.29;
fr.1 Vitelli 91,31; **fr.2 Vitelli**
93,15-16; *tessara sômata*, four
elemental bodies, **3.14** 108,36
sômatikos, of body, corporeal, **3.2**
81,28; **3.9** 98,4
sophisma, sophism, **fr.1 Vitelli**
90,2-3.5; 91,27
sôreitês, sorites, **fr.1 Vitelli** 90,1
sôros, heap, **fr.1 Vitelli** 91,12
sôstikos, preserving, preserve, **3.2**
81,23
sôtêria, preservation, **2.21**
68,21.24.31-4; 69,4
sôzein, preserve, **2.17** 62,10; **2.20**
64,36; 65,2.9; **2.24** 75,16; **2.28** 78,23;
3.3 83,35; 86,21; **fr.2 Vitelli** 93,18
span, draw, draw in, **2.23**
74,7.11-13.17
spanios, infrequent, **2.21** 67,4
sperma, seed, **2.20** 64,6; **2.23** 74,15;
2.26 76,25.31
sphairikos, spherical, **2.18** 63,4
sphodra, strongly, **2.21** 70,34
stagón, drop of water, **fr.1 Vitelli**
91,10
stasis, rest, being at rest, **2.18** 62,30;
63,2.6; **2.25** 76,14.16-18.21-2
stateusis, scorching, **3.14** 111,6.16;
112,2
stena, straits, **3.10** 99,1
stereos, solid, **2.23** 73,29
stereotês, solidity, **2.17** 62,3
sterêsis, privation, **3.7** 92,25-6
sterêtikos, of privation, **3.3** 84,33
stigmê, point, **3.9** 94,20; 96,10; **3.12**
103,29
Stoa, Stoa, Stoic, **fr.2 Vitelli** 93,3.9
stoikheion, element, elemental,
45,11; **2.17** 61,30.32; 62,5.13; **2.20**
64,18; 65,1.5-6; **2.24** 75,9; **3.10** 99,7;
3.12 104,12; **3.14** 108,19.24.29;
112,16; letter, **3.11** 101,5.7
Stôïkos, Stoic, Stoics, **fr.1 Vitelli**
90,1; **fr.2 Vitelli** 92,2-3
stokhastikos, stochastic, 45,8; **2.16**
61,1.4.6-7.17
stratêgein, be a general, **3.3** 85,23

subôtês, swineherd, **2.21** 67,34
sullabê, syllable, **3.11** 101,7
sullambanein, include, take
together, **2.28** 79,3-4; **fr.1 Vitelli**
91,8-10.13-14
sullogismos, syllogism, **3.15**
115,28-9; **fr.1 Vitelli** 91,5
sumbainein, happen, result, **2.21**
66,27-8; **3.10** 100,21; **3.12** 103,27;
fr.1 Vitelli 91,3.24
sumbainein, be property, **3.12**
103,30; be accident, belong per
accidens **3.8** 93,28; **3.12** 106,10
sumbebêkos, accident, **2.28** 78,25;
3.12 104,28; 105,6.16; 106,15; *kata
sumbebêkos*, accidental, *per
accidens*, 45,19; **2.21**
65,17.23.25-6.28-30.35;
66,1.5-6.10.19.25.29.30-1.34;
67,2-3.7.9.12.16.<18>.19.22.[24-7];
68,6-7.14.19; 70,9; **2.23** 74,17; **3**
80,16; **3.8** 93,23.25-7.29-31;
94,1-4.6-9
sumboulos, adviser, **3.13** 108,11.13
summetria, proportioning,
commensurateness, **2.20**
64,25.31.33.34-5; 65,4.6.15; **2.23**
73,31
summetros, commensurate, **2.23**
72,11.16.25
sumphtheiresthai, pass away along
with, **2.20** 64,14-15; **2.28** 79,7
sumphutos, in one's nature, **3.14**
112,33
sumplêroun, complete, **2.28** 79,5
sumptôma, accompaniment, **3.13**
107,27
sunaidein, be in harmony, **2.21**
70,28; **fr.2 Vitelli** 93,12
sunaisthanesthai, be self-aware, **3.7**
93,20
sunaisthêsis, self-awareness, 80,13;
3.7 91,25.28.30-1; 92,16-17;
93,12.15.18
sunamphoteros, compound,
compounded, **2.24** 75,27-8.30.34;
76,5.7; **2.27** 77,4-5; **2.28**
78,3.22.23.25.27.30; 79,12
sunanapheresthai, be carried up
with, **3.10** 100,8
sunauxanein, increase, **3.14** 110,19

Index of Passages Cited

Numbers in **bold** type refer to the works cited; numbers in ordinary type refer to the pages of this book. Cross-references to one *quaestio* from the notes on another are indexed, but not the main translation and discussion of each *quaestio*.

Subject Index

See also the Glossary, Greek-English Index and Index of Passages Cited: the Subject Index is selective and complementary to these. The Appendix (pp. 151-60) has been indexed only for topics that concern Alexander and the *Quaestiones*. References are to the pages of this book.

accident, accidents, 37, 56-7
action, is in thing affected, 55-6;
   action at a distance, 123 n.132
active and passive powers, 78-9, 81-3
activity, actuality, 35, 55, 59, 95-6,
   111 n.33, 128 n.198, 129 n.211, 135
   n.274; *see* potentiality
advisers, 77
affection, being affected, 40-3, 45-6,
   59-63, 95
air, 86; as intermediary of sensation,
   51-2
Alexander of Aphrodisias, 1, 153; life
   and dates, 110 n.3; and earlier
   philosophers, 158; criticised by
   Plutarch of Athens, 159; Michael of
   Ephesus and, 155; minor works
   attributed to, 1-3; school, 110 n.5
alteration, 38-43, 45-6
amber, 29, 31
an with optative, 6
antiperistasis, 142 n.383
appearance, 76-7; *see* image
appetite, 31
Arabic versions, 2, 7, 89, 95-6, 98, 110
   n.6; *see* Index of Passages Cited
   under 'Alexander – texts surviving
   in Arabic'
Archytas, 138 n.317
Aristotelianism, 1
Aristotle, 1, 92-4; Alexander's doctrine
   and Aristotle, 118 nn.99-100, 121
   n.116; Aristotle on providence, 25-6
art, arts, 13-14, 17, 39, 44, 112-14
ash, 64-6
assent, 76-7

atomism, atomists, 139 nn.330, 333,
   143 nn.391-3
atoms, 29
Atticus, 119 n.104, 120 n.113, 121
   n.118
attraction, 30-1
authenticity, of works attributed to
   Alexander, 2-3

Bessarion, 5
bladder, 64
blame, 77
blending, total, in Stoicism, 114 n.61
blood, 86
body, 74-5; natural bodies, 15-16;
   simple and composite bodies, 18-19;
   body passing through body (two
   bodies in same place), 94, 145 n.418;
   god and soul bodies for Stoics, 94
boiling, 82
breath, *pneuma*, 82, 84
bronze, 30

capacity, 112 n.33
carelessness, grammatical, 6, 135
   n.277
categories, 95-6
chaff, 29
chance, 69; and frequency, 119 n.106
change, 17-19, 38-43, 45, 61, 95-6, 112
   n.33, 135 n.275, 142 n.371
character, and view of end, 141 n.365
choice, 78
circle, 60
codex Ambros. gr. Q 74 supp., 97
codex Florent. Riccard. 63, 89-90
cold, 78-87